Praise for *The Sponsorship Seeker's Toolkit,* Fourth Edition

"Finding sponsorship is an honorable job, but sometimes it can also be a tough one. You need persistence, passion, and knowledge. And you need this book! It's not a guarantee, but it helps you to decide on your right strategy and leads you step-by-step in the choices you have to make in the whole process, from gathering internal support to renewal. It's so unique, detailed, and complete. I never read a better how-to book on seeking sponsors."

—Ad Maatjens, Founder and Director, Sponsorreport

"This essential, practical, and easy-to-use guide to sponsorship is one of the best and most thorough 'how to' books in fund-raising! Using real-world examples and case studies, easy-to-use checklists, and templates, *The Sponsorship Seeker's Toolkit,* fourth edition, offers clear, step-by-step guidance through the process, from internal planning to proposal development to sales and negotiation to servicing. The authors provide the knowledge and the tools for successful implementation based on their many years of experience in the field. A must-read orientation for nonprofits considering transforming their approach or venturing into the exciting world of sponsorship!"

—Kyla Shawyer, Chair of the International Fundraising Congress (IFC),
Chief Operating Officer, SCIA—International Alliance

"In every field of endeavor there's one book you must read, the go-to guide that you just can't do without. For sponsorship seekers, that book is *The Sponsorship Seeker's Toolkit,* fourth edition, by Kim Skildum-Reid and Anne-Marie Grey."

"Gone are the days of sticking logos on things and putting your hand out for a donation. Today's sponsors are more sophisticated than ever and expect you to develop a sponsorship program that provides unique marketing opportunities and a return on investment.

"For all you serious sponsorship seekers out there, *The Sponsorship Seeker's Toolkit* contains all the information you'll need to successfully develop, deliver, and manage a best-practice sponsorship program, using an easy-to-understand, step-by-step process supported by useful case studies and example templates."

—Kym Oberauer, founder of PracticalSponsorshipIdeas.com

The Sponsorship Seeker's Toolkit

The Sponsorship Seeker's Toolkit

Fourth Edition

Kim Skildum-Reid & Anne-Marie Grey

New York Chicago San Francisco
Athens London Madrid
Mexico City Milan New Delhi
Singapore Sydney Toronto

1 2 3 4 5 6 7 8 9 0   QFR/QFR   1 2 0 9 8 7 6 5 4

ISBN   978-0-07-182579-5
MHID   0-07-182579-7

e-ISBN   978-0-07-182313-5
e-MHID   0-07-182313-1

Library of Congress Cataloging-in-Publication Data
Grey, Anne-Marie, author.
  Sponsorship seeker's toolkit. — Fourth edition / by Kim Skildum-Reid and Anne-Marie Grey.
     pages cm
  Includes bibliographical references and index.
  ISBN-13: 978-0-07-182579-5 (paperback)
  ISBN-10: 0-07-182579-7
  1. Corporate sponsorship. 2. Fund raising—Management. 3. Marketing—Management. 4. Corporate sponsorship—Australia. 5. Fund raising—Australia—Management. 6. Marketing—Australia—Management. I. Skildum-Reid, Kim, author. II. Title.
  HD59.35.G74 2014
  658.15'224—dc23
                                                                          2014003639

Contents

Foreword

The books Kim and Anne-Marie have written are referred to at length in the ESA Diploma—a professional qualification for those working (or wishing to work) in the sponsorship industry. They are known for their practical, straightforward approach.

This newest edition of *The Sponsorship Seeker's Toolkit* marks the place in the sponsorship industry's history when there is no longer any excuse for a below-par sponsorship proposal. I couldn't recommend it more highly to each and every sponsorship seeker out there.

In their straight-talking, sensible, and structured book, Kim and her coauthor Anne-Marie Grey have provided a comprehensive road map for every professional seeking sponsorship on behalf of his or her organization—whether that be an event, a sport or art governing body, an art gallery—whatever.

All anyone has to do is follow their straightforward and practical approach. The process—planning, sales, and servicing—couldn't be more logically set out. And in the fourth section there are a number of useful resources to make the job as simple as possible.

The book is a veritable bible for every sponsorship seeker and should ensure that there are far more "win, win, win" sponsorship programs out there, benefiting both sponsor and sponsee and, thus, proving the business value of sponsorship.

I like the honesty in the book. No one, least of all the authors, is pretending that it's easy to find sponsors. But difficult questions are not avoided. They are tackled head-on. And logical, practical tips are provided as to how to best resolve awkward issues and turn them into pluses rather than minuses.

The planning section really underlines the value of homework prior to putting any sponsorship proposal together. Not only that, but it highlights to the reader the steps that need to be taken to gather all the necessary information, proving that a "quick hit" just doesn't work.

I especially like the brainstorming process and suspect that a number of people reading this book will find it exciting, different, and productive—and probably a world away from the way in which ideas have been generated in the past.

The sales pages provide logical steps to the best way to approach potential sponsors. I could almost feel the breadth of the armory the authors were providing the reader! But, best of all, there's no waffle. Just practical, logical, and rational thinking that adds up to a really professional approach that sponsors will appreciate and that should lead to the best results.

Last, the prolific amount of case studies are the proof of the pudding. They demonstrate successful sponsorship programs and show the reader just how it can best be done. What more could sponsorship seekers want or need? It's all in the book—they just have to go out and follow the road map.

Well done, Kim and Anne-Marie. The sponsorship industry becomes ever more professional and owes you both a debt in showing the way.

Karen Earl
Chairman
The European Sponsorship Association

Foreword

On a recent trip to Dubai, while clearing customs, I noticed a large advertising poster informing visitors that in 1991 there was only one high-rise building in the city, while today (only a brief 20-plus years later) there are nearly 1,000, a clear testament to the speed of evolution and development happening all around us every day. Comparatively, in 1990 I coauthored, with Robert Jackson, one of the early books to come out in our field (*Special Events: Inside and Out*), which featured a dedicated (cutting-edge at the time) section about how to research potential sponsors—before the advent of the Internet, along with a variety of well-intentioned guidance about sponsorship sales and service. Today, you hold in your hands the evolutionary sponsorship equivalent of 1,000 new high-rise buildings in Dubai!

After decades of my own career in festival and event management, from a global perspective, I have been fascinated to note that sponsorship continues (by far) to be the leading topic of interest for conferences, conventions, webinars, et al. throughout our industry. Perhaps this is because it touches and supports everything we do or dream of doing. As we continue to learn and evolve—events and sponsors alike—there is a clear understanding that we must all keep pace in this all-important arena if we are to succeed.

In this latest update of the top-selling resource *The Sponsorship Seeker's Toolkit*, Kim Skildum-Reid and Anne-Marie Grey have continued to refine this critically important topic and lead our industry evolution in all areas of sponsorship—from planning and process to measurement and evaluation, and everything in between—providing readers with an unprecedented plethora of downloadable templates, examples, checklists, pro formas, case studies, and resource recommendations, plus direct access to the authors themselves. They have effectively taken away all of our excuses.

In a world of information overload, Skildum-Reid and Grey have simplified both process and explanation to provide the equivalent of a degree in sponsorship within the pages of a single book. Well beyond illuminating the pathway, they have provided a virtual GPS to sponsorship success for professionals at every level of experience. Follow their directions, and they will help you to evolve your own organization's efforts to ensure that you are maximizing sponsorship returns for everyone—event/organization, sponsors, and attendees. And don't let their "down-under" accents fool you—this is a must-have global resource for anyone currently managing or planning to implement a successful sponsorship program.

If you have ever felt the palpable energy when a new idea, vision, or tool is introduced into your own world, within your own team and organization, that allows you to see new opportunities, imagine new possibilities, or create new processes that will streamline current methods and expand returns exponentially, you already understand the difference that sharing *The Sponsor Seeker's Toolkit* (4th edition) with all those in your organization can have. From there I encourage you to spread that value further along the many spokes of your professional network to help move us all forward as an industry.

Pearl Buck (1892–1973), winner of both the Pulitzer Prize and Nobel Prize for her writing, once noted, "The secret of joy in work is contained in one word—excellence. To know how to do something well is to enjoy it." Kim Skildum-Reid and Anne-Marie Grey obviously understand where she was coming from on both fronts, and it is our good fortune that they have chosen to take us along that continuing and evolutionary path.

Steven Wood Schmader, CFEE
President & CEO
International Festivals & Events Association (IFEA World)

How to Use This Book

There are a lot of people who think creating sponsorship requires some kind of mystical, magic power. We're here to tell you that as surely as the beautiful assistant doesn't really get sawn in half, there is no magic behind developing strong, lasting, and mutually beneficial partnerships with sponsors.

We fully believe that building and maintaining these partnerships can be achieved by people with little or no sponsorship experience, so long as they have two things: enthusiasm and a road map. The enthusiasm you will have to supply yourself, but this book is your road map.

We suggest using the book as follows:

- Read through the book once first, taking notes as you go. This will help you to understand the desired outcome when you start to implement the strategies that we have outlined.
- Ensure that key stakeholders within your organization know what you are doing (reading the book themselves may help). The system we advocate is a big departure from the approach many organizations are currently taking to sponsorship—you need to ensure you have support for the change.
- Check out the resources we have outlined in Appendix 2. Start increasing your knowledge level right away.
- Go through the book, doing the exercises outlined along the way. Don't get hung up on the formats. The ones we have used are those that work for us, but feel free to alter them so that they work for you.
- Use the exercises collaboratively whenever possible. There are a number of places where two or more heads are definitely better than one.
- Be proactive with potential sponsors. The assumption is often that because they have the money, they know what they are doing. This is often not the case at all. Once you have completed this book, you may very well know more about doing sponsorship right than many sponsors do, and it may be

an educational process for them, too.
- Pay attention to the case studies—you never know what they may inspire!
- Have fun with it. Good sponsorship is a highly creative process. If you don't allow yourself to have big, creative, sometimes silly ideas, you'll never hit upon the really great ones.

Special note: Throughout this book, we will sometimes generically use the word *event* to describe the property for which you are seeking sponsorship, whether that is an event, venue, cause, organization, program, individual, or team. Also, if you don't understand a term, be sure to check out the Glossary in Appendix 1.

If you don't understand a term, check the Glossary in Appendix 1.

Overview of Sections

The book is broken into four general sections. Here is an overview of what is included in each of them.

Part 1: Planning

In this section, you will look closely at both your property and your organization to determine what you need to plan and implement a sponsorship program effectively. Long before the selling process begins, you need to determine whether you and your organization are prepared to engage in long-term relationships with the corporate sector. We will guide you through creating internal policies, undertaking market and corporate research, creating a marketing plan, and negotiating promotional media.

Part 2: Sales

In this section, you will learn about preparation and persistence. Both are required to guide your proposals successfully through to the negotiation stage. This section shows you how to identify potential sponsors, research them, create a customized proposal for every potential sponsor, and negotiate a mutually beneficial deal. Included to assist you are a number of detailed checklists and forms, as well as a sponsorship proposal template.

Part 3: Servicing

This section outlines how to create and implement innovative sponsorship servicing programs that ensure your partnerships are creating "wins" for all parties concerned. Covered are steps that will get your relationship off on the right foot, quantification and reporting mechanisms, and a wide range of maximization options, which will assist your sponsors in achieving all they can from their investments.

Part 4: Appendices

It is essential that you continue to develop your sponsorship and marketing skills and build up your resources. To this end, we have included a listing of resources, including associations, Internet sites, and publications that will assist you in creating and developing a sponsorship portfolio that will bring your organization and your sponsors the results you desire. Also included is a comprehensive glossary of terms and an outstanding Sponsorship Agreement Pro Forma template, provided by one of Australia's foremost experts on sponsorship law.

Downloadable Tools

This book comes with a series of tools and templates to help you implement our approach. Tools are marked in the book text by this symbol: ⬇.

To download the tools, you will need a computer with an Internet connection and this book (hard copy or e-book). Go to www.sponsorshipseekers toolkit.com.

- Answer five simple questions about the book. All questions can be easily answered if you are looking at the book, particularly if you use the Contents pages as a quick reference.
- After answering all five questions correctly, you will be asked to enter your email address. A link to a one-time download will be emailed to you straightaway.
- When you receive the email, click the link to download the zip file containing the templates. All templates are in MS Word format (docx).

If you have any difficulties, contact details are on the download site.

Warning

These tools are copyrighted and provided as an added value to owners of this book. If you return or sell the book, you no longer have a license to use the tools and they, and any derivative works, must be deleted or destroyed immediately. If you continue to use them, you will be breaching copyright and we may exercise legal options. Plus, they will be very difficult to use without the context provided in the book.

We've gone to a lot of effort to provide you with a book that will make seeking sponsorship as easy as it can be. Please, do the right thing.

Acknowledgments

When we wrote the first manuscript for *The Sponsorship Seeker's Toolkit* way back in 1998, we had no idea that 15 years later, we'd be working on the fourth edition. The assistance and support we've received from so many people is humbling, and it makes all those hours in front of the computer typing and doing research worth it.

First and foremost, we need to thank our readers around the world who have made this book the success it has become. We have lost track of the number of emails you've sent about how the books have transformed your approach, and we appreciate every one of them. Your support in blogs and social media has been nothing short of amazing. You have inspired nearly every change we've made through three new editions, and we couldn't have done this without you.

We would also like to thank all of the people who have attended our workshops and keynotes all over the world. We appreciate your openness about the challenges you face, and all of your input that allows us to continually improve our skills.

We would also like to acknowledge the following people and organizations for their assistance in the development and production of this book: Steven Schmader and Karen Earl for gracing us with their wonderful forewords, Lionel Hogg for going above and beyond the call of duty with the agreement pro forma, and Michelle Norris for her assistance in finding great case studies. We would also like to thank all of our colleagues and clients who have allowed us to share their experiences with our readers, as well as all of the sponsorship and marketing associations and media that have supported our books.

Thank you to all of the family and friends who have supported us through all of this author craziness for so many years. You'd think this would get easier after a while, but it doesn't, and we can always count on you to remind us that there is life outside of sponsorship and writing books.

This isn't done until we've extended our thanks to the team at McGraw-Hill Australia for taking a chance on us way back when. And thanks to McGraw-Hill USA for continuing the support of our vision, for their patience in the face of our crippling work schedules, and for letting us continue to sound like Aussies.

The Sponsorship Seeker's Toolkit

Part 1

Planning

CHAPTER 1

Internal Planning

Before your organization begins the sponsorship acquisition process, it is essential to consider your organization's ability to enter wholeheartedly into a marketing partnership with a corporation. Too many organizations turn to sponsorship as a last-minute resort for raising much-needed funds. Sponsorship, however, is no longer a fundraising activity but, rather, a joint marketing activity involving both your organization and a corporate partner. If you are not prepared to be part of a win-win partnership and share the "ownership" and glory of your programs, your sponsorship efforts will fail. You may be successful in raising sponsorship, but retaining your sponsors will be very difficult.

Understanding Your New Role

Your job as a sponsee has changed dramatically over the past few years, driven primarily by sponsors' increasingly sophisticated expectations. They want to achieve multiple objectives, integrate sponsorships across a myriad of marketing activities, and, more than anything else, truly connect with their target markets. That last one is often a hard pill to swallow for sponsorship seekers, but it is true. Sponsors are no longer interested in being "associated with" your event. They don't want to connect their brand with football or the arts or whatever. They want to connect with the target markets on a personal level, fostering relationships and creating a degree of relevance that a less passionate marketing medium, like television, could never equal.

Historically, sponsorship has been all about connecting a brand with your property, and the very clear focus of negotiations and sponsorship leverage has been about enhancing that connection—bigger logos, more signage, players

Sponsors don't want to connect with your event. They want to connect with your target market.

using the brand on TV commercials, event logos on product packaging, on and on and on. The assumption that went along with all of this was that if the two organizations were connected in a highly visible, thorough way, then the target market would just get it—that the guy in the pub watching football would say to himself, "That's my favorite team, and it's sponsored by XYZ Beer, so I should drink XYZ Beer" (Figure 1.1). That delusion was nice while it lasted, but a lot of research has shown that this approach is only minimally effective.

Don't believe us? Ask yourself, or better yet, a friend, the following questions:

- What was the last major sporting event you attended in person (with which you weren't professionally associated)?
- How many logos do you think you saw that day?
- Just give me a number—how many do you think you could name right now?
- Okay, name them . . .
- Of the sponsors you've named, have any of them changed your perception of their brands? Have any of them made you behave any differently with their brands—trying the brand, becoming more loyal, telling other people about it, or whatever?

We've asked these questions hundreds of times, and the answers are virtually always the same: people claim to have seen somewhere between 15 and 100 logos, think they can name 8 to 10, can actually name 2 or 3, and none of the sponsorships by those brands have affected their brand perceptions or behaviors in any way. That's traditional sponsorship thinking at work, and it's not very effective.

Modern, best-practice sponsorship turns this thinking on its head. Best-practice sponsorship starts from the premise that sponsors don't want to connect with you, they want to connect with your audience, and they want to use

Figure 1.1 Traditional sponsorship model

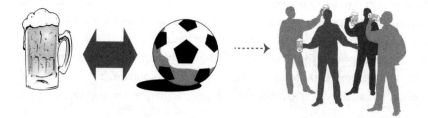

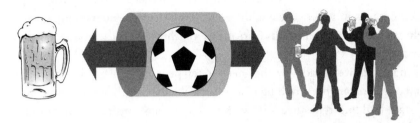

Figure 1.2
Best-practice
sponsorship model

their sponsorship of your property to deepen their connection with their audience. Given that, the new model of sponsorship looks like Figure 1.2.

Best-practice sponsorship makes the relationship between the sponsor and the target market the primary focal point and changes the sponsor's goal from getting "in front of" an audience to adding value to the target market's experiences with the event and the brand, demonstrating their understanding of and alignment with the target market's values, motivations, and passions, and deepening their relevance and relationships with key markets.

Your role as a sponsee has changed from being a flag-waver to being a conduit, providing a variety of benefits and opportunities that will help your sponsors achieve that level of connection. They now also count on you to help them understand your audience's values, motivations, and desires in a much deeper way than ever before. They don't just want to know age and gender any more, they want to know why people attend your event, join your association, or donate to your cause, what are the drawcards and downsides, and how they, as sponsors, can improve or enhance that experience.

This does mean more work for your organization, but this is not such a bad thing. Back when sponsorships were selected based on the amount of exposure they could deliver or the exclusiveness of the hospitality program, there was always another event that could deliver more. Events, teams, causes, and all of the other sponsorship options were interchangeable commodities, making your sponsorship income very unreliable. The new model of sponsorship is based on partnership and produces strong, multifaceted results that any sponsor will find difficult to leave.

How Sponsorship Fits with Brand Marketing

Before you will be successful in selling sponsorship, the very first thing you need to know is how it fits with brand marketing. Every brand has a life cycle—

The sponsor's primary goal is adding value to the target markets' experiences with the event and with their brand.

some short, some long—and for each, what the brand needs from sponsorship at different stages in its life cycle is different (Figure 1.3). Understanding this will help you to understand brand priorities and find the focal point of your sponsorship offer.

When brands are brand new, they need to tell people they exist. But nobody buys, or considers buying, anything just because it exists, so they need to immediately start building relevance—Why should someone consider their brand? How will it benefit them? What does it say about you if you choose this brand?

Once they have established their relevance, and most of their target market knows and understands their brand, their primary objective is to build relationships. It's far easier for a brand to nurture its current relationships, figure out ways to sell them more, and create avenues for advocacy than it is to chase new business. Of course, sponsors are still trying to develop relevance with new

Case Studies: Win-Win-Win Sponsorship

NAB (National Australia Bank) used their sponsorship of the Australian Football League to make Australia's national sport accessible to everyone—even the estimated 25 percent of Aussies who were born overseas. They created www.footify.com to teach those first-generation immigrants and other AFL newbies about the lingo (like calling it "footy"). They then went further, training people to expertly commentate the game in a wide variety of languages, and creating an online "radio station" during the Australian Rules Grand Final so even non-English speakers could enjoy the biggest game of the year live on TV, while listening to live commentary in their native languages. Inspired!

Time Warner Cable customers in the Carolinas got a four-day window to buy Charlotte Bobcats play-off tickets before they went on sale to the general public.

At the **Toyota** Owners Hospitality Tent at NASCAR races, Toyota, Lexus, and Scion owners simply have to show their Toyota key to

allow access for them and a guest. Inside the tent, owners will find a relaxing place to hang out before the race with complimentary refreshments, giveaways, and a chance to meet Toyota NASCAR drivers. Toyota partners with the local dealerships to identify and invite current owners to events. One dealership out of Tennessee has so far reported three sales as a direct result of the program.

Canon used sponsorship of the London Fashion Week to showcase their range and quality to pro photographers and consumers alike. Among their huge array of leverage activities, they provided product loans, servicing, and repairs to pro photographers at the event; ran Canon Studio, a studio where 5,000 attendees were photographed by a pro and prints provided to take away; and showcased their projection products in the Canon Cinema, projecting live fashion shows and on-demand fashion content; they also created six short films (unique content) featuring fashion heavyweights.

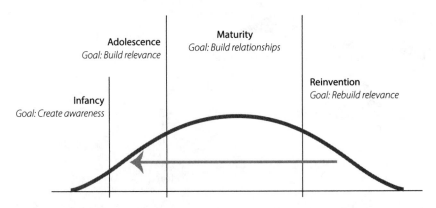

Figure 1.3
Sponsorship priorities
at each stage of the
brand life cycle

or emerging markets, but what they're not trying to do is create awareness. Think of this next time you promote "exposure" as your biggest benefit to McDonald's or Sony or Ford.

Brands also have a customer cycle, representing their relationships with customers and their increasing value as that relationship deepens.

The entry point is simply being aware of the brand, but lacking any understanding or context. This is very low value. Slightly higher is someone who understands the relevance of the brand, but hasn't really considered it. An example might be most of our relationships with Ferrari. We get it, but we really haven't considered buying the car.

Trying a brand is a big step up because it represents the first time a person moves toward the brand under his or her own power. This can be actually buying the brand or checking it out online, test-driving a car, comparison shopping, or liking/following on social media.

At that point, some of those trialers will add that brand to their repertoire in the category: the collection of beers brands they drink, the financial services providers they use, the cereal brands they buy, etc. This is an even bigger step up because the customers have now decided they like and trust the brand, and the brand can now set about to increasing their preference within that repertoire.

The next level is generally thought to be loyalty, and while some categories do get 100 percent loyalty, most don't. So, instead of engendering loyalty, most brands concentrate on both increasing preference and driving advocacy, so their customers are creating relevance in a more credible way than any amount of ads could ever achieve.

Why do you need to know this? Because most sponsorships are sold only on the basis of creating awareness, delivering some kind of relevance message,

Figure 1.4
Customer cycle

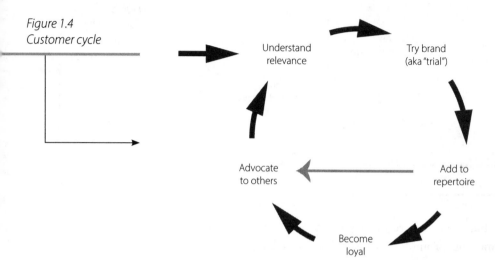

and driving people to try the brand—impacting only the least valuable customers of a brand. What brands really want are sponsorships that work all the way around, with advocacy being a must-have feature (Figure 1.4).

Creating a Sponsorship-Friendly Organization

If you want to succeed in modern-day sponsorship, it is important that everyone within your organization understands that sponsorship is about creating a win-win-win partnership. It used to be just win-win, with you and the sponsor achieving your objectives without undue strife. Best-practice sponsorship has introduced the third "win"—the target market. They must get a meaningful benefit, however small, from the sponsorship if it is going to really work for anyone.

This shift from the neediness of a fundraising mindset (just one "win") or the objective orientation of a traditional sponsorship ("win-win") and into a holistic, market-driven approach is the major point of difference from sponsorship programs in the seventies through to the midnoughties, to the best-practice sponsorship in today's marketplace.

Throughout this book, there will be ample case studies that showcase this thinking, and it will be critical for you to engender this win-win-win mindset within your organization if you want to position your organization to take advantage of the vast opportunities that best practice can present.

The majority of organizations that seek sponsorship do so from a position of need—the need for funds is continual and ever pressing. Many organizations are concerned that corporate partnerships and sponsorship will threaten their credibility and integrity. And this is just the tip of the iceberg. In fact, there are often several hurdles that you will need to overcome in order to gain the support of your staff and board.

Some typical areas of concern with sponsorship include

- Being seen as "going commercial"
- Perceived ownership of an organization or event
- Selling out to the corporate sector
- Compromising the integrity of programs and services
- Placing financial objectives before programming objectives
- Allocation of much-needed resources to marketing activities
- Placing consumer needs ahead of staff needs
- Lack of recognition as to the value of sponsorship to the organization
- Refusal to deal with particular industries or specific companies

Your goal should be to create a win-win-win partnership.

What's in a Name?

In this industry, there is plenty of jargon—some of it confusing and a lot of it interchangeable. Although we cover all of this in the Glossary, we thought it would be useful to go through a few of the most common (and commonly interchanged) terms here:

Sponsorship seeker, sponsee, right-sholder, property, event. If your organization is looking for sponsorship, that's you.

Sponsor, brand. While not all brands are sponsors, all sponsors are brands. If someone references a brand in relation to sponsorship, he or she is talking about a sponsor.

Leverage, activation. This is what a sponsor does with the sponsorship. You sell them opportunity; it is leverage that provides the results.

Broker, agency. Someone who sells sponsorship on your behalf for a commission.

And a special note on sponsorship versus partnership . . . While there is a move by properties to start calling their sponsors partners, we're not fans. It is absolutely true that sponsorship has become much more partnership-oriented, but that shift in focus has basically redefined what sponsorship is about, not changed it from sponsorship to something else. Plus, for sponsors, the word *partnership* can be problematic. Their legal department will baulk, as what you're offering does not meet the legal definition of a business partnership, and the word *partnership* means something different to every department in a company. Everyone knows what sponsorship is, so we recommend just sticking with that and doing it really well.

- "Government should fund this program, and we should not be seen to be absolving them from their responsibility."
- "We tried it before and it didn't work."

As a sponsorship manager, you will need to determine what the critical issues of concern are within your organization and devise strategies to deal with them. Interviews with staff throughout your organization, as well as interviews and surveys with board members, clients, and customers, are efficient methods for determining the critical issues of concern. Many of these issues may not appear to be legitimate to you. However, perceptions and issues are always real, even if they are not accurate. You will need to address these perceptions nonetheless.

Often you will need to phrase your questions or lead the conversation in order to pull out the specific area of concern or the exact nature of the issue. Reluctance to engage or support sponsorship activities is often highly emotive. Exercise great care, compassion, and consideration in your interviews. As a start, you may want to consider asking the following questions:

- How do you feel about corporate sponsorship, generally? Is it a good or bad thing?
- Do you think it is appropriate for our organization to be working with corporate sponsors?
- How is sponsorship currently affecting what you do? How involved are you in sponsorship? How much do you know about what we do in sponsorship?
- Are you having any sponsorship-related challenges? Have you in the past?
- Which of our sponsors reflects the best partnership? Why?
- Describe the ideal sponsorship for our organization.
- Sponsors provide funds, but can provide a lot of other things, as well. Is there anything besides money that a sponsor could provide that would make your job easier, cheaper, or more effective?
- Is there anything else I should know?

We should acknowledge that most sporting organizations have long held a commercial outlook on sponsorship. If you are in the sporting area, you will probably have a much easier time garnering internal support for your activities. This does not make you immune from internal dissension and questioning, particularly if you are expanding your sponsorship program to include grassroots or community service activities.

> There are often several hurdles to overcome in order to gain staff support.

Once you have determined what issues are relevant to your planned sponsorship programs, you are better able to develop and implement strategies to confront them or to take corrective action.

In order to develop a sponsorship-friendly organization, we recommend a multipronged approach:

- Stay in contact with your staff and board.
- Educate all internal stakeholders.
- Provide reports, case studies and so on to all staff.
- Create a sponsorship team.
- Ask better questions.

Stay in Contact

Just as you need to keep in close and constant contact with your sponsors, you also need to communicate continually with your staff, members, and board. You want to cultivate an appreciation of sponsorship marketing principles and create an organization that will fully maximize every partnership.

Educate Staff

We have found that conducting staff workshops, explaining sponsorship marketing principles and organizational approaches to sponsorship, is an effective strategy for engaging staff in a sponsorship program. Regular presentations to the board outlining policies, strategies, and results are not only effective but also politically necessary.

Report Results to All Staff

Regular case studies, progress reports, and interviews with sponsors should be included in all staff communications. Remember to involve all staff, not just marketing and public relations people, in your communications program.

Create a Team

Creating a sponsorship team of decision makers from across departments and outside resources is a great step in creating a shared sense of responsibility for sponsorship across your organization.

Monthly meetings with your sponsorship team are almost guaranteed to provide you with additional opportunities for building a commitment to sponsorship within your organization, while maximizing your sponsorships and

> Sporting organizations are not immune to staff dissension on sponsorship.

minimizing your costs. For the investment of a couple of hours and a tray full of sandwiches, you will gain insight into many untapped resources and unearth potential trouble spots that could cause problems further down the track. Most important, though, you will gain the support, cooperation, and understanding that it takes to create a fantastic sponsorship program.

When putting together your team, remember not to overwhelm the group with "marketing people." The point is to create a multifaceted think tank. Consider including representatives from the following areas:

- Advertising agency
- Media partners
- Social media
- Corporate communications
- Customer service
- Human resources
- Market research
- Merchandising
- Tourism
- Packaging/production
- Product management
- Public relations
- Membership
- Ticket and group sales
- Concession sales
- Sales promotion
- Program or event production
- Sponsorship consultants

Remember to keep the team up to date on all developments throughout the process—a one- or two-page update a couple of weeks after each meeting should be adequate.

Ask Better Questions

Our guess is that you will have a lot to say to your colleagues about sponsorship as you go through this book, and by all means, share. Just as important, however, is using every appropriate opportunity to ask a few key questions. For instance:

- "Great idea! Now, how can we turn that into a win for our sponsors?"
- "How can we make this a win for the fans?"
- "How does that get Sponsor X closer to their target market? Is there some way we can tweak this so it's more about that relationship?"

These aren't difficult questions, they are just *different*, and if you ask them enough, your colleagues will start asking them, too.

Planning Your Sponsorship Programs

As is the case with any successful program, outstanding sponsorship programs require thorough research, careful planning, and flawless execution. There are two critical strategic planning documents that should be the linchpin of your sponsorship activities: a sponsorship policy and a sponsorship strategy. Both documents dovetail with your organization's mission statement and business plan. See Figure 1.5.

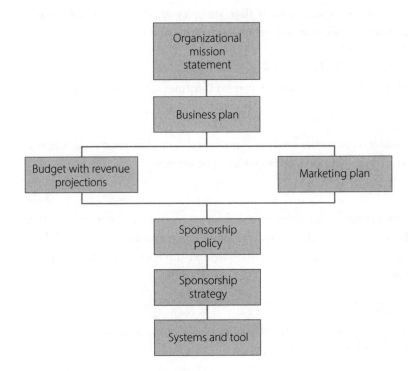

Figure 1.5
Internal planning
process

Sponsorship Policy

Find out if your organization has a sponsorship policy in place. If it has, ensure it is updated to reflect your current situation. If not, start developing one as a matter of urgency.

A sponsorship policy is a necessity for every organization seeking sponsorship, even traditional sponsorship seekers such as sporting groups. It is one of the most often overlooked components of a sponsorship program despite compelling reasons for having one. For example:

- Any program generating or distributing substantial funds should define the principal objectives and administrative processes of the sponsorship program.
- A sponsorship policy will ensure that your organization has a uniform approach to sponsorship.
- A policy outlines accountability and responsibility. This point is particularly important if your organization is in receipt of government funds or enjoys nonprofit status.
- A policy outlines specific issues that are relevant to your organization's approach to sponsorship and details exclusions and limitations.

Components of a Sponsorship Policy

A sponsorship policy should contain certain information as outlined here.

Background

The background outlines the history of sponsorship within your organization, as well as your organization's approach to sponsorship.

Definitions

The definitions state what does and does not constitute sponsorship (this is particularly important if you receive government funding and/or philanthropic donations). They also define the internal stakeholders in the sponsorship program.

Situational Analysis

The situational analysis identifies all current issues that may impact on your sponsorship program.

Exclusions

The exclusions section clarifies and describes fully what companies and industry sectors you will not engage with in a partnership arrangement. For example, many health-related organizations will not accept funds from alcohol or tobacco companies, and environmental organizations may be opposed to working with oil-companies.

For each exclusion, provide a rationale as to why a partnership with this company or industry sector is unacceptable. You may find over time that the issues prohibiting partnerships are no longer valid. You will also be prepared to answer questions from the board and members of the public as to why partnerships with these companies are unacceptable.

Processes and Procedures

The processes and procedures that your department will use to secure sponsorship agreements and manage your sponsorship programs are specified here.

If your sponsorship acquisition process is to be centralized, explain why. Outline the processes by which you will follow up sponsorship leads or provide comments and progress reports to the senior management, financial management, and auditors. If you are an organization with a national office and state branches, describe how information and leads will be shared and benefits negotiated across the organization as a whole.

This section will describe how you are actually going to manage the sponsorship acquisition program and service your sponsors.

Delegations

Delegations describe who within your organization is delegated to sell, receive, and approve sponsorships, and to what dollar level.

Many organizations are required to have board approvals on delegations related to the distribution of organizational information and financial transactions. Preapproved delegations can certainly make the audit process smoother for everyone involved.

Approvals and Contracts

This section explains who can approve a sponsorship and clarifies when a contract is required.

Accountability and Responsibility

Accountability and responsibility describes who within your organization is responsible for your sponsorship programs. Responsibilities will include seeking and reporting sponsorship funds; processing, banking, and investing funds; and servicing sponsorship relationships.

Unrelated Business Income Tax (UBIT)

A special note for US-based nonprofits: It is critically important that you work with your finance officer and legal team to determine if sponsorship income will attract unrelated business income tax (UBIT). The IRS can tax nonprofit organizations on proceeds from business activities that generate unrelated business income if the activities fail to relate sufficiently to the tax-exempt purpose of the tax-exempt organization. It is very important that your organization is aware of UBIT and the implications it may have on your sponsorship revenues.

For additional information, please refer to IRS Publication 598, *Tax on Unrelated Business Income of Exempt Organizations*.

Review and Evaluation

Review and evaluation defines when the policy will be reviewed and evaluated. Review your policy at least every six months. Publicize the results of the review process and encourage input from staff and members.

Frequently Asked Questions About Sponsorship Policy

Who Should Create the Sponsorship Policy?

If your aim is to create a policy that your staff and members feel they own, involve as many of the staff and members as possible.

Some smart sponsorship managers create a draft policy after discussions with staff, sponsors, and members and then present the draft policy to staff for comment. Other managers form a working party to develop the draft document. Whatever method you choose, ensure that you involve your chief executive officer, as well as your financial and human resources managers. Without their backing, your policy is going nowhere. Finally, you will want to have your policy formally accepted by your board.

Alternatively, secure the services of a sponsorship consultant to guide your organization through this process. Sometimes it can be easier and far more effective to have a consultant do the work for you. Ensure that the consultant works closely with your organizational stakeholders, or the organization will not feel ownership for the policy.

How Long Should the Policy Be?

Your sponsorship policy should be as long as is required to outline your organization's sponsorship principles, processes, and accountability procedures. Some sponsorship policies are as short as 2 pages, while others are closer to 10 pages.

Is a Sponsorship Policy Necessary?

Shouldn't you be concentrating on getting the money in and not worrying about documenting processes and systems? Nonprofit organizations, in particular, are under increasing scrutiny from their boards, their members, the media, auditors, and government departments as to their source of funds. The time you invest in creating and documenting your guidelines, systems, and processes is never wasted. A policy, endorsed by your board, ensures that your organization is credible, legitimate, and strategic. You have a responsibility to your stakeholders to ensure that your processes and accounting procedures are as transparent as possible. Taking the time to plan and document today may save you significant time and heartache in the future.

How Do You Motivate Staff to Create a Policy?

Staff in your organization may have been through many of these exercises previously. How do you motivate them to go through one more of these planning sessions?

If the issue is important to them, they will participate. You need to listen carefully to what issues are of concern and be prepared to engage in a relevant discussion of these issues. The bottom line is increased revenue and marketing expertise for your organization. Staff might not be particularly interested in how you obtain expertise and funds, but they are bound to have ideas on how to distribute the proceeds. Find the sweet spot and work from there.

Sponsorship Policy Questionnaire

Go through the following sponsorship policy questionnaire to ensure you have covered all issues. At the end of this process, you should be ready to draft your sponsorship policy. Take the time to consult as widely as possible before drafting your policy.

List the key stakeholders that will be affected by this policy, and then ensure you speak with a representative from each stakeholder group. Include staff and union representatives, marketing and public relations staff, front of house staff, sales staff, finance and resource officers, auditors, board members and senior staff. Also include program staff and recipients of sponsorship funds, along with members of your organization if appropriate.

Background
- Why does your organization want to engage in sponsorship?
- Do you see sponsorship as a fundraising exercise or a marketing activity?
- Do you want to develop long-term win-win-win partnerships?
- What are the overall principles of your approach to sponsorship?

Definitions
- How does your organization define sponsorship?
- How does this differ from philanthropy, cause-related marketing, and/or government support?
- Who are the internal stakeholders? (Board, sponsorship department, marketing department, etc.)

Situational Analysis
- How many people are currently engaged in seeking sponsorship for the organization?
- Is this their only responsibility, or are they responsible for several other major activities?
- Where does the sponsorship office fit into the organizational structure?
- To whom do the sponsorship staff report, and how frequently?
- What resources are presently allocated to the sponsorship department? Are the funds sufficient?
- What training and professional development are available to the sponsorship department?
- Have there been any changes to the organizational structure or staff changes that impact on the department?
- Are there any political issues that affect your programs?
- How does our business strategy or organizational plan affect the sponsorship?

- Does our organizational culture embrace sponsorship and win-win-win partnerships, or does work need to be done in this area?
- What issues will affect your sponsorship program?
- What issues do staff and your board need to be aware of?

Exclusions

- What companies and industries does your organization refuse to work with in a partnership? List each company or industry sector and provide a detailed rationale as to why they appear on the exclusion list. Indicate when your organization will review or repeal this decision.
- If corporate responsibility is important to your organization (e.g., you run an environmental education program), consult ethical investment firms or corporate social responsibility (CSR) advisors to get up-to-date information on companies' CSR policies, practices, and risk assessments.

Processes and Procedures

- What are your organization's principles guiding the selling of sponsorships?
- How will your organization ensure that sponsorship does not influence tendering processes and program activities (in the case of government and nonprofit organizations)?
- How will your organization manage sales rights within your purchasing processes?
- How will your organization ensure that a sponsor does not exert control over your organization or sponsored event?
- How will your organization protect and maintain its integrity and credibility?
- How will your organization value in-kind or contra sponsorships?
- How will your organization keep staff and other departments or sponsors informed?
- How will your sponsorship manager train staff?
- How will your sponsorship manager report to the board and to staff, and how frequently?
- How will your organization evaluate sponsorships for your organization and for your sponsors?
- What procedures are in place for:
  - Selling sponsorship?
  - Maintaining and servicing sponsors?

- Evaluating the effectiveness and return on investment for sponsorship activities and programs?
- Determining what projects will attract sponsorship?
- Ensuring that all funds are accounted for?
- Distributing funds?
- Ensuring that the public interest is best served?
- Reporting on the program to the board, members, and staff?
- Handling inquiries from auditors, accountants, taxation officials, media, and the general public?
- How will your organization handle a controversial sponsorship?

Delegations
- Has your resource management section ensured that the relevant financial delegations are in place for receiving, selling, and approving sponsorships?
- State the specific delegations and approvals within the policy.

Accountability and Responsibility
- Who is responsible for:
  - Selling sponsorship?
  - Maintaining and servicing sponsors?
  - Analyzing the effectiveness of sponsorship activities?
  - Determining what projects will attract sponsorship?
  - Ensuring that all funds are accounted for?
  - Distributing funds?
  - Ensuring that the public interest is best served?
  - Acquitting sponsorship funds?
  - Reporting on the program to the board, members, and staff?
  - Handling inquiries from auditors, accountants, media, and the general public?
  - Determining UBIT implications?

Approvals and Contracts
- Who determines what benefits are available to potential sponsors?
- How is this determined?
- How often do you review your benefits list?
- Who can negotiate a sponsorship deal?

- Who can approve a sponsorship?
- What is the process for approving sponsorships?
- Who can sign final contracts?
- Will your organization use a letter of agreement or a contract?
- When will your organization consult a lawyer?

Review and Evaluation
- When and how often will this policy be reviewed?
- Who will be involved in the review process?
- How will the policy be reviewed?
- How will your organization communicate policy amendments to your stakeholders?

Sponsorship Strategy

Your sponsorship strategy is, very simply, the process that you will take to gain and retain sponsorship, and the attitude you take with every aspect of your sponsorship program.

The bulk of this book is about sponsorship strategy. When you finish the book and all of the exercises in it, you will have developed an approach—a personalized system that works for you. Document it—this is your sponsorship strategy.

CHAPTER 2

Marketing Plan

If you want to succeed in your quest for sponsorship funds and strong sponsor relationships, you must ensure that you have access to people with the relevant marketing skills, sufficient resources, a good strategic plan, a marketing plan, market research information, and a commitment to applying that market research.

Your organization must be able to demonstrate to potential sponsors that it can capture and retain its audiences. Your products and services must be based on genuine market needs and values as opposed to what your staff think your clients want or what your organization thinks its clients need.

As part of your organization's strategic planning process, you will need to create a marketing plan. This is not a plan for marketing the sponsorships but rather is a plan for marketing your organization and its events or products. In the case of an event or a property, every marketing plan must have a media plan and an evaluation plan to measure performance. Every marketing plan must be based on audience market research as it needs to reflect your audience profile, the number of people who will attend your event, and your ability to reach out and connect with your audiences. Developing your marketing plan will help you to determine what makes your organization valuable to sponsors.

This chapter will take you through a series of worksheets, many in a question and answer format, that will assist you in completing the marketing plan template found at the end of the chapter. Tip sheets and checklists are scattered throughout the worksheets to assist you in your planning. The result will be that you will be better placed to get more from your audience (more money, more participation, more heartshare) and create a far more valuable proposition for sponsors.

Every marketing plan will have its base in market research.

23

Defining Your Brand

Realistically,
no event will
appeal to
everyone.

In previous editions, we started this chapter with developing your target market profile. While that is still an absolutely essential part of getting your marketing plan right, we have realized that many of the difficulties organizations have with getting their marketing plans right—including their target market definitions—go straight back to how they define their brand.

Companies have brand managers, there are brand marketing agencies, and many a magazine and website are dedicated to the cult of "the brand." All of that makes it seem like brand development is terribly complicated and only for big corporations with a lot of money. Not so! Brand development isn't complicated at all, is within reach of even the smallest organizations, and can be the difference between financial success and failure.

Going through this process will benefit your organization in many ways:

- You will differentiate yourself from your competition on every level.
- Your marketing messages will be more specific and compelling.
- Your sponsor hit list will be more concise and effective.

Unfortunately, most sponsorship seekers tend to define who they are and what they do in very general terms, creating virtually no differentiation in how they present themselves, even when there may be some very important differences. What strong brand development boils down to is understanding, in very specific terms, what constitutes the personalities of your organization and your events. The easiest way we've found to do this is to create brand bullseyes for each of your "brands." There are a number of ways to do this, but we've developed a method that is effective and doesn't overcomplicate the process.

Creating a Brand Bullseye

Your organization is a brand, and so is each of your events. This process will need to be replicated for each of them, but for your first go at this, just pick one reasonably uncomplicated event to practice the skills. This is a directed brainstorming exercise, so it is much more effective if you do it in a group. Invite people from across your organization and, ideally, interested parties from outside, like your sponsors.

Before you start, rather than putting a lot of pressure on yourself, try to imagine this as a very straightforward process of describing the personality of your event or organization. It's that simple. In fact, if you find yourself struggling with this process, try practicing all of the steps below using your best friend or spouse as the subject first, and then move on to your event.

Step 1: Get Over Yourself

Accept that, as much as you'd like to think you do, you don't control your brand definition. Your audience does. Yes, we know, that's a bit of a hit to the ego, but it's true. Think about it this way: when the biggest bank in your country or region runs advertising that says they care about you, that they're with you in good times and bad, and that they want to make your life better, do you believe them? If you're like most people, the answer is probably no. So, what do you believe about that bank, and which is a more powerful brand definition—the one you've built based on your experience or the one they talk about in their advertising?

We hope there isn't that much of a disconnect between your brand as you see it and your brand as your audience sees it, but there are probably some aspects that you haven't really thought about that could create opportunities or obstacles for you and your marketing program.

Step 2: Create a Benchmark

Imagine someone has just left your event or otherwise finished an experience with your organization (such as making a donation, volunteering, becoming a member). What are the three things you would like them to think about that experience? Don't spend more than a couple of minutes on this and then set those three things aside for later review.

Step 3: Draw a Bullseye

On a whiteboard or piece of butcher's paper, draw a large bullseye that looks like Figure 2.1. It may look a little complicated, but taking it step-by-step, you should find this quite a simple process.

Step 4: The Outer Ring

On a brand bullseye, we work from the outside in. In our version, this outer circle is for perceptions—how people perceive your event or organization, whether they are involved in it or not. We want you to fill up this outer circle with perceptions. These perceptions may be good, bad, or ugly, accurate or untrue, complimentary or painful to admit. The point is, you want to capture it all.

> The first step in defining your brand is realizing that *you* don't define it.

Figure 2.1
Brand bullseye

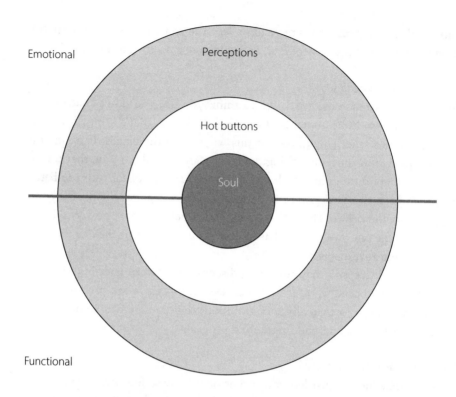

You will notice that there is a horizontal line cutting your bullseye in half. The upper part is for emotional aspects, the lower part is for functional aspects. Do your best to put every perception into the correct half of the bullseye, as this will assist with your analysis later. A few examples are below:

Functional	**Emotional**
Expensive	Elitist
Good entertainment	Inspiring
Family oriented	Quality family time
Boating	A dream/aspirational
International	Eye-opening
Disease	Depressing
Safe for kids	Peace of mind

You will notice that some of your functional aspects are also related to the emotional aspects, as with most that we've listed here. In some cases, you may even find an aspect that sits comfortably in both halves, like "inconvenient."

That's fine. You can put it on the line, write it twice, or indicate that it is in both with arrows—whatever works for you. The point here isn't that it's neat—in fact, the best bullseye brainstorms end up very messy!—but that what you capture is as complete and powerful as possible.

You also want it to be very specific. There are some aspects of your event that may well be true, but they aren't very useful. The end result of this exercise is that you will have a brand definition that really captures what your event or organization is all about, creating a strong differentiation from competitors. You will not achieve that if you allow yourself or your team to populate your bullseye with bland terms that could be used to describe hundreds or thousands of other events. Some examples are "fun," "community," "excellence/excellent," "entertaining," "family," and "exciting." Again, these may be true, but they aren't really that useful. It's like sending someone to the airport to pick up your brother and describing him as a male wearing blue jeans. It may be true, but it's not going to help that person locate your brother. And neither are generic terms going to get you to the most powerful and useful brand definition.

If your team is stuck in these generic terms, just keep asking questions until they get specific. For instance, if someone wants to put "fun" on the bullseye, that's fine, but be sure to ask the team for more detail. Ask, "What kind of fun?" "How do people feel when they are having fun at our event?" "How does our brand of fun differ from, say, going to a baseball game?" Keep drilling down and you will start to get much more powerful and specific perceptions.

Step 5: The Middle Ring

Once you've captured as many perceptions as you can in the outer ring, it's time to move in. The middle ring is for hot buttons—the aspects of your event or organization that actually motivated people to get involved, attend, buy a ticket, donate, volunteer, change their behavior (e.g., eat more vegetables or stop wasting water), or whatever you are trying to get them to do.

If you are struggling to understand the term "hot button," try this:

1. Think of the last time you went to an event (not one of your events!).
2. Why did you attend that event and not some other event? What was the experience you wanted to have? Write down as many reasons as you can in one minute.
3. Now, circle the absolute most important one or two—the ones that really led you to making that choice. Those were your hot buttons.

The fact that a charity is tax deductible makes it a reasonably financial decision to donate to anyone. But why do you choose to donate to the one(s) that you do? Again, those reasons are your hot buttons.

Many of these things will be the same or related to perceptions in the outer ring. Use arrows to "move" perceptions into the middle ring and write anything else that comes to mind. If you get stuck, pretend your team are a bunch of people who just attended, donated, or whatever you wanted them to do, and ask them why they did it. Those were their hot buttons.

Step 6: Take It All In

Before moving to the center, take a look at what you've accomplished. The bullseye you have just created will be invaluable in developing many aspects of your marketing plan, but it should be telling you a few things already:

- **Functional hot buttons are threshold needs.** The items that appear as functional hot buttons may be important, but they are probably not the primary reason someone got involved. For instance, your event may be safe, local, and have good parking—all important to parents of young children, and reasons for them not to go if you didn't have those things covered— but they are not compelling enough to have made them choose your event over going to another event, the park or some other safe, local, convenient activity.
- **The real motivations are emotional.** Once you have ticked all of the functional boxes (the threshold needs), people make decisions about their time and money for emotional reasons.
- **There is no one-size-fits-all marketing message.** People make their decisions to attend your event, donate, or whatever it is that you want them to do, for very different reasons. The message that works on one group won't even register a blip with another.
- **Part of your job as a marketer is to manage the negatives.** If there are negatives that are turning off key parts of your target audience, you need to determine if their perception is founded in reality. If the negative is a real problem with your event, you need to fix the problem and communicate that in your marketing messages ("Twice as much parking this year!"); if not, you need to address the misconception ("100 percent of funds raised benefit Canadian communities").

- **You can do an even better job creating a bullseye if you get feedback from your actual audience.** We're sure you've done a great job, and the bullseye you have created is probably miles ahead of your current brand understanding, but no one can tell you about their perceptions and motivations better than the audience itself. Resolve to spend a few hundred dollars (up to a couple thousand) for some focus group or interview research after your next event. Use the feedback to augment what you've already done and fine-tune it going forward.

Step 7: The Center

The center of your bullseye is where you define the soul, or the essence, of your event. The "soul" of your event will consist of a maximum of three aspects or concepts around your event that capture what it is about in powerful, specific wording. Now is not the time to fall back on generic terms like "fun" and "family." Imagine if you were trying to capture the essence of your very best friend using just three concepts, would you say "fun, smart, female"? Unlikely. We bet it would look more like, "irreverent, whip smart, fashion mad"—much more specific and much more powerful. That's your aim.

After all of the fast-paced brainstorming leading up to this point, there is a tendency to rush this part of the process, but we don't recommend it. If there is something that obviously needs to go in the center, by all means put it there. If you agree that a concept is 90 percent there, but not quite, put the concept in there with a question mark, so it operates as a placeholder while you mull it over. Even if they are all placeholders, put two or three concepts in the center and agree that you and your team will keep working on it.

Even if all you've got are placeholders, compare the bullseye to the three things you wrote down and put aside back in Step 2 of this process. We've found that there is usually a marked difference in the before and after. If not, you are more in touch with your brand essence than most.

As an example, have a look at the brand bullseye developed by New Zealand Fashion Week in a brainstorming session with their sponsors (Figure 2.2). As the focus of that event has shifted from an industry-only event to one that involves the fashion-loving public, their brand has also changed. What you will notice is that the bullseye takes into account a variety of perceptions, opinions, and hot buttons—some counter to each other—all contributing to a brand soul and an understanding of their target markets that is far deeper

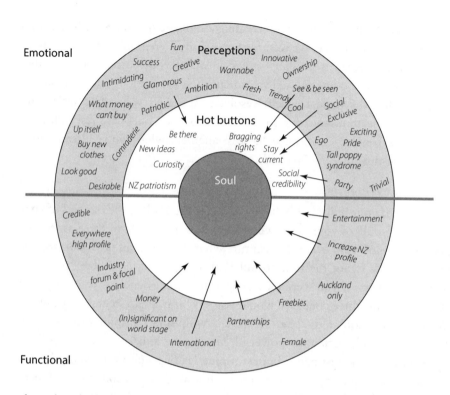

Figure 2.2
New Zealand Fashion
Week bullseye

than they had previously. For more about New Zealand Fashion Week, see www.nzfashionweek.com.

Step 8: Get More Input

Post the bullseye somewhere obvious and invite anyone in your organization or visiting your offices to add their thoughts. Do this for a week, and we're 99 percent sure your "soul" will have developed to a point where it really reflects what your organization does and who you are, powerfully and in a way that differentiates you from all or most of your competition.

Defining Your Target Markets

It is often a temptation to define your target market as a "general audience"— you *want* everyone to come to your event and you are sure that if they do they will enjoy themselves. You may even receive government funding or a grant that tells you that your event/organization or whatever has to serve the whole community.

Unfortunately, in a marketing sense, virtually no organization has the money or other resources to reach the entire marketplace effectively. The job, then, becomes how to determine and prioritize your target markets so that you maximize the effectiveness of your marketing program. Your target markets, sometimes called "segments," are determined by two general criteria:

1. **Demographics.** This is the hard data about a person or a marketplace, such as age, sex, marital status, whether they have children, where they live, income, and employment status, as well as more specific information, such as whether they own a computer, how old their car is, or how often they travel on business.

2. **Psychographics.** This is the softer data on your market and relates to why people do what they do, what motivates them to prefer one product to another, and lifestyle questions. Examples of words used to describe a marketplace psychographically include "active," "value-for-money oriented," "quality oriented," "feminist," "risk taker," "strong environmental responsibility," "macho," "saver" and "adrenalin junkie." Psychographics have clearly overtaken demographics as the most important factor in defining a target market.

A target market is a group of people with very similar demographic and psychographic profiles. You will probably have several target markets, some of which will be very different from each other. All of your target markets put together are called your audience. Try not to confuse these terms, as the distinction will become very important when it comes time to targeting potential sponsors.

There are also two types of target market.

1. **End users.** These are the people we normally consider as customers—the people who come to the event or venue, buy tickets, join, donate, or use your service. These people could also be exhibitors, in the case of an expo, show, or convention, or event participants, such as runners registering for a marathon. The target market exercise below will help you to prioritize these markets.

2. **Intermediary markets.** Intermediary markets are the organizations that the end user will go through or take the advice of in order to participate. These are many and varied but could include
    *   Ticket sellers

> Target markets must be defined both demographically and psychographically.

- Exhibition space sellers
- Venues
- Retailers (e.g., "get your entry form at Foot Locker")
- Convention and visitor bureaus
- Schools
- Reviewers
- Public transportation and/or parking facilities.

The importance of intermediary markets will vary from one event to another. If you have a large number of intermediary markets, it may be useful to prioritize them using the following target market exercise.

Target Market Assessment Worksheet

Using your brand bullseye as a starting point, look for related terms in the emotional perceptions and hot buttons and pull out three or four types of people who attend your event. As an example, people who attend the Melbourne Cup or the Kentucky Derby could be segmented by the following perceptions/motivations:

- **Segment 1**—See and be seen, ego, elite, bragging rights, "in" crowd
- **Segment 2**—Excuse to party, social, drinking, group bonding, pilgrimage
- **Segment 3**—Gambling, money, best races, best horses, winning
- **Segment 4**—Glamor, fashion, excuse to shop, competitive (fashion-wise)

Using your brand bullseye as a starting place, segment your audience using their primary motivation(s) as the main differentiating factor (not factors such as gender or age). You should complete an assessment worksheet for each group, whether they are end users or intermediary markets. Leave naming your target market segments until last.

What is the prime motivation for this segment to attend your event?

_____

_____

What else makes your event appealing to this segment? (Note: Oftentimes, something that is a primary motivation for one target market will be a secondary motivation for another. Don't worry if there is some crossover.)

_____

_____

_____

What proportion of your audience does this segment make up? (Estimate, if required.)

_____

_____

Is this segment growing or shrinking? What is its potential for growth?

_____

_____

Who will this segment attend with (if it is an event)?

_____

_____

Does this segment influence the attendance or participation of others? (For example, highly social, well-connected people who will encourage their friends to donate.)

_____

_____

Do geographic or logistical challenges affect the appeal of your event to this segment? Get specific.

_____

_____

What are the five things that have to go right in order for this segment to consider their experience to be a success? (Note: You do not necessarily have control over every one of these things.)

1. _____

2. _____

3. _____

4. _____

5. _____

Describe this segment as if it were one person. Be complete—name, job, family, lifestyle, etc. Don't make it just a list of attributes. Tell a story, such as the example in the box. The more fun you have with this, the better. Really let yourself get to know this person.

_____

_____

_____

_____

What media are likely to appeal to this segment—specific newspapers and sections, radio and television programs, specialty pay TV channels, magazines, websites, social media?

_____

_____

_____

_____

_____

What message(s) will this market be receptive to? (What will make them attend?)

_____

_____

_____

_____

Name this segment. Make it something that has meaning to you and something that you and your staff can use to refer to this segment.

_____

_____

Example: One-Person Description

Steven is a veterinarian in inner-suburban Manchester, specializing in small animals. He has an unassuming but successful practice and is known for the genuine affection he shows for the animals under his care, as well as for their concerned owners. He lives not far away with his partner, Donald, in a terminally half-renovated eighteenth-century cottage. He recently purchased a new VW four-wheel-drive—a compromise between the style he wanted and the practicality demanded of his work. He loves music, especially the crop of new blues and soul artists breathing new life into the genre, and mourned the passing of Amy Winehouse like an old friend. At 41, he looks after himself and has no plans to grow old gracefully. He's stylishly dressed, without being flashy—you'd have to look closely to notice that his watch is a Tag. Steven has a wide social circle and enjoys trying—and critiquing—new restaurants and bars. His Facebook and Instagram are brimming with his reviews, happy snaps taken while out with friends, and endless food photos. He and Donald love to travel and have seen most of Europe, but never during football season—Go Man U!—although he always worries about his patients when he's gone.

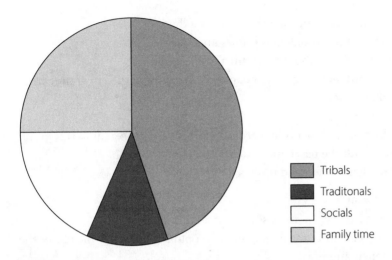

Figure 2.3
Target markets of
a football team

Once you have completed these questions and analyzed your customer markets in depth, including research, you should have a more complete understanding of your current and potential customers. There are a number of ways to segment a marketplace. Some organizations see clear divisions between segments, while others see a lot of overlap.

Following is an abbreviated sample of how a football team may segment and define its target markets (Figure 2.3). As you can see, the motivations and interests are very different from one segment to another. People don't experience your event in the same way or for the same reasons, nor can you effectively reach them all with the same marketing message or mechanisms.

Tribals—45 percent
- Motivated by atmosphere of the game
- Love being part of the crowd
- Very emotional about their experience
- Opportunities for participation are important, such as singing the team song
- If not at the game, prefer to view it in a crowd atmosphere, such as a pub
- Fickle—lose interest if the team doesn't perform
- Equally divided between males and females

Traditionals—10 percent
- Supporting the team is a family tradition passed down from one generation to the next

- See attending and/or viewing the game as a duty
- Support the team through good times and bad
- Know a lot of detail about the team and the game
- Skewed toward male and older people, often having shifted over time from being Tribal or Social
- Strong loyalty
- Acknowledgment of their long-term support is very important to this group
- Interaction with the team and coaches is a big hot button
- If not attending game, tend to watch at home

Socials—20 percent
- Use games as an excuse for a social day with friends
- Day starts well before the game, often at a pub, and finishes long after the game, often at a pub
- Logistics of meeting and getting from one place to another is the biggest concern
- Attend games in groups
- If not attending, watch games in groups, often at a pub
- See strong team performance as a bonus, not a requirement for a good day
- Skewed to people who are male and under 35

Family time—25 percent
- Quality time with family is the strong motivating factor
- Have school-age children
- Attend games with family only, or possibly with another family
- Watch games together at home
- Make an effort to make games a "special time" for the family
- The whole experience is important, no matter where they see the game
- Cost is important—they see a cost approximately equivalent to a family movie pass and associated concessions as being acceptable

> All of your target markets put together are called your "target audience."

Prioritizing Your Target Markets

We have found the following exercise useful in prioritizing the key target markets that make up your audience.

Step 1

Try to imagine that the entire marketplace is represented by the graph shown in Figure 2.4. You will see three things:

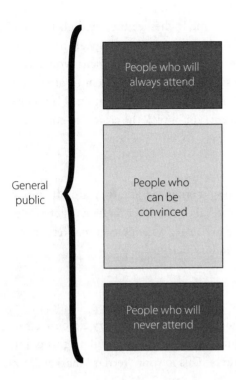

General
public

People who will
always attend

People who
can be
convinced

People who will
never attend

Figure 2.4
Who is your marketing
plan targeting?

1. There is a certain percentage of people who will always come to your event—they just need to know when and where it is and they will be there.
2. There is also a certain percentage of people who will never come, no matter what you do.
3. The people in the middle—the people who can be convinced—are your opportunity. They haven't made up their minds yet, so you can influence their decision. This is still a lot of people, though, so it needs to be assessed and prioritized.

Some of these people can be convinced relatively easily. It makes sense that it is most cost-effective to address your marketing activities to this group first. The less likely people are to come, the more difficult and expensive it will be to market to them. You may choose not to market to people who probably won't be convinced at all.

Step 2

Imagine that the "always" group is already at your event. In front of you is a ballroom full of people—100 people from each of the target market segments that you've defined—and they haven't decided whether they will go to your event or not. It will cost you $100 for the opportunity to speak to one of those target markets to convince them to attend. Which segment would you choose—the one where it will be easiest to convince all of them to attend or the one where you will be lucky to get 10 percent of them to attend? If you're trying to get the most people to your event, you'll pick the easiest to convince. That is your primary target market.

Step 3
Congratulations, the whole group has been convinced and they are off enjoying themselves at your event. Now you can talk to another target market group of 100, but it will cost you $200 for the privilege. Which target market would you choose this time? This is your "secondary market."

Step 4
Keep doing this until you reach a point where you either run out of money or you determine that your marketing efforts will probably be very expensive for the return in terms of participants (Figure 2.5). Usually, you will hit this point somewhere between three and five markets. This is your "tertiary market."

*Figure 2.5
Prioritizing your
markets based on
relative costs*

The goal is that, over time, your "always" group will grow by pulling in some of the people in your primary and secondary markets as they become what we call "true believers." This will allow you to invest in the tertiary markets, expanding your audience year by year.

Researching Your Target Markets

You need to know a lot about your audience in order to reach them effectively. The best way to gather that type of data is very simple—ask them. The benefits of conducting comprehensive research and truly understanding your markets are twofold.

1. **Marketing plan.** The research will give you not only an understanding of who your audience is but also of what motivates the different segments of it. This will enable you to create a marketing plan that will reach them effectively and at the lowest possible cost because you won't be paying to reach people who are not in your catchment groups.
2. **Targeting sponsors.** The most powerful things you can deliver to a sponsor are your audience and information about how they can connect to the various target markets. Thus, it follows that the better you know your audience, the stronger your understanding of your audience, the more valuable that sponsorship will be to a sponsor. This will help you to target your sponsors more effectively.

What Do You Need to Know?

When conducting research of your market you will need to ask a number of specific questions to obtain the type of information you will need to know. The questions you ask may relate to information from current customers and potential customers on any number of things.

We have divided this list into psychographic and demographic factors, which are both important for different reasons. Understanding a target market's psychographic profile is essential in knowing how to market to them—to convince them to do what you want them to do—and providing meaningful opportunities for sponsors to connect with them. Demographic factors are great for excluding markets. If you are trying to get people to have regular mammograms, it is unlikely that your target market will include men; if you're running a local festival, it's probably a waste of time marketing to people overseas or even in the next state; and if you're trying to sell tickets to a $1,500 a plate fundraising dinner, there is no use in targeting people who could never afford to pay that much.

Psychographic

- How would they describe themselves? (A valuable open-ended question best asked in qualitative research, but possibly using multiple choices on a survey.)
- Top three priorities in their lives? (Ditto above.)
- What do they do for recreation and/or hobbies?
- Do they donate or volunteer? How much and to whom?
- What are their travel and vacation preferences?
- Are they investors, savers, or spenders?
- Are they trendsetters/opinion leaders or followers?
- Are they active in social media? What are their main reasons? (E.g., staying in touch with far-flung friends and family, sharing their adventures, or staying in touch with the latest news, jokes, etc.)
- Are they fashion-conscious?
- Are they sports fans? Favorite teams?
- Are they involved in their community? How?
- Are they interested in gardening or do-it-yourself activities?
- Are they fit and healthy? Do they exercise?
- What is their interest in the arts?
- What is their attitude toward corporate sponsorship
- How would they describe your event to a friend or colleague?
- Why did they or didn't they attend your most recent event?

The last two are very important to understand a target market's specific perceptions and motivations concerning your event. Again, this is probably a quantitative question, but far too valuable not to ask.

Demographic

- Age and/or life stage (kids in school, grown-up kids, retired, etc.)
- Marital status
- Income
- Renter or homeowner
- Number and ages of children
- Occupation
- Education

- Car ownership—age of car, make, and model
- Location (often the easiest way is to get a postcode or zip code)
- Length of time at present address
- Internet use and type (dial-up, broadband, wireless)
- Mail order and online buying
- Television viewing preferences
- Club, organization, and affiliation memberships
- Public transportation use
- Purchasing habits
- Frequent flyer membership
- Pet ownership
- Political activity
- Movie- or theater-going habits
- Beverage preferences
- Food preferences

Remember that information on product usage, propensity to buy, and sponsorship attitudes may greatly assist your sponsorship sales process. If you can demonstrate that your customers actively seek out a sponsor's product, a potential sponsor is likely to be far more interested in you. If you approach a car manufacturer with research on the average age of your customers' cars, their car purchasing habits, and their attitudes toward the car manufacturer, your potential sponsor is far more likely to consider your proposal seriously.

Before conducting your research, you must understand that it will require an investment of time, money, or both, although newer web-based applications have reduced the cost for some kinds of research by quite a lot. Once you have decided what information you are seeking, be sure to create a strategy and budget to achieve your research goals.

Our Three Favorite Research Questions

Three of the most valuable questions you can ask are often the most overlooked:

- What were the three best things about your experience with [event/program] today?
- What were the three worst things about your experience with [event/program] today?
- What were the three main reasons you decided to attend/participate?

These questions will net you a ton of useful information. As they are qualitative, they are fantastic for helping you flesh out your brand bullseye. You could identify positives about the experience that may be great marketing hooks for you. You could identify issues that you weren't aware of. You can use the answers to help you build sponsor offers . . . but more on that later!

Primary Versus Secondary Research

So, how do you get all of that information about your target markets so that you can create the strongest possible marketing plan? There are two main sources—primary and secondary.

Primary information is research that you conduct (or commission) with your target markets. Secondary information comes from an outside resource— such as a tourism body, governing body, media, and industry research firms. Secondary information is aggregated from across a whole sector, so while it may have some general relevance, it isn't going to be nearly as useful as research that is specific to your property and your target market.

Also important to take on is that sponsors are looking for primary research. They don't need to know about all festivals in Oregon, they need to know about *your* festival, *your* target markets, and what that means to them. If you've got some compelling secondary figures, you can always include them, but they are support players only.

Types of Primary Information

As we stated earlier, if you want information about people in your target markets, ask them. Your potential audience is the best possible source for information about what will appeal to them and what kind of marketing will interest them enough to bring them to your event. This is primary information.

Primary information can be obtained by conducting: interviews with participants (such as runners in a 10K race), attendees, and potential attendees; surveys, including web-based and telephone surveys, entrance and exit surveys, target market perception surveys, and focus groups.

Target Market Surveys.   Target market surveys are done across your identified target market segments, whether they participate in your event or program or not. This is great for understanding perceptions and hot buttons alongside other key demographic and psychographic information.

If you want information about your target markets, ask them.

Entrance and Exit Surveys. Entrance and exit surveys are used to gather demographic and psychographic data, and other sponsorship-related data, as outlined earlier.

Focus Groups. Focus groups are a highly effective method for gaining qualitative information on target markets and they are really easy and inexpensive to do. They involve getting together a group of 10 to 18 people who are representative of your target audience and asking them a range of questions about their opinions, preferences, and lifestyles. This is a goldmine for information that will help you to develop your brand (and fill in your brand bullseye). If you do embark upon a program of focus groups, be sure to enlist an experienced moderator and preplan all questions to ensure you find out everything you need to know.

Interviews. Conducting a series of interviews with competitors, peers, industry specialists, and individual customers is a valuable way of gathering primary information on your markets that will assist in the development of your brand, your event, your overall marketing plan, and your sponsorship strategy.

How to Get Primary Information

A well-executed survey program need not be expensive. One of the cheapest ways to gather information is to utilize the services of a class at a business school, technical school, or university. As part of their studies, they need the opportunity to gather and analyze data, as well as presenting it, and you can provide that opportunity. The key here is not to treat them like research slaves but to work with them on both the methodology and reporting of results.

If you are going to use students, do make the commitment to rent tablet computers and software, allowing for easy collection, automated collation of data, and professionalism.

The cheapest way to get primary information is to use online survey sites, such as SurveyMonkey.com. You can fully customize a survey, and even make it a mix of multiple-choice (quantitative) and open-ended (qualitative) questions. The trick is always how you get people to participate. You'll often find that your more committed fans are happy to participate, while your less committed fans, or a target market that doesn't consider themselves fans yet, may need an incentive, such as a discount to your next event or other token, for their time.

The cheapest option for research is to use online survey tools, like Survey Monkey.com.

Audience Profile Questionnaire

Here is an example of a survey that could be carried out on people who have just attended a women's professional basketball game to determine the demographic and psychographic features of the audience market.

1. Is this your first visit to a women's professional basketball game?
- ❑ Yes
- ❑ No

2. How many games have you attended this season?
- ❑ This is my first
- ❑ 2–4
- ❑ 5–10
- ❑ More than 10

3. Where did you hear about tonight's game? Check all that apply:
- ❑ I have season tickets
- ❑ Friend or relative
- ❑ Radio ad
- ❑ TV ad
- ❑ Newspaper ad
- ❑ Internet
- ❑ Another sporting event
- ❑ TV or radio program or print article (please specify)
  - ❑ TV
  - ❑ Radio
  - ❑ Press
  - ❑ Magazine
- ❑ Other (please specify) _____

4. What did you think of the stadium? Check all that apply:
- ❑ Good visibility
- ❑ Comfortable
- ❑ Easy to get to
- ❑ Good food/drinks
- ❑ Too many sponsor signs
- ❑ Not enough food outlets or staff
- ❑ Parking difficult/expensive
- ❑ Public transportation difficult

❑ Food/drinks too expensive
❑ Food/drinks poor quality
❑ Adequate food outlets and staff

5. What are the top three reasons you decided to attend this game?

_____

_____

_____

6. What were the three best things about attending the game tonight?

_____

_____

_____

7. What were the three worst things about attending the game tonight?

_____

_____

_____

8. Did the game live up to your expectations?
❑ Yes
❑ Mostly
❑ No

9. If you could change one thing about your experience, what would it be?

_____

_____

_____

10. Including yourself, how many people are in your group today?
❑ 1
❑ 2
❑ 3–4
❑ 5–9
❑ 10 or more

11. Who are you here with?
❑ Family adult(s)
❑ Nonfamily adult(s)
❑ Child/children
❑ School group
❑ Other organized group

12. What is your post/zip code?

Questions 13–16 for Non-Tri-State residents only

13. How long are you staying in the Tri-State area?

14. Are you staying in paid accommodation?
- ❏ Yes
- ❏ No

15. What other activities have you done/do you plan to do during your stay?
- ❏ Attend another sporting event
- ❏ Football
- ❏ Baseball
- ❏ Ice hockey
- ❏ Other
- ❏ Attend a non-sporting event
- ❏ Basketball
- ❏ Visit a museum or gallery
- ❏ See a concert, play or show
- ❏ Sightseeing
- ❏ Shopping
- ❏ Other (please specify) _____

16. What are your three favorite ways of spending your free time?

_____

_____

_____

17. If you could use three words to describe yourself, what would they be?

_____

_____

_____

18. Are you in paid employment? What is your occupation?
- ❏ Yes
- ❏ No
- ❏ Occupation _____

19. How old are you?
- ❏ Under 18 years
- ❏ 18–24 years

    ❑ 25–34 years

    ❑ 35–49 years

    ❑ 50+ years

20. What is the highest level of school you have completed?

    ❑ High school

    ❑ Trade/technical or business college

    ❑ University degree (undergraduate)

    ❑ Advanced university degree

21. Which of these categories does your total annual household income fall into?

    ❑ Under $25,000

    ❑ $25,001–$40,000

    ❑ $40,001–$60,000

    ❑ $60,001–$80,000

    ❑ $80,001–$100,000

    ❑ Over $100,000

22. How likely are you to attend a women's professional basketball game again in the next 12 months?

    ❑ Very likely

    ❑ Somewhat likely

    ❑ Not very likely

    ❑ Not at all likely

    ❑ Do not know

Thank you for your help.

23. Record gender of respondent

    ❑ Female

    ❑ Male

Date of interview _____ I certify that this interview was conducted in accordance with briefing instructions and the Code of Professional Behavior, and that the information gathered is true and accurate.

Signed by interviewer:_____

Developing the Marketing Plan

Now that you understand who your audience is, it is time to create a plan that will bring them to your event, venue, organization, or service.

SWOT Analysis

SWOT stands for **Strengths**, **Weaknesses**, **Opportunities**, and **Threats**. The SWOT analysis is a tool that allows you to identify the internal and external issues that may impact on your ability to market your event or product.

Strengths and Weaknesses

In order to identify the strengths and weaknesses of your event or products, you must examine the issues *within* your organization that impact on your ability to sell your event or property to your target markets and to sponsors.

Strengths and weaknesses are generally issues within your organization's control.

An important area to explore is how your organization perceives the value of the event or product. If your organization sees your event as a priority and an opportunity to raise the profile of the organization, the event is considered a strength. However, if your board sees your event as a drain on resources, then the event is a weakness.

Exercise. Consider the following list of internal organizational factors and determine how these will affect the success of your event. For each factor, determine whether its effect is a strength or a weakness and place your specific factors under either the strengths or weaknesses headings in the **SWOT Analysis Worksheet** later in this section.

The internal factors that may influence your event include

Every weakness provides an opportunity.

- Staff attitudes and opinions
- Staff experience and expertise
- The organization's track record in staging and promoting similar events
- Booster clubs, membership programs, databases
- How your corporate plan and your corporate objectives impact on your event
- Key stakeholder analysis
- Resources—money, people, assets, facilities, volunteers
- Existing media profile
- Media partners

- New organizational initiatives
- Board and/or head office support
- Your location

Opportunities and Threats

The next step is to analyze all factors *outside* your organization that may affect your event. The external analysis will assist you in identifying the opportunities and threats related to your event. Once you have determined the threats to your event, you can reassess the situation and analyze how you can make these threats into opportunities.

For example, if you are holding an outdoor children's community festival, the following external factors may influence your event:

- Weather
- Major sporting finals on the same day
- Poor attendance at last year's event
- Fewer children in the relevant age group in your community

It is imperative that you address each threat to your event when conducting your planning to ensure the success of your event. Each threat can be further categorized into one of four types of threat to help you determine its importance to your event's success. Categorizing the threat determines how you will respond to the threat to minimize its effect.

1. **Monitor.** You may decide only to monitor some threats for which there is little that you can do to change or plan for, nevertheless you want to know what is happening. Examples might include any low-risk threats.
2. **Monitor and analyze.** You may decide to monitor and analyze threats that you can do little to reduce but you need to determine how they might impact on your event.
3. **Prepare contingency strategies.** You should prepare a contingency strategy for threats whose impact you can reduce with planning. For example, if bad weather is a threat to your outdoor event, you can determine how you will handle it—postpone the event, move to an indoor facility, or take out insurance.
4. **Prepare in-depth analysis and strategy development.** You will want to prepare an in-depth analysis and strategy development for those threats that

Generally, threats are beyond the control of your organization. You can anticipate and even plan for them, but there is little you can actually do to stop them happening.

have the greatest likelihood of impacting on your event. Technological, competitor, and legislative factors are examples of threats that may require more detailed analysis and strategy development.

Exercise. Look at the following list of external factors that may influence your event and consider how these offer opportunities and threats to your event. Place your specific factors under either the opportunities or threats headings in the **SWOT Analysis Worksheet** later in this section. Keep in mind that threats can often be turned into opportunities.

The external factors that may affect your event may be:

- Political
- Competitor related
- Environmental
- Customer perception related
- Geographic
- Economic
- Demographic
- Consumer confidence related
- Historical
- Technological
- Industrial
- Legal
- International
- Natural
- Local

Look at the list of threats you have compiled in the **SWOT Analysis Worksheet.** Determine which of these threats require your attention. What do you need to do in order to maximize or minimize the effects of each factor?

SWOT Analysis Worksheet

Strengths

_____

_____

_____

_____

_____

_____

Weaknesses

_____

_____

_____

_____

_____

_____

Opportunities

_____

_____

_____

_____

Threats

_____

_____

_____

_____

You are competing for your audience with anything they could do with their leisure time, money, and care.

Competitor Analysis

As with any company, you have competitors. It used to be that events only really competed for their audience against other events, but as more leisure options have come into play and leisure time has become more limited, this is no longer the case. In fact, you are competing against anything that potential customers could do with their leisure time and money.

Competitor Analysis Worksheet

Use the following worksheet to analyze your competition.

1. Who are my direct competitors (similar events or organizations)?

_____

_____

2. Who are my indirect competitors (other activities or events that are compelling to your audience)?

_____

_____

3. What do my potential and existing customers like about my competitors' events, products, and services?

_____

_____

4. How much are customers paying for my competitors' events, products, or services?

_____

_____

5. What makes my competitors successful and why? What are they doing right?

_____

_____

6. How do my competitors communicate with their customers?

_____

_____

7. How do my competitors position their events, products, and services within the market?

_____

_____

8. Who are my least successful competitors and why? What are they doing wrong?

_____

_____

9. What are my competitors' major strengths and weaknesses?

_____

_____

10. Are my competitors implementing any changes to their fees, products, marketing programs, or operations?

_____

_____

11. Who are my potential competitors in the short and long term?

_____

_____

12. How does my product or service differ from my competitors' events, products, and services? This is your unique selling point! A great way to find it is to do a quick competitor footprint.

_____

_____

_____

Competitor Footprint

Create a Venn diagram with your organization and your two biggest competitors (you can add other competitors later) showing attributes you share and those you don't. We recommend that you use butcher's paper—you need some space—and work in a group setting. You already have most of the content for this—just pull the information straight off of your brand bullseye to start.

What this process will show is whether you are marketing yourself in ways that you share with your competitors, or whether you are (or could be) marketing yourself based on your unique selling points (Figure 2.6).

Marketing Strategies

Now that you have completed your SWOT analysis and you know who your competition is, it's time to plan your marketing strategy.

In order to ensure your marketing strategy remains on track, you need to include the following information:

- Objectives

Figure 2.6
Competitor footprint

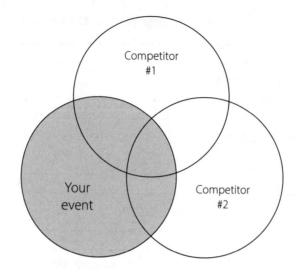

Remember
to keep your
objectives
SMART—
Specific,
Measurable,
Achievable,
Results
oriented, and
Time bound.

- Rationale for each objective
- Strategies for achieving each objective
- Measurement mechanisms to determine the outcome of each objective

Objectives
Your objectives indicate what you want to achieve. They should be SMART objectives:

- **Specific**
- **Measurable**
- **Achievable**
- **Results oriented**
- **Time bound**

For example, if your stated objective is to obtain media coverage of your event, you have not been specific enough. Try, instead, "to obtain a major article in *The Daily Express* and two major news stories on Channel 8 News and Radio Station 9CN by the second week of the festival."

Rationale
The rationale must be a brief statement outlining why a particular objective or strategy has been chosen.

Strategies

Strategies indicate how you will meet an objective. Strategies are the specific actions that will be undertaken to achieve a desired outcome.

Measurement Mechanisms

Measurement mechanisms are ways in which you will determine whether you have achieved your objectives and your audience's critical success factors. Measurement mechanisms may include, but are not limited to:

- Sales figures (tickets, donations, memberships, etc.)
- Sales growth
- Propensity to buy or preference
- Customer intent to return to the next event
- Advance ticket sales
- Wholesale ticket sales
- Group bookings
- Quality of media coverage
- Number of attendees
- Fan opinion and satisfaction
- Social media activity (shares, views, retweets, comments)
- Social media followers
- Sponsorship sales (new, renewals)

Sample

Objective

To obtain a major article with a color photo in *The Daily Express*, as well as two major news stories on Channel 8 News and Radio Station 9CN during the second week of the festival.

Rationale

This will achieve an 80 percent market penetration in our target markets and will give an added boost to ticket sales beyond the opening week rush.

Strategies

- Create a media kit for distribution to local media representatives.
- Create media interview opportunities with celebrity festival guests.
- Provide DVDs of last year's event and highlights of the first week to local television stations for ease of coverage.

Measurement Mechanism

- Quality and acceptance of media kit
- Number of media interviews
- Number of broadcasts that utilize video material

- New sponsor enquiries
- Database growth
- Database activity
- Profit or revenue
- Number and quality of cross-promotions

Resources

All plans require resources. The resources required to implement your plan might include information, time, advertising expertise, graphic design skills, media talent, equipment, office space, and staff, as well as funds. In many cases, your marketing and promotional plans will be designed with a specific budget in mind.

Ask yourself the following questions to ensure you have addressed all your resource requirements.

1. What resources do you need to implement the marketing strategies? Sponsors can often provide nonmonetary resources to a project. These should be clearly identified in your marketing plan.
2. How much funding do you require for these items? Include the number of hours, space required, training, and administration support when budgeting for resources. Some examples include
   - Staff time (include overtime)
   - Advertising
   - Equipment
   - Office space
   - Maintenance and storage
   - Printing
   - Distribution
   - Volunteer costs
   - Travel
3. What sources of information, data, knowledge, and research do you need?

Develop an Action List

Having a plan does not mean anything unless you put it into action. These points are designed to enable you to create a master timeline and action list for your marketing plan.

1. Phase the strategies and timeline for each and every strategy. Ensure that each strategy has specific start and stop dates.
2. Identify who will be responsible for each step of every strategy.
3. Determine how each strategy will be evaluated, measured, and reported. Identify who will be responsible for these tasks. Schedule all evaluations, approvals, meetings, and reports into your master timeline and action list.

Remember to consider reports, in-house experience, surveys, and consultant studies that already exist within your organization. No one needs to reinvent the wheel.

Marketing Plan Template

This template can be used to develop your own marketing plan. In the worksheets in this chapter you have been asked key questions and should have answered them comprehensively. If you haven't, go back to these worksheets and your research and do so now. Summarize and transfer this information by answering the questions in this template to develop your marketing plan.

Background
Why are we preparing this document? What do we want this document to achieve?

Target Audiences
Who are we trying to reach? What do we know about them?

Critical Success Factors
What are the key things we need to achieve in order for this plan to be a success?

Market Research
What are our strategies based on? (Summarize your research in bullet points.)

Internal Analysis
What within my organization can affect this plan, both positively and negatively?

Environmental Analysis
What factors in my environment can affect my purpose? What changes must we plan for? (State the assumptions you are making about the future.)

Competitor Analysis
Who are our competitors?

Marketing SWOT Analysis
What factors are hindering or restraining our purpose? What environmental factors are driving or assisting our purpose? (List here your strengths, weaknesses, opportunities, and threats.)

Marketing Objectives
Where do we want to go?

Marketing Strategies
How are we going to get there? (Put these in bullet points underneath your objectives; follow the "Sample" earlier in this section.)

Evaluation
How will we know that we have achieved our objective? (Indicate how you will evaluate, measure, and report against your key quantification mechanisms.)

Master Timetable and Action List
When will we get there? (Complete the following table to assist you in your planning.)

Strategy	Time frame	Action officer
Objective 1: (provide details)		
Strategy 1 detail	Start and completion date	Person responsible
Strategy 2 detail	Start and completion date	Person responsible
Strategy 3 detail	Start and completion date	Person responsible
Objective 2: (provide details)		
Strategy 1 detail	Start and completion date	Person responsible
Strategy 2 detail	Start and completion date	Person responsible
Strategy 3 detail	Start and completion date	Person responsible

Resources

How much is it going to cost us to get there? How much time? What other resources do we need?

Review and Continually Reassess the Marketing Plan

Now that your plan is complete, you need to look back on it to double-check that you have covered all of the key aspects. Consider the following questions as you review your marketing plan. Do you have a clear vision of what the completed marketing campaign will look like? Have you identified the critical success factors and measurement mechanisms? Have you identified the key elements that need to be organized within your master timetable and action plan? Have you clearly identified all resources, including financial, human, and training, that need to be planned for? Do you have a contingency strategy if parts of the plan don't work? Have you addressed all possible threats to your plan and event? Have you identified internal communication strategies within your plan? How will you report on progress to staff, members, and your Board?

A marketing plan is a living document. Ensure that you have scheduled review periods into your plan so that you can fine-tune your plan throughout the implementation phase.

Calculating Overhead

When calculating your staff costs, you need to take into account your additional overhead. Adding these to the salary or hourly rate will give you the "real cost" of employment.

You have two choices for calculating these costs. One is to calculate actual costs for all overheads (rent, equipment, utilities, insurance, etc.) and divide these by the number of staff and their hours. This is very time consuming and generally unnecessary.

The other option is to use a standard multiplier on salary or hourly rates. Most companies that approach real costs of employment this way use a multiplier between 1.4 and 2.6. In our example, we have used 1.9, meaning that if an activity will take an employee paid $10 per hour 100 hours to complete, the real cost of those hours will be $1,900.

CHAPTER 3

Implementing the Marketing Plan

You have written your marketing plan, and it's looking good. Now we need to make that plan work for you.

Although there may be a number of other aspects to implementing your marketing plan, the most common components are

- Media promotion
- Online promotion
- Publicity
- Database/loyalty marketing
- Signage

We have included information about each of these components.

Media Promotion

Although you can go out and simply purchase media, like any other company, this is not all that common, primarily because it ignores the fact that you have a lot to offer a potential media partner. Instead, most sponsees embark upon media promotion to achieve their objectives without spending a fortune.

Generally, media promotions are created with one or more media partners. You provide them with co-ownership of the promotion and either a paid schedule or sponsorship of your event (and all ensuing benefits), and they provide several times that investment in media value. This can be an extremely cost-effective way for you to get your message out into the marketplace.

Who Should Create the Promotion?

Generally speaking, the sponsee is much more likely to achieve its goals if it is intrinsically involved in creating the promotion. See "The Ten Steps of Promotional Media" in the next section for some hints.

Do You Go to One or More Media Outlets?

If you have determined that you can achieve your objectives with either of two competing media outlets, our suggestion is that you brief them both on the promotion and ask them both to come back to you with a package that meets the brief.

If you have determined that there is only one media outlet that will suit your needs perfectly, you should negotiate closely with them to create a partnership. Do not let them hold you to ransom—you can always walk away and rethink your approach for a different type of media.

How Much Value Should You Get?

If your proposal is structured correctly (see "The Ten Steps of Promotional Media" in the next section), you should be receiving substantially more value from the media partner than the funds you invest. This is usually expressed as a value-to-cost ratio.

The table below outlines some value-to-cost ratios and what that value includes.

Media	Target value-to-cost ratio	Value Includes
Television	3:1 to 8:1	Paid spots
		Bonus spots (confirmed)
		Bonus spots (space available)
		Promotional spots (co-branded by the television station)
		News coverage
		Other editorial coverage (lifestyle, sporting, or news magazine programs)
		Website, app, and/or social media promotion
		Advertising production
		Use of on-air personality for endorsement, appearances, voice-overs, or as a spokesperson

Media	Target value-to-cost ratio	Value Includes
Radio	3:1 to 10:1	Paid spots
		Bonus spots (confirmed)
		Bonus spots (space available)
		Prerecorded promotional spots (co-branded by the television station)
		Live promotional spots
		Live liners (very short promotional spots)
		News coverage
		On-air interviews
		Remote broadcasts
		Website, app, and/or social media promotion
		Advertising production
		Use of on-air personality for endorsement, appearances, voice-overs, or as a spokesperson
Newspaper	3:1 to 8:1	Paid advertising
		Bonus advertising (confirmed)
		Bonus advertising (space available)
		Insertion of program, poster, or other promotional material that you supply
		Website, app, and/or social media promotion
		Printing and/or design of program or poster
		Special supplement (can often be used as the official program)
		Advertorial coverage
Magazine	2:1 to 5:1	Paid advertising
		Bonus advertising (confirmed)
		Bonus advertising (space available)
		Special section
		Insertion of program, poster, or other promotional material
		Advertorial coverage
		Website, app, and/or social media promotion
Outdoor	2:1	Paid advertising
		Bonus advertising

Is There Any Downside to Media Promotions?

Sometimes there can be a downside to media promotions. If you work with, say, one radio station, it will provide much greater value for your investment if you agree not to work with any other radio stations. But this could severely limit the number of people in your target market that you can reach. In that case, you have two choices:

1. Offer paid and promotional exclusivity to the one radio station and get maximum value from it. Use other types of media to increase your reach.
2. Offer promotional exclusivity but not sales exclusivity, explaining that in order to achieve your objectives you need greater numbers than it can deliver alone. You will probably get less value from it as a result.

The Ten Steps of Promotional Media

Buying promotional media is very much the same as any other kind of marketing transaction. It is part science, part street smart, part creative, and a lot of common sense. Here are nine easy steps to make the task easier.

1. Set Your Objectives for Media

Establish your specific goals. What are you trying to do? Are you promoting an event, selling tickets, or building up your profile? Know what you want to accomplish, who you want to communicate with, and how much you have to spend before you begin the media buying process.

2. Target Your Media Correctly

As with above-the-line media, the key to success is to choose the media partner(s) that will deliver the largest portion of your target market for the least amount of money. For instance, the number one radio station may deliver you 115,000 listeners in your target market, but you will pay to reach their total audience, which may be many times your core market.

On the other hand, if you select a lower rating radio station, magazine, or television program where their core market is your core market, the likelihood is that:

- You will spend less money to reach more of your core audience with less media coverage waste.
- Their listeners/readers/viewers will be more receptive to your marketing message.

3. Understand Why Media Run Promotions

Competition within the media for the attention of consumers is increasing exponentially, and the fact is that most media are virtually interchangeable in terms of content.

In addition to making a sale to you, most media groups want one or more of the following things from a media promotional opportunity: to create a point-of-difference from their competition through the creative use of promotions. This will attract more listeners/viewers/readers and make them more attractive for regular advertisers. Creative is the key word here—if it looks or sounds like every other enter-to-win promotion in the marketplace, it isn't worth anything in a media negotiation to increase the profile of their shows, personalities, stars, etc. or to create new advertising vehicles. An example would be a newspaper creating the official program for your event in exchange for the right to sell advertising in it.

4. Create a Proposal That Helps Them to Achieve That Goal

In order to maximize the media value you achieve for your investment, it is imperative that you go to your target media with a plan that will achieve your objectives and will create a strong point-of-difference for them and assist them with attracting their audience. Do not fall into the trap of thinking that your promotional spend is their driving force, because it is not.

5. The More Creative the Better

Think outside the square, push the envelope, think laterally—whatever you call it, it is about thinking creatively.

Make your proposal relevant to the audience—really think about what this audience is interested in and what they want, and then give them that and more.

Ensure your proposal really is creative. Sure, everyone wants a vacation, but open up any magazine and you can enter five different contests to win a holiday at a beach resort and, with discount travel packages in every newspaper, most people know that it is not that great a deal. Be sure that what you offer is special—go to the extra effort to make this something that they could not do without you.

6. Involve Your Advertising Agency

This is really your call, but we strongly suggest that you utilize the creative resources of your advertising agency to ensure that what you propose to your target media is fully developed and creatively executed.

7. Negotiate for Control of Scheduling

Negotiate for time slots in programs that consistently deliver ratings and the demographics you are seeking. Bargain for newspaper and magazine placements in sections that have proven circulation and the readership demographics you need.

Many media sponsorships provide advertising time at the discretion of the station. This is of absolutely no value to you. If you can't match the demographics of your audience with programs and publications that deliver to these groups, the sponsorship is of little value to you or other sponsors.

8. Never Pay More than Your Volume Rate

There are some media groups that will tell you that, since they are giving away a lot of unpaid promotion, the buy must be made at casual or "rack" rates, even if you are a regular advertiser who normally gets a discount. This is a lot of rubbish.

Media Lingo

Although some of this terminology is specifically about television, most of the terms can be applied to other media (e.g., print, radio) as well.

Rating A measure (expressed as a percentage) of viewers watching TV within a specific demographic.

Target Audience Rating Point (TARP) A measure of audience level at a given time on TV. This is expressed as a percentage of the potential audience available of a given demographic.

Example: If there are 1 million adults aged 25 to 39 in your market and 250,000 of them see your advertisement, then you have reached 25 percent of the potential audience and the spot would have a TARP of 25.

Gross Rating Point (GRP) This is a summary of all TARPs on a TV schedule and can also be referred to as total TARPs. Often, your media plan may state that you will purchase,

for example, 250 TARPs per week. This figure is an expression of GRPs and will comprise a number of separate advertising spots.

Audience Share This is often quoted by TV networks to express the percentage of people using television that watched the particular program or event. Remember—it only refers to percentage of those watching any TV and not potential of a demographic. You can have a TARP that is different from the share figure.

Reach/Coverage The percentage of total potential audience reached over a given period of time.

Frequency This refers to how many times the people see the advertisement. Frequency is often measured in "bands." These numbers will often be quoted as being 1+, 2+, or 3+, which refers to people who have "been reached" one or more times, two or more times, or three or more times.

If you structure your promotional offer correctly, you are actually doing them a favor—you are helping them to create a strong point of difference and paying their costs to do it. You should never pay more than the rate negotiated by you or your media buyer for the paid portion of the deal.

9. Keep Your Ear to the Ground

Make time to meet and network with people in the media industry. These people are approachable. Learn the lingo, read industry publications, and speak to your contacts to find out about the media buying process. If there is a media campaign that you feel has been particularly successful or innovative, contact the organization and arrange to discuss the campaign with the relevant people.

Keep your ear to the ground on how radio, television, and newspapers are performing. Listen to the radio and keep an eye out for industry trends, new programs, and industry developments. Become an active media watcher.

10. A Little Cash Goes a Long Way

If you are trying to secure a media partner on a strictly contra basis—they provide media value, you provide sponsorship benefits—you will usually be working with a promotions manager. The problem with that is that most promotions managers have little influence in the organization. They only have a certain amount and type of media inventory to work with, and it's often not that high quality.

Rather than hoping the promotions manager will be able to work a miracle and get you exactly what you need, it's a much better idea to have a small cash budget. As soon as you bring money to the negotiation—even if it's just a very modest amount—you are no longer working with the promotions manager, but the sales manager, and the sales manager has a lot of clout and flexibility.

Online Marketing

Within this section, we are addressing a while range of web-based marketing options. Please keep in mind that what is available—and even possible—is increasing all the time, so take this section as a guide only. Although the mindset we recommend is likely to be relevant for a number of years to come, as new tech becomes available, assess it to see if it will meet your needs and ensure your approach is consistent throughout.

Social Media

Facebook, LinkedIn, Twitter, Google+, Tumblr, YouTube, Reddit . . . it feels like a new social media site is launched every day. Social media has revolutionized our lives, providing new ways for people to connect and use word of mouth to promote everything from events to causes to campaigns to products. It's this advocacy that makes social media one of the most powerful and cost-effective ways that you can market yourself.

To be successful in social media, you first need to understand its power. Social media puts the control into the hands of the users. While losing some control over your content, the two-way and infinitely shareable nature of social media means that if what you're doing is worth talking about, they'll talk about it to hundreds and thousands and sometimes millions of people.

More than that, you can involve your sponsors, allowing them the privilege of accessing and connecting with your passionate fans.

The two most important factors in successful social media marketing are having relevant, shareable content and using an authentic voice.

Shareable Content

The main drawcard for properties to use social media is that the message can spread exponentially through sharing and participation. But that doesn't happen just because you post it; you have to either create something that is worth their interest or allow them to create relevant content and share it with you.

If what you need is to get word out about your event or season ticket sales or an exhibition, don't just hammer people with that message. They will feel like their trust has been abused and stop engaging with you. Instead, decide on a target ratio for messages and content you generate. For instance, you could post four items that are interesting (useful, funny, how-to, behind the scenes, etc.) for every call-to-action, and you won't do a call-to-action post more than once every couple of days on each of your social media pages. You've probably got tons of content to share—do that, build trust, and people will be much more receptive to your calls-to-action.

If this advice is true for you, it's doubly true for your sponsors. Straight promotion of your sponsors in social media just looks like an ad that you were paid to place, and your audience will tune out. Instead, encourage your sponsors to come up with some great leverage ideas (more on that later) with a strong social, real-time, social media component. If their ideas are creative

Don't overdo your social media calls-to-action. You'll lose your audience.

and participatory and social, they will look right at home alongside your social media activity.

Authentic Voice

In social media, it is imperative to speak with the voice of a human—a fellow fan—not an organization. It's the difference between:

> "Monster Truck Madness tickets on sale now—Johannesburg, Durban, Cape Town."

> *And*

> "Mud? You want mud?! We've got the biggest mud pit ever seen in the Southern Hemisphere! Guess how many liters—closest gets a pair of weekend passes and behind-the-scenes tour! 20 minutes—go!"

Yes, you have to have details about what you're doing, but you can put that in the main image of your Facebook page, in the background of your Twitter page, and reference getting all of the details with a link—still maintaining an authentic voice.

You want to sound as excited and passionate about what you're doing as the fans are. You want to give them insider or behind-the-scenes information that they're hungry for—and do it with enthusiasm. You don't want to be unprofessional, but being professional doesn't mean passionless!

What Can Social Media Accomplish?

Social media is a marketing jack-of-many-trades. Used well, it can

- Drive interest
- Drive intent and/or preference
- Sell tickets
- Sell merchandise
- Garner donations or volunteers
- Drive people to participate in research
- Get fan feedback
- Drive fan advocacy
- Extend your sponsors' leverage activities
- And so much more!

Social media is no longer a nice "extra" within your marketing plan but an essential component that your sponsors and audiences expect you to have well developed.

Going Viral

The real brass ring is if you can get your social media activities to "go viral"—that is, to spread from person to person, expanding their impact exponentially, like a virus.

If that's the goal, you can achieve it in a number of ways:

- Be funny, outrageous, or surprising—go out on a limb with a video, spoof something familiar (and do it well), create a social media app or meme that will capture people's attention.
- Offer insights or context that creates relevance to individuals that they may not have understood. This is particularly effective for causes, which can often suffer from an understanding and/or relevance gap with potential donors.
- Crowdsource content—ask people to submit ideas, videos, photos, solutions to a problem, or whatever. They'll share it. You can share the best.
- Ask your celebrity or athlete spokespeople to forward and promote your content to their followers.
- Simply ask people to spread the word. If your content is compelling, just ask for the retweet or for people to share on Facebook or other platforms.
- Ask your sponsors to share select content with their followers.

Case Studies: Going Viral

To highlight the importance of, and need for, clean water and toilets in the developing world, the cofounder of Water.org made a call to action. Matt Damon called a press conference to go on strike—not using the toilet until everyone in the world had access to clean water and a toilet. See the press conference and more on www.strikewithme .org, a site encouraging others to "strike" . . . at least in spirit.

Nickelodeon Australia partnered with Kids Help Line to create the Dare to be Square initiative. Australian superstar Guy Sebastian wrote the song and invited kids across Australia to submit videos of themselves singing the chorus. Many of those videos were incorporated into his performance of the song at the Nickelodeon Slimefest, and the video was made available on YouTube. See more at www.daretobesquare.com.au.

Your Website

We are assuming that your organization or event already has a website. If not, you really need to set one up. The web is now a major, and for some, the primary, tool for gathering information on topics of interest, events, causes, and more. If you're not online, you're not in the game. In addition, your online presence, and how it is presented, says a lot to sponsors about your professionalism.

At a minimum, your website should feature the following:

- What the event or organization is and what it's about.
- Location.
- Dates and times.
- Pricing.
- Transportation and parking information.
- Schedule of events (if applicable).
- Special offers.
- Sponsor recognition (at minimum, logos linked to their sites).
- Logos of all endorsing bodies (linked to their sites).
- Key marketing messages—tell visitors how this event relates to them. Push those hot buttons!
- Links to connect/follow/like you in social media.
- Share buttons, so it's easy for people to share your site content with their own networks.

How you feature all of this is very important, and although we make no claim to being website gurus, we do have a few suggestions:

- Get the website professionally designed and built. A good web designer will know where to put the most important information, how to make it user friendly, and will be able to make the whole thing reflect your image. This doesn't have to be expensive. You can use resources like Elance.com, Odesk.com, Guru.com, or Crowdspring.com to get strong design for a very fair price.
- It doesn't have to be huge—a credible-looking 4- to 5-page site with the right information is better than 20 pages of fluff.
- It also doesn't have to be flashy (literally). Flash animations have fallen well out of favor, along with music and other purely cosmetic additions to an otherwise useful website.

- If there is content that would be useful for people to have around or bring with them to your event, such as an event map or schedule of activities, either provide a printer-friendly version or create a downloadable PDF.
- Give away information—a great way to get people to welcome contact from you is to ensure you are giving them useful information, such as how-tos, checklists, articles, and white papers, and more.
- Start a blog. If you can commit to blogging once every couple of weeks (at least), or hire someone who can, a blog is a great way to ensure your site has fresh, topical, shareable content.

Other Websites

Be sure to get your event or program listed on complementary websites. These will vary greatly from one property to another, but here are a few suggestions:

- Convention and visitors bureau schedule of events
- Convention and visitors bureau listing of local cultural and/or sporting organizations
- City council schedule of events
- Governing body schedule of events (e.g., if it is a golf event, ensure that your state and national endorsing golf bodies list your event on their calendar), newspaper "what's on" sites (some radio and television stations have this type of listing on their sites, too!)
- Related directories (e.g., listings of causes serving your geographic area)
- Your sponsors' websites
- Sites specific to your target market (e.g., gamers, football fans, retirees)

Apps

Unless you've been living under a rock, you are familiar with the idea of apps. There are apps for smartphones, apps for Facebook, apps for computer operating systems, and more types coming all the time.

In our world, how apps are delivered is less important than how meaningful they are to the experience around your event or program. There are three main types of apps: helpful, amplifying, and games.

Helpful Apps

As the heading implies, these apps are about getting helpful information into the hands (literally) of people who need it, and they're a great way to make whatever it is that you do even more relevant and accessible to your target markets. Whether it's an interactive event or exhibition information, a festival map, team stats, artist profiles, workout plans, or other how-to skills relating to what you do, they can be wrapped into an app.

Amplifying Apps

These apps are about amplifying and personalizing the fan experience. You can give fans a platform for sharing their love for your team or allow culture buffs to re-create their social media avatars in the style of great painters from a blockbuster exhibition.

Games Apps

Gamification—enhancing and augmenting the fan experience through social gaming—is a huge trend for events and other properties. It deepens your bonds with your target markets by making them feel like participants, not spectators.

Search Engines

The fact that google is now officially a verb should tell you how important search engine positioning is. Again, we're not experts, but here are some suggestions.

- Double-check to see that your site is indexed on Google, Yahoo!, and DMOZ. (Dmoz.org is the indexer behind hundreds of smaller search engines.) If it's not, follow the instructions and submit your site.
- Get a business Google+ page and share content from your website and/or blog. This has been shown to increase your Google search ranking.

> Gamification is a big trend . . . and yes, that is a word.

Examples

Following in the footsteps of fantasy football and baseball, **NASCAR** has launched NASCAR Fantasy Live on their website, allowing people to pick drivers and amass points live during a race, augmenting the viewing experience of fans who aren't in attendance: http://fantasygames.nascar.com/live.

Same idea, totally different execution. SPARX is a game initiated by the **New** **Zealand Ministry of Health** and the **University of Auckland**. This role-playing game's mission is to provide insight, advice, and cognitive behavior therapy to young people dealing with depression. By taking this angle, they avoid the sometimes confronting aspects of seeking help: www.youtube.com/watch?v=wgocT0YyV8M.

- Up your positioning—if you get your event listed and include a link to your home page on a number of complementary websites, you are far more likely to come up higher in a search engine results list.
- Consider search engine advertising—products like Google's AdWords allow you to pay for advertising alongside searches for keywords you specify. If you specify "cancer research," then whenever someone searches for that topic, your ad will come up. You can target specific geographic regions and only run the ad during certain time frames or times of day. It works on a pay-per-click basis and is a science unto itself, but it gets easier pretty quickly.

If all of this is starting to sound like gobbledygook, don't despair. Every half-decent website in cyberspace has gone through the same thing. There are plenty of good books available, including "For Dummies" books on search engine optimization and AdWords, and there are lots of online tutorials. That's how we did it!

Emails

Email marketing can be very powerful, or it can be perceived as very annoying. It is, basically, database marketing, but the immediacy and personal contact has its own benefits.

If you want to get into email marketing and have absolutely no experience, you will probably want to find yourself an expert to develop the strategy and help you build your list. Whether you are currently doing email marketing or not, we have a few suggestions:

- Send a regular newsletter. Make it a mix of useful information—links to pertinent blogs, white papers, advice—and promotion of your event or program.
- Focus on the customer. When you are trying to market something (sell tickets, increase donations, etc.), talk about the specific benefit to the customer. Email is personal. Keep the message personal, as well.
- Segment your list—categorize the people on your list based on various factors so you don't send every communication to every person. If you've got a community event in Texas, they don't need to hear about it in Connecticut. If you are selling tickets to a $1,000-a-plate dinner, your $15 one-off donors probably don't want to know about it.
- Don't spam. If the people on your list haven't asked to be on your list, it is unethical and, in many jurisdictions, illegal to send unsolicited bulk mail

messages to them. Plus, it will give you really bad karma, and no sponsorship seeker needs that.

- Respect your customers. Do not ever, ever loan, sell, or rent your list. Also, if someone doesn't want to hear from you by email, be sure the person is removed permanently from the list and apologize for any inconvenience.

Podcasting

Whether this pertains to your event or not depends entirely on the scope of your event. But if you've got content that people want to see or hear, this is a very interesting marketing medium that is only set to grow.

The gist of it is that you can create content, put it on iTunes, other MP3 sites, or your own site, and people can download it and listen or watch on their smartphones or MP3 players. This is not just limited to music—if you can record it in audio or video format, and it's useful or entertaining, it's worth distributing.

Below are just a few examples of content that might be compelling. Many of these could be done in serial form.

- Business advice from a professional association
- Training program from a marathon organizer
- Concert footage or behind-the-scenes footage from a concert promoter or band
- Infant first aid basics from a children's hospital
- How to fix a flat tire from a racing team

You can charge for the content—possibly using it as a fundraiser—or let it out there for free. The key is to make it compelling and credible.

Publicity

Publicity includes editorial media coverage in newspaper and magazine articles, and television and radio coverage. It is also known as public relations. Public relations will probably be very important to your event. That said, it is the only facet of a marketing plan that is out of your control—you can't make the newspaper write what you want them to write—so be sure that PR isn't your only marketing strategy. There are some key strategies that you can follow that will help you gain better results from your activities.

- Be sure that your public relations program is handled by a reputable public relations professional, preferably a member of your national public

> Use technology to extend the event experience for your audience and your sponsors.

relations institute. Hiring an independent public relations professional is probably a lot less expensive than you think. Do not dismiss spending this money until you have analyzed the value against the cost.

- If you are handling public relations internally, do ensure that whoever handles it is an active member of the public relations community.

- Whether internal or external, be sure your publicist understands what is expected, the resources available to him or her, and how success will be judged.

- Understand that not all media are equal. One spread in a national magazine could be worth dozens of smaller placements, but if you have a niche market, the right coverage in a niche publication or broadcast could be worth a lot more than something aimed at a broader market.

- Understand that, in order to get coverage, an event has to be newsworthy.

- Spend some time developing a variety of interesting angles. This will not only increase your potential for coverage, but it will also allow you to go to the same media outlets again and again with different stories.

- Do not discount the value of smaller, more targeted media outlets. They may be more receptive to your story and the readers may be more avid.

> Whether your publicity is handled internally or externally, be sure to brief whoever handles your PR fully in writing.

Database Marketing

One of the best ways to communicate large amounts of information to a specific target market is to embark upon a campaign of database marketing.

Databases come in all shapes and sizes, and you probably have access to several. Below we have listed several sources, in order of their probable receptiveness to your marketing message:

1. Members
2. Season ticket holders
3. Previous attendees or ticket purchasers
4. People who have signed up for your mailing list
5. Databases provided by industry organizations (e.g., your local arts governing body)
6. Databases that you rent from outside sources (demographically and geographically targeted)

Once you have settled on the database(s) to be used for your communications, you will need to determine how you will reach this group. Keep in mind that different types of databases represent different groups that may be receptive to varying methods of communication. You have many options for communication, including:

- Email announcements and e-newsletters (ensure your list is highly targeted, opt-in, and run in an ethical manner)
- Newsletters or other publications
- Inserting information in regular mailings
- Special mailings (specific to this event)
- Telemarketing
- Promotional material in member gathering places (clubhouse, etc.)

In addition to informing target markets about your event or organization, you may also want to include some type of enticement for them to attend. Some suggestions include

- Priority seating
- Early ticketing
- Special pricing or offers
- Merchandise discounts
- Invitations to special events

> You probably have more access to databases than you realize.

Signage

Signage includes signs that are made specifically for an event, such as banners, A-frames, and scoreboards. Pre-event and event signage can be a strong communication vehicle. Think broadly about your options, which could include

- Venue signage (facing a roadway or public area)
- Signage on your office building (if it is in a good location)
- Street banners or flags around your town
- Electronic billboards (many cities and towns have electronic reader boards that show upcoming events)
- Signage at convention and visitor bureau kiosks
- Perimeter signage
- Airport signage
- Vehicle signage

> Any surface that can be painted, bannered, or hung from can support signage.

Sponsor Leverage

We will talk extensively about sponsor leverage and its strategic importance to both the sponsors and your organization a bit later on, but there is also a marketing plan angle to it. Everything your sponsors do to leverage their sponsorship—to use it to enhance connections with their target markets and promote their brand—also promotes what you do. And if you are collaborative in the process of leverage development, you can suggest ways that they can achieve their objectives and augment your marketing plan.

One very simple example is to encourage your sponsors to extend their leverage into social media. In the very simple example below, American Express employees volunteered with the New York City branch of City Year. @CityYearNewYork tweeted about it to their 2,500-ish followers and American Express retweeted the message to their nearly 650,000 followers.

Figure 3.1
Get sponsors to help
spread the word

CityYearNewYork @CityYearNewYork   22 Jul
.@AmericanExpress employees joined us to add inspiration to a
West Harlem school bit.ly/15bS68W #service #CSR

Retweeted by American Express

Case Studies: You or the Sponsor?

You could come up with some amazing content for your website or social media activities, or a fantastic idea for an app, but are you best placed to deliver it? Oftentimes, providing that idea to a sponsor as a leverage idea can make your offer a lot more compelling. You can still promote it to your target markets, but the sponsor will create the activity and promote it to their target markets, as well. Depending on who they are, a sponsor could have many times the social media audience you do.

For example, European brewer **Carlsberg** developed an app around the fun, crazy culture of attending the Hong Kong Sevens rugby tournament. In the app, you could virtually streak across the ground. It was both irreverent and entertaining and ended up

going viral. That was great for the Sevens as well, as many people heard about the Sevens and put the event onto their sports bucket lists that may never before have considered flying to Asia for a rugby event.

Blackberry sponsored the Rugby World Cup in 2011 and created an app where fans could virtually face-paint their countries' flags on their social media profile pictures. Simple, effective, and definitely amplifying the fan experience, whether those fans made it to New Zealand or not.

Virtually everything **Red Bull** sponsors (and all of the events Red Bull owns) has their own games, making fans feel more a part of the experience and building stronger affinity between fans and sports: www.redbull.com.

Part 2

Sales

CHAPTER 4

Understand What You Have to Offer

When most sponsorship seekers, particularly nonsporting organizations, are asked to define what they have to offer, they either start listing all of the places where they can place a sponsor's logo or they talk at great length about all of the good corporate citizenship a company will foster by supporting them. Either way, it's the wrong answer.

In general terms, a sponsor wants three things from a sponsee:

1. To use the sponsee's brand attributes and hot buttons to underpin or introduce those attributes within the sponsor's own brand. (Note: this is about reinforcing authentic sponsor attributes, not making them look like something they're not.)
2. To access one or more of the target markets of a sponsee and to connect with these people in a meaningful way.
3. To gain a range of tangible benefits from the sponsee that they can use to add value to their relationships with their target markets—improving those target markets' experience with the event or organization they care about and/or improving their experience with the brand.

If you want to maximize your chances of creating a strong match with a sponsor, it is imperative that you understand fully what you offer in each of these areas. The more precisely you can define these benefits, the better.

Define Your Brand and Hot Buttons

The good news is that, if you've created a brand bullseye to better market your organization or event to your potential audience, you've already defined your brand and hot buttons. This time, though, we are going to look at the bullseye as a *sponsorship tool*.

If you haven't created a brand bullseye yet, now is the time to do it. The information it will provide will assist you to:

- Identify potential sponsors
- Create a compelling and creative offer
- Provide the sponsor with ideas and insights that will help them get the most from the sponsorship

Define Your Audience

Define your audience in terms of everyone who cares about what you do and the larger theme, not just the people who will attend.

You have already defined your target markets when you developed your marketing plan. Now, you need to look at your target markets from the sponsor's perspective.

Your marketing objective is to get people to your event. This is quite different from the sponsor's marketing objective, which is to effectively connect with and add value to as many of their target markets as possible. Thus, when defining your target markets in terms of what you can offer a sponsor, you need to be absolutely certain that you don't fixate on the people who actually come to your event. No matter how many people attend, or how well suited they are to your potential sponsor, they still reflect only a fraction of the sponsor's target marketplace.

Through your marketing efforts, you will reach a lot of people who will not attend your event for one reason or another but who are still receptive to the marketing message. These people could include people who experience your:

- Social media activities
- Blogs and e-newsletters
- Other publications
- Podcasts
- YouTube channel
- Pre-event advertising
- Pre-event promotions

- Pre-event publicity
- Street, venue, or event signage
- Media or online coverage of the event
- Post-event wrap-up coverage.

Now that you're thinking more broadly about your target markets, it's time to really think big.

Punching Above Your Weight

"Punching above your weight" is a great old boxing term, and it means to have such a strong punch you would be a contender against bigger opponents. If you're going to be competitive in a crowded sponsorship marketplace, being able to position what you offer as being bigger, lasting longer, and being more meaningful than other opportunities is a critical skill to have.

A very smart way to think about extending the functional target markets is to look at the larger relevance of what you're doing and develop ways for a sponsor to use that relevance with their target markets. For instance, your event may be a marathon, which is directly relevant to participating marathon runners and fans. The larger themes could include fitness, endurance, dedication, personal bests, goal setting, and lots more, which are all things that a sponsor could use to make their marketing to their own target markets more effective.

The following illustration shows what we're talking about (Figure 4.1). For most sponsorship seekers, your audience is smaller than the total marketplace the sponsor is targeting. What sponsorship seekers tend to do is sell the overlap—the proportion of your audience that you share with the sponsor. Even if what you're offering is fantastic, it can look pretty small in relation to the larger market objectives of a sponsor.

By extending your thinking to that larger relevance, you can create ways for a sponsor to authentically use that relevance to people who may not be interested in your specific event or program. Using the marathon example, a bank could use the larger themes of dedication and goal setting to underpin their entry-level investment products. You could assist them in developing content around how top marathon runners set goals and milestones, how they make themselves train when they sometimes don't want to, and how they recover from setbacks. Suddenly, your sponsor sees what you're offering as not just a marathon that lasts one day and impacts 30,000 people, but a marketing platform that they can use for months and impact millions.

Making your sponsorships look and work like much bigger opportunities is a critical skill in a crowded marketplace.

Figure 4.1
Punching above
your weight

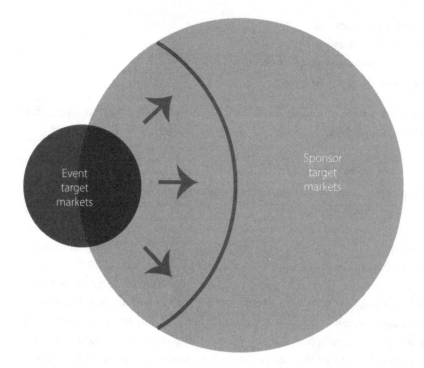

The two most important factors to make this work are credibility and willingness to share information. If your organization is credible and you either have or can access relevant information, advice, or other content, there is no reason you can't genuinely impact an audience much larger than your own.

Take Inventory

In order to understand the full range of tangible benefits your organization has to offer, you need to prepare an inventory of your assets. Make a list of every promotional and marketing opportunity that could possibly be of value to a potential sponsor. List everything, even if you wouldn't sell it. This helps you to think expansively, and you can sort them out later.

During this process, you need to look at your organization as a sponsor would. You will no doubt be astounded at the wide range of benefits that you have to offer that you never thought of before. This should allow you to show-case the value of your organization to a much broader range of sponsors.

Once you have prepared this list, do not make the mistake of offering your entire inventory to sponsors (we have seen this done). Instead, think

Never offer
a sponsor
everything on
your inventory.

of your inventory as your kitchen. It is a list of everything you have in your kitchen that could be used to make a meal—the food, the spices, the utensils, appliances, and even the electricity in the wall. Imagine what a mess you would get in if you tried to make a meal using everything in your kitchen. That's the same kind of mess you will get in if you try to create an offer using every item on your inventory. What you need is a recipe, and we'll provide you with one.

The **Generic Inventory** in the following tool will get you started. Just keep adding to and subtracting from it, as well as fine-tuning specific benefits, until it reflects what your organization has to offer. Remember, this is a living document—update it regularly.

Do not delete items from the inventory just because it might be unlikely that you'd offer those benefits. We recommend using the "million dollar rule": if you would at least consider providing that benefit (or figuring out how you could provide it) if the perfect sponsor offered you a million dollars, then leave it on the list. You still may never offer it (but you never know!), but keeping the list big, creative, and even a little outlandish will spark even more creative new ideas into the future than if you made the list very conservative. Sponsors love creativity, so you need to work at keeping an open mind.

> When creating your inventory, use the "million dollar rule."

Generic Inventory

What follows is a generic inventory. This is a starting point for you to prepare an inventory of your own property. The point of this exercise is to ensure you catalog everything you control that could be of value to a potential sponsor. You will probably not use all or even most of these items, but this inventory creates a menu from which to develop customized proposals for your potential sponsors.

The types of benefits that are most valuable to smart sponsors who take a best-practice approach to connecting with their target markets—the blue-chip benefits that create win-win-win sponsorships—are marked with an asterisk (*). This is not to say that the other benefits should be ignored or minimized, but that you should endeavor to include at least some blue-chip benefits in every proposal.

Sponsorship Types
- Naming rights sponsorship (perceived "ownership" of the event)
- Presenting sponsorship

- Naming rights or presenting sponsorship of a section, area, entry, or team
- Naming rights or presenting sponsorship of a day, weekend, or week at the event
- Naming rights or presenting sponsorship of an event-driven award, trophy, or scholarship
- Naming rights or presenting sponsorship of a related or subordinated event
- Major sponsorship
- Supporting sponsorship
- Official product status
- Preferred supplier status

_____

_____

_____

Exclusivity

- Category exclusivity among sponsors at or below a given level
- Category exclusivity among sponsors at any level
- Category exclusivity in event-driven advertising or promotional media
- Category exclusivity as a supplier or seller at the event

_____

_____

_____

License and Endorsements

- License to use sponsee or event logo(s), images, and/or trademark(s) for the sponsor's promotion, advertising, or other leverage activities
- Merchandising rights (the right to create co-branded merchandise to sell)
- Product endorsement (your event or organization endorsing the sponsor's product)

_____

_____

_____

Contracts

- Discounts for multiyear contracts
- First right of refusal for renewal at conclusion of contract
- Last right of refusal for renewal at conclusion of contract (not recommended)

- Performance incentives

_____

_____

_____

On-Site
- Dedicated space to carry out on-site leverage activities
- Sampling opportunities
- Demonstration/display opportunities
- Exhibition space
- Opportunity to sell product on-site (exclusive or nonexclusive)
- Coupon, information or premium (gift) distribution
- Merchandising (sponsor selling dual-branded products)

_____

_____

_____

Exclusive Content*
Note: When we reference content, this could be used by the sponsors in social media, websites, apps, customer and staff communications, videos, advertising, or more.

- Provision of content for sponsor activities (for example, weekly health tips, star athlete's training diary, pertinent articles, podcasts, other exclusive download-able content, etc.)
- Provision of online "events" (for example, online chat with a star, webcast, webinar)
- Access to venue, athletes, celebrities, artist, curator, etc. for creation of new, exclu-sive, "ownable" content
- Access to background information, statistics, photos, video clips, autographs, Q&As, etc. for creation of new, exclusive, "ownable" content

_____

_____

_____

Other Online*
- Promotion of relevant sponsor leverage activities through sponsee's social media activities, e-newsletter, and/or website

- Promotion of sponsor through sponsee's social media activities, e-newsletter, and/or website
- Ability for sponsor to add value to sponsee fans/followers via sponsee-controlled social media
- "Signage" on sponsee website and/or e-newsletter
- Promotion or contest on sponsee social media, e-newsletter, and/or website
- Links to sponsor website from sponsee website
- Sponsor profile on sponsee website

_____

_____

_____

Customer Added-Value*

This section is about providing benefits that the sponsor can pass on to their target markets in order to reinforce their relationships.

- Access to event, parking, or merchandise discounts for customers or a specific customer group (for example, frequent flyers, Gold Card holders)
- Access to event, parking or merchandise discounts, or other perks for customers
- Exclusive access to an event, area, contest/prize, service, celebrity, or experience for all or a specific group of customers
- Early access to tickets (before they go on sale to the general public)
- Block of tickets, parking, etc. that the sponsor can provide to loyal customers. Can be provided with or without naming rights to that section (for example, the Acme Energy Best Seats in the House).
- Proofs of purchase for discount admission
- Proofs of purchase for discount or free parking
- Proofs of purchase for premium item (for example, people can trade three proofs of purchase for a free program)

_____

_____

_____

Signage

- Venue signage (full, partial, or non-broadcast view)
- Inclusion in on-site event signage (exclusive or nonexclusive)
- Inclusion on pre-event street banners, flags, etc.

- Press conference signage
- Vehicle signage
- Event participant uniforms
- Event staff shirts/caps/uniforms

_____

_____

_____

Hospitality

- Tickets to the event (luxury boxes, preferred seating, reserved seating, or general admission)
- VIP tickets/passes (backstage, sideline, pit passes, press box, etc.)
- Celebrity/participant meet-and-greets
- Sponsorship-related travel arrangements, administration, and chaperone (consumer prizes, VIP or trade incentives)
- Access to or creation of what-money-can't-buy experiences*
- Development of customized hospitality events to suit the interests of the target market (high-end, adventurous, behind-the-scenes, for their families or kids, etc.).*

_____

_____

_____

Venue

- Input in venue, route, and/or timing
- Use of sponsor venue for launch, main event, or supporting event

_____

_____

_____

Database Marketing

- Unlimited access to event-generated database(s), such as member lists, for direct marketing follow-up (be careful not to breach privacy laws, which vary from country to country)
- Opportunity to provide inserts in sponsee mailings
- Rental/loan of sponsee database for one-off communication with people who have opted into third-party promotions

- Opportunity to run database-generating activities on-site
- Opportunity to run database-generating activities on-site as a requirement for attendee admission

_____

_____

_____

Employees/Shareholders*

- Participation in the event by employees or shareholders
- Access to discounts, merchandise, or other sponsorship-oriented perks
- "Ownership" of part of the event by employees (for example, creating an employee-built and run water station as part of a marathon sponsorship)
- Provision of a celebrity or spokesperson for meet-and-greets or employee motivation
- Creation of an event, day, or program specifically for employees
- Creation of an employee donation or volunteer program
- Opportunity to set up an employee recruitment station at your event
- Distribution of employee recruitment information

_____

_____

_____

Public Relations

- Inclusion in all press releases and other media activities
- Inclusion in sponsor-related and media activities
- Public relations campaign designed for sponsor's market (consumer or trade)

_____

_____

_____

Ancillary or Supporting Events

- Tickets or invitations to ancillary parties, receptions, shows, launches, etc.
- Signage, sampling, and other benefits at ancillary parties, receptions, shows, launches, etc.

_____

_____

_____

Other Promotional Opportunities

- Custom design of a new event, program, award, or other activity that meets the sponsor's specific needs
- Securing and administration of entertainment, celebrity appearances, etc. to appear on sponsors' behalf
- Provision by sponsor of spokesperson/people, celebrity appearances, costumed character, etc. for sponsored event
- Opportunity to provide prizes for media or event promotions
- Couponing/advertising on ticket backs

_____

_____

_____

Media Profile

- Inclusion in all print, outdoor, and/or broadcast advertising (logo or name)
- Inclusion on event promotional pieces (posters, fliers, brochures, buttons, apparel, etc.—logo or name)
- Ad time during televised event
- Event-driven promotional radio or television schedule (you provide them with part of your advertising)
- Event-driven outdoor (billboards, vehicle, public transport)
- Sponsor/retailer share media (themed display ads, 30/30 or 15/15 broadcast)
- Ad space in event program, catalog, etc.

_____

_____

_____

Research

- Access to pre- and/or post-event research
- Opportunity to provide sponsorship- or industry-oriented questions on event research

_____

_____

_____

Pass-Through Rights

- Right for sponsor to on-sell sponsorship benefits to another organization (this is always pending sponsee approval). An example would be a telecommunications company on-selling part of a sponsorship to Nokia. They would then usually leverage the sponsorship jointly.
- Right for retailer sponsor to on-sell sponsorship benefits to vendors in specific product categories.
- Right for retailer sponsor to involve vendors in sponsorship-driven in-store promotions.

_____
_____
_____

Contra

- Opportunity for sponsor to provide equipment, services, technology, expertise, or personnel useful to the success of the event in trade for part of sponsorship fee
- Opportunity for sponsor to provide media value, in-store/in-house promotion in trade for part of sponsorship fee
- Opportunity for sponsor to provide access to discounted media, travel, printing, or other products or services in trade for part of sponsorship fee

_____
_____
_____

Production

- Design and/or production of key sponsor events (hospitality, awards, etc.)
- Hiring and/or administration of temporary or contract personnel, services, and vendors for key sponsor events
- Logistical assistance, including technical or creative expertise

_____
_____
_____

Cause Tie-in

- Opportunity to involve sponsor's preferred charitable organization or cause
- Donation of a percentage of ticket or product sales to charity

_____

CHAPTER 5

Creating a Hit List

Once you understand your target markets and what you have to offer, you should start developing a preliminary hit list of potential sponsors. In fact, you will often start thinking of companies when you go through the previous exercises.

When creating a list of potential sponsors, be sure to pay attention to *specific brands, products or services*, not just the overall corporation. We cannot emphasize this enough. There are three reasons for this.

1. Very few companies have only one product or brand and, where there are multiple brands, they are often very different from each other. Their differing attributes and target markets will fit with varying types of sponsorships.
2. Corporate sponsorship departments are usually the first place that sponsees go with their proposals, and hence they are inundated with requests. Going directly to a well-matched brand area can minimize the competition you will face for both attention and money. Plus, many sponsorship departments do not have the authority to make major sponsorship decisions, with sponsorship managers operating largely as gatekeepers. More and more, that authority is falling to the brand team anyway.
3. The brand areas will almost always have their own marketing budgets, and those budgets are often reasonably flexible. These areas are most closely accountable for the performance of their brands, rather than where the money is spent, and are often willing to put marketing funds that are not specifically committed to something else into sponsorship if they believe they will get a positive result.

When looking at potential sponsors, look at specific brands, products, or services, not just the corporation.

Sponsor Matching

A good hit list will be based upon matching your event or property with a sponsor. There are three ways of doing this:

- By target markets
- By objectives
- By attributes/values

The power is where two or more of these matches intersect (Figure 5.1).

Audience Matching

The starting point for sponsor matching is ensuring that your event or product targets one or more of the sponsor's core audiences. The more of your target markets that match the sponsor's target markets, the more potential there is for a strong sponsorship. If you don't match any of the potential sponsor's target markets, then it does not matter how well you match objectives or attributes, you are wasting your time.

There are several types of sponsor audiences that you could match:

- Current customers
- Potential customers that fit one of the sponsor's current customer profiles

Figure 5.1
The best sponsorships are matched three ways

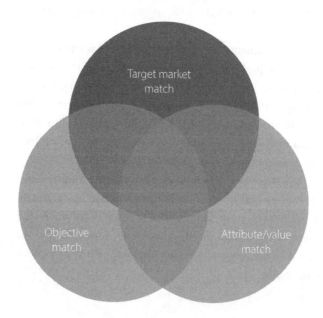

- Newly targeted potential customer groups
- Intermediary customers (retailers, trade, distribution)
- Internal customers (sponsor employees and/or shareholders)

There is one common pitfall surrounding newly targeted customer groups. Often, sponsorship seekers will realize that their event does not target any of a company's different markets. Instead, they try to make a case that they can deliver new markets. Although this approach is very proactive, it rarely works.

When a company targets a new group of customers, the initiative is usually developed through market research and accompanied by a comprehensive marketing campaign. If the company has not already identified your marketplace as having a potential for them, it is unlikely that they will be receptive to your approach, particularly within your time frame. In addition, one sponsorship on its own is unlikely to deliver the critical mass of people needed to make the new marketplace desirable for the potential sponsor.

Exercise

We have developed an easy way to develop your hit list based on target market matching. Starting with the "one person" descriptions from your **Target Market Assessment Worksheet** (Chapter 2), for each of your segments, write down any brands or categories of product/service that would feature reasonably prominently in their lives.

Aim for a big list—at least a couple of dozen brands for each target market. What you will notice is that the better and more complete your one-person description is, the easier it will be to find potential sponsors for your hit list. There will definitely be some red herrings on your hit list, but don't be deterred. This is a brainstorming exercise and you will find some genuine prospects. Plus, you will be finding out a lot of information about these potential sponsors before approaching them. If they aren't right for your organization or the event, it will be obvious long before you commit yourself to anything.

Attribute Matching

Strong attribute matching is one of the hallmarks of great sponsorship. It creates relevance between the sponsor and your event, which carries through, creating relevance and interest in the sponsorship to your target markets.

Look at the brand bullseye that you prepared in Chapter 2. Just as there are different levels to your organization's personality, there are also different levels in how you can match with a potential sponsor.

- Your "soul," in the center circle, is the core of what you are about. Matching one or more of these with a sponsor is absolutely essential in order to create an authentic match that a sponsor can use to underpin their own brand.
- Attributes, found in the "perceptions" and "hot buttons" part of your bullseye, are the areas where you can define yourself to best match a potential sponsor. This is where you can be somewhat of a chameleon, creating a strong and relevant appeal to a wide range of potential sponsors.

When identifying potential attribute matches, remember that there are two different ways of matching:

1. **Attribute equals attribute.** For example, a women's contemporary art exhibition has the attributes of being smart, strong, sexy, and original. This may be a good match with Calvin Klein fragrances, which markets itself in the same way.
2. **Sponsor attribute solves sponsee attribute.** For example, being a member of a rally driving team has to be one of the world's dirtiest occupations. This may be a good match for a laundry soap, car wash, personal care products, or Black and Decker's Dustbuster.

Promoting a strong attribute match can be a big selling point. When used in an interesting or humorous way, attribute matching can lead to new approaches to creative advertising and is a great way for a company to cut through the clutter of a heavily sponsored event.

Keep in mind that who you don't target can be just as important as who you do. Be sure you take into account the impact on your organization's image and target market before you approach any potential sponsor.

A case in point is the National Education Association in the United States. The NEA decided against accepting sponsorship from Hyundai, as most of the teachers who make up the membership are unionized and Hyundai is not. The NEA realized that taking sponsorship from a nonunionized manufacturer would undermine its credibility with its membership and could spark a major backlash.

Vetting

At this point, it's likely you have two big, messy lists of possible sponsors, and we find it very useful to do a quick assessment of your best candidates. How? Easy. Just look at the specific brands and specific categories of brands (e.g., "work boots," not "shoes") that appear on both lists. Brands that feature on both lists can be considered your A-list, and you need to look at objective matching.

Objective Matching

This type of matching does not always happen, but it can be a very powerful tool for gaining sponsorship if it does. Objective matching happens when you and your sponsor share actual objectives, such as "promoting good health and nutrition to primary school students," or when your objectives are mutually complementary.

Extending Your Hit List

By now, you should have a nice, tight A-list of sponsors to approach in your first tranche, but you can probably extend that a bit.

Go for 2nd, 3rd, 4th . . .

Oftentimes, sponsees target only the biggest companies in a given category: The market-leading telecommunications company, the biggest airline, the biggest bank. We're not saying that those brands might not be great sponsors, but there is a strong case for looking at their direct competitors.

They Are More Motivated to Do Something Innovative

Market leaders can tend to be conservative in their marketing approach, landing somewhere along the lines of, "If it ain't broke, don't fix it." On the other hand, brands that are trying to become market leaders tend to do more interesting, innovative marketing, and best-practice sponsorship definitely qualifies.

They Get Fewer Approaches

So many sponsorship seekers make the assumption that the market leader will be the best or most cashed-up sponsor that these companies get inundated with proposals. The same can't be said for many of their competitors. On a number of occasions, we've had competing sponsors in the same public workshop and asked how many approaches they get in a month, and the answers can be shocking. It's not uncommon to hear that the market leader gets 15 to 20 times more proposals in a month, and in one instance, the market-leading telecom thought they received 6,000 to 7,000 proposals and other unsolicited requests a month, where the number two telecom got about 200.

They Move Faster

This is not a hard-and-fast rule, but if you're approaching a company that has a culture of innovation and they receive far fewer proposals, there is likely to be less red tape and fewer hurdles for a genuinely great offer to be approved.

Get Referrals

A lot of corporate sponsors know each other, and you should use that to your advantage. If you have happy sponsors, ask them for referrals to other potential sponsors. Just use the direct approach, and ask if they know of any other sponsors that would be a good match for your organization. Some sponsors won't be a lot of help, but others will be a wealth of information, not only about who may be interested, but what their hot buttons are and how best to approach them.

If you have any doubts as to the satisfaction level of a sponsor, don't ask them for a referral. You will only make yourself look silly. Take some time to improve your relationship and their results before you ask.

> If you have happy sponsors, ask them for referrals.

Research Your Potential Sponsors

If you ask a sponsor, any sponsor, what they want from a sponsorship proposal, they will invariably say one thing: "We want a proposal that is tailored to our needs." The big question is, how do you know what they need?

Now that you know how you can match with a potential sponsor, you need to get the information that will allow you to assess their suitability—do you match?—as well as allowing you to create an offer that meets their needs.

Your *job* as a sponsee is to assist your sponsor in meeting their needs. In order to do that, you should know your potential sponsor's:

- Long-term marketing objectives (over 12 months)
- Short-term or tactical marketing objectives
- Product or brand attributes

- Target markets
- Needs—absolute requirements
- Wants—these are things that would be nice
- Exclusions—many companies, for instance, will not sponsor individuals, and some will not be involved if an alcohol company is a prime sponsor, so you need to know these things.
- Special emphases—basically everything else, such as new product launches, new services being offered, a new logo, their competitive situation

In Chapter 4, when we discussed creating an inventory of your assets, we compared the inventory to a kitchen. Well, the research you gather about your potential sponsor is your recipe.

The **Sponsor Information Checklist** that can be found later in this chapter will help you to compile and organize this information. Completing this checklist will provide you with a strong understanding of what a potential sponsor requires from a sponsorship investment. It should be completed in full prior to developing your offer.

As you complete the checklist for each of the companies on your preliminary hit list, you will notice that a number of potential sponsors will emerge as being very strongly matched with your event, some less so, and many companies will be excluded altogether. This process will save you a lot of time, as you will then only approach the most likely sponsors. It will also demonstrate to potential sponsors that your primary aim in sponsorship is to understand what they need to achieve and to help them achieve it.

The sources for obtaining the information for the Sponsor Information Checklist are outlined below in the order in which they should be utilized or approached.

First, Use Other Sources

Before you even bother picking up the telephone to call a company, you need to research them thoroughly through other sources. If you have a list of prospects, a couple of afternoons spent on the Internet and at the library can provide you with a lot of information.

Use this information to fill out, as completely as possible, the **Sponsor Information Checklist** for each of your potential sponsors.

A range of research, news, and networking resources is included in Appendix 2.

> Do not develop your offer until you have completed the Sponsor Information Checklist for your potential sponsor.

Sponsorship Guidelines

The fastest, cleanest, and usually most complete way to get the required information from a sponsor is to request a copy of their sponsorship guidelines. This is (usually) a short document that outlines all of their needs, exclusions, target markets, and the process by which they make investment decisions.

Although sponsorship guidelines are gaining popularity with sponsors, not all companies have them. If you come across one that does not, you can make yourself look great and add value to your relationship by providing our version of this valuable tool to them. Clearly, the **Sponsorship Guidelines Template** that we have provided later in this chapter is just an example that the sponsor will need to customize to reflect their unique needs and positioning.

Website(s)

Have a good look at their company website in your country, as well as any pages or websites devoted to the specific brand(s) you're targeting. For instance, you could check out the Unilever's UK website, but if you're targeting their Dove brand, you'd also check out the Dove page on the Unilever website, as well as Dove's stand-alone brand website.

What you're looking for:

- Messages that indicate their brand values and attributes
- Who they appear to be targeting
- Clues as to their current priorities
- Information about their sponsorship-driven or promotional activity, which will tell you how they like to use their sponsorships
- Any brand cross-promotions: Are they cross-promoting with other brands owned by the same company? Different companies? Specific retailers?

If your target brand has headquarters or major markets overseas, do check out the global website and websites in other major markets. What you're looking for:

- Insight as to new initiatives, products, or brand extensions that may be coming to your region
- Information on how they use sponsorship in other markets

If your target has headquarters or major markets overseas, be sure to check the global website.

Social Media

If you're researching a brand, definitely "Like" the brand Facebook page and follow them on Twitter, Instagram, YouTube, and other key social media. You will get real-time insights as to what their priorities are, but you'll also get a very strong indication of how they interact with their target markets. Is it all one-way sales messaging, or do they interact on a more human level? Do they run contests? Ask for fans to create content or give suggestions? All of this will give you a strong feeling for the tone, innovation, and responsiveness of their marketing activities.

Television Ad Aggregators

There are dozens of websites around the world that collect television ads for your viewing pleasure. A quick way to get an understanding of a brand that you may not be personally familiar with is to do an Internet search on "[brand] television ads [your country/region]". Check out the most recent ads, which should give you some insight as to what they're focusing on, their target markets (who they're talking to), and their key messages.

ABI/Inform Full-Text Online

This is an essential (and free) resource for people in this industry and a must-have for sponsorship seekers. You can enter keywords—search engine style—and it will search thousands of business publications around the world and bring you back the whole articles relating to that topic. You can mark the ones that are interesting to you and email them to yourself. The kinds of things you will find are

- Background on how sponsors you're targeting use their sponsorship investments
- Background on what multinational sponsors do in other countries
- Background on how sponsors use their sponsorships of properties like yours around the world
- Examples of best-practice sponsorship—win-win-win!
- Examples of interesting, out-of-the-box sponsorships
- Examples of interesting, out-of-the-box sponsorship benefits
- Precedent to add weight to that great sponsorship idea you have

The kicker is that mostly only university and major public libraries have a license to this. The good news is that you should be able to get a library card and PIN number to remotely log into the online materials from your office. Just call and ask your closest major library about the process to get a card and PIN number because you want to access ProQuest databases. (ABI/Inform is a ProQuest service.)

> For real-time insights on a sponsor's tone, innovation, and responsiveness to target markets, pay attention to their social media.

Annual Report

When we wrote the first edition of this book, reviewing a company's annual report was considered an essential part of understanding their organizational and brand culture. With the prevalence of information available online, it has faded in relevance.

That said, you may find it useful to download an online copy of the most recent financial report, as it could give you some or all of the following:

- An understanding of the corporate mission and vision
- A list of all products and brand lines
- The overall financial performance of the company (and often specific product categories)
- Annual expenditure on sponsorship
- A list of all (or sometimes only major) sponsorships
- New company initiatives
- Income and expenditure trends

. . . Then Talk to the Sponsor

By this time, you should have your **Sponsor Information Checklist** about 80 percent completed and should be prepared to speak to the sponsor to fine-tune your understanding of their goals and markets.

In-Person Meetings

No matter how much information you find about a company from other sources, it is always ideal to meet with a potential sponsor prior to developing a proposal. There are several reasons for this:

- You will gain a lot more insight from a conversation than from even the best proposal guidelines.
- You will develop a personal relationship with the brand or sponsorship manager.
- Your enthusiasm and belief in the project will often be infectious.
- It is more difficult for someone to brush you off if you are sitting there in person.

Be sure to do your homework before your in-person meeting. Again, you should endeavor to fill out as much as possible of your **Sponsor Information Checklist** before making contact. This will allow you to demonstrate your professionalism and commitment to understanding their needs. You can also use what you know about the company and its sponsorship program to find out what has and has not worked for them in the past, how sponsorships were utilized, and other pertinent pieces of information.

Example
Instead of . . .

"What are your top five marketing objectives?"

Say . . .

"You seem to be targeting an increasingly younger, cooler marketplace. Is that reflective of where your brand is going, or are you simply extending your existing markets to include them?"

Or . . .

"In my research, I noticed that the brand is extending into premium ice cream flavors in America. Is that something that's likely to happen in Canada? Any idea on time frame, as we may be able to assist with your launch activities?"

What you absolutely don't want to do is go straight into a sales pitch. You need to ask great questions and understand their needs before you're ready to sell to that sponsor. Keep any sales rhetoric right out of your conversation during this meeting. Your goal is to understand their needs and showcase that you're different from the sponsorship sales people they usually meet, and someone they want to work with. If you can do that, they'll invite a proposal from you.

For specific meeting techniques, see the **Sales Checklist** in Chapter 7.

Telephone Interview

If you cannot have a meeting in person with the potential sponsor, a telephone interview is definitely the next best thing. Again, it is imperative to do your homework prior to picking up the telephone, or you could do more harm than good.

Do make an appointment for the interview, just as if you were there in person, and stick to your allotted time.

What If You Can't Reach the Sponsor?

Brand managers are busy and can be hard to reach—though they are usually easier to reach than sponsorship managers. In any case, if you can't reach the

> Do your homework on the company before the meeting.

brand manager and are confident that the sponsorship is a good match for them, you can use all that you have researched about a sponsor to create a customized proposal without their input.

Do note, this is your fallback position and not ideal. Don't make this your primary strategy just because you're nervous about making the call or going to the meeting. Doing that hard stuff is as much a part of your job as the rest of this, so take a deep breath and pick up the phone.

Sponsor Information Checklist

The idea of the **Sponsor Information Checklist** is to provide you with a format so that you can obtain as much information about your target sponsor as you possibly can, by giving you all of the clues you need to make your best shot at gaining their sponsorship. Do not worry if you cannot get all of the information, but do try to get most of it before creating your offer.

If you speak to your potential sponsor, be reasonable about the amount of information you request and the time you need to gather this information. Know the basics and ask about objectives, target markets, and new initiatives first. Also, get the correct address, name, and title from the receptionist or assistant, not from your target contact.

Sponsor: _____

Address: _____

Phone: _____

Website: _____

Contact name: _____

Contact phone: _____

Contact email: _____

Assistant name (if applicable): _____

First step, check sponsor website for sponsorship guidelines.   ❏ Done

Key Brand/Product Attributes

1. _____
2. _____
3. _____
4. _____
5. _____

Objectives

What perceptions are they trying to change about this brand? What behaviors?

1. _____
2. _____
3. _____
4. _____
5. _____

Relevant Product Lines and Target Markets

Product	Target markets

New Initiatives

Have they recently or are they planning to add to or extend their brand lines, change their logo, relaunch a product, merge with another company, or enter into a new or distinctive marketing campaign? Please describe.

_____
_____
_____
_____
_____

Key Direct Competitors in Their Category

1. _____
2. _____
3. _____
4. _____
5. _____

Key Indirect Competitors

(Other categories that may compete with their category)

1. _____
2. _____
3. _____
4. _____
5. _____

How Do They Utilize Their Sponsorships?

_____
_____
_____

Precedent

Has this company ever sponsored a similar property? Can you get any information on how that went? (Speak to the other sponsee if you feel it is appropriate.)

_____
_____
_____

Is there any national or overseas precedent for a relationship such as this? Do you have a copy of any supporting magazine or newspaper articles?

_____

_____

Exclusions

Do they have any exclusions in the area of sponsorship?

_____

_____

Approvals

How long should approval take, and what is the approval procedure for sponsorship?

_____

_____

Date: _____

Information gathered by: _____

Sponsorship Guidelines Template

Hawk Brewing receives dozens of proposals every year, many of which we reject because they do not adequately meet our needs. We have developed this document to make our requirements clear to potential sponsorship seekers and to encourage the presentation of proposals that meet those needs.

General

- We will consider proposals in all categories except [insert exclusions here].
- We require sponsorship and sales (if applicable) exclusivity in the category of beer and premixed alcoholic beverages.
- We generally need a minimum of six months lead time to effectively plan and implement our leverage activities.
- Logo and/or name exposure is considered a bonus but is not the primary goal of sponsorship.
- We prefer to invest in sponsorships that carry out audience research during and/or after the event, including questions relating to our industry, and provide results to Hawk Brewing.

- We expect that our sponsorship partners will invest a minimum of 10 percent of the total value of the sponsorship to proactively add value to the sponsorship.

[Sponsor] Brand Positioning

Here is a short overview to assist you in understanding our brand positioning. Our goal is to partner with organizations and events that are a strong, natural match to at least some aspects of our brand positioning. For example,

- "Not everyone can be a Hawk" (tag line)
- Premium beers (including brands for true beer connoisseurs)
- Smart, witty, irreverent
- Cool, sexy
- An American status product
- "Drink Responsibly" message

As we expand overseas, our goal is to become known as an American status brand that retains its desirability independent of any prevailing or cultural attitudes toward America (think "Levi's").

Target Markets by Product

Hawk Beer	Males, highly social, into music and sports, consider themselves to be "cool."
Light Hawk *(reduced alcohol)*	Primary: Designated drivers, responsible, socially oriented, consider drinking a premium light beer to be a good compromise. Secondary: Single, young women, active, tomboyish, highly social, out-and-about, somewhat fashion-conscious.
Raven Ale	Mature men, upscale, status and quality-oriented, highly brand aware, want to be seen with cool brands but not impressed by fads.
Raven Special	Upscale bars, pubs, and restaurants, available East Coast only.
Mad Vulture	Young adults (18–25-ish), single, music- and fashion-oriented (pop culture), party/rave-oriented, not generally alternative types, introducing new flavor in October 2015.

Sponsorships must provide at least six of the following:
[These should be tied to both your overall objectives and key attributes/values and should number 10 to 15.]

- A natural link with our brand positioning (see above)
- Provision of exclusive and meaningful content for our website, social media, app development, etc.
- Onsite sales
- Exclusive event, access, or area for members of Hawk's Hawkeye Club (1.2 million members worldwide, 84 percent in North America)
- Provide opportunity for key customer hospitality ("what money cannot buy" activities are particularly good)
- Opportunities to host pre- or post-event parties, concerts, or other over-21 social activities
- Celebrity appearances at key pubs and clubs (or "virtual" appearances in video web chats or webcasts)
- Other event-related benefits that we can pass along to a large proportion of our customer base (both consumers and trade). Feel free to use your imagination.
- Product placement (using one or more of our brands in a meaningful way as part of the event)
- Ticket discounts, premium tickets, or access to an exclusive ticket line for customers with proof-of-purchase
- Ability for Hawk Brewing staff to participate in a meaningful way

To be considered, proposals must include
- Key details of the opportunity
- Overview of your marketing plan, including what is and is not confirmed
- List of sponsors who have committed to date
- Comprehensive list of benefits, including how they relate to us and our products
- Creative ideas as to how we can use this sponsorship and those benefits to connect with our target markets
- Timeline, including important deadlines
- Credentials of your company and key subcontractors (publicist, event producer, etc.)

Process for Consideration:
- All proposals are reviewed by Sponsorship Manager to assess suitability, feasibility, and resources required (human and monetary)
- Recommended proposals are presented to [insert title] for approval
- Sponsee is notified of the disposition of the proposal within [X] weeks.

Submit Proposal to:
[Insert full contact details]

CHAPTER 6

Creating the Offer

Most sponsorship sales efforts start with a template proposal. It has several levels—often gold-silver-bronze—and the entire customization process includes using search-and-replace to create 200 identical proposals for 200 different potential sponsors. Then the next three months are spent trying to get those sponsors to call you back, and the lion's share of them never will.

Sponsors hate those proposals, and what these boilerplate proposals say about you is that you are inflexible and unimaginative and don't care what they are trying to achieve. Do yourself a favor and vow never to send another of those proposals. Instead, take the time to craft a customized offer that is not only worthy of their attention and consideration, but genuinely worth a bigger fee.

Customized offers are built around leverage ideas that you come up with that will achieve the sponsor's objectives. We will say that coming up with leverage ideas isn't your responsibility, it is the sponsor's. That said, providing specific, creative ideas that they can use to make the opportunity you're selling turn into the results they want is totally in your best interest. It makes saying yes much easier for them.

So, as much as you think you're selling benefits, you're not. You're selling a vision for what sponsoring your organization can mean to their brands, and to the people they target. That's what offer development is all about.

This chapter is full of great case studies to inspire you. You'll find even more in Chapter 11, "Leverage."

More than anything else, you're selling a vision.

The Event Versus the Event Experience

Before you start developing offers, we need to break something to you: As fantastic as your organization/event/whatever may be, functionally, you're not really selling very much.

You're selling a package including some rights to a sponsor designation and some intellectual property (IP) and/or some content, some tickets, hospitality, visibility, and maybe some space or time to do some on-site activity. That's the start of a leverageable sponsorship platform, but if that's all you use when creating the offer, you're selling yourself short. You're selling your event (or whatever) and missing the huge sponsor opportunities around the event experience.

Let's just take a baseball team, for example. People don't stop being fans at the end of the game. They don't even stop being fans at the end of a season. There is an entire fan experience that sits around the baseball games they attend or watch on television. It starts when they start anticipating the new season and doesn't stop until the last memory has faded. Fans don't have to ever attend a game or event or visit your museum to have an experience around that, and if you show sponsors how they can add value to their bond with their target markets within both the event and the much larger event experience, you're extending the effective time frame, the geographic footprint, the depth and number of "wins" the sponsor can provide to the target market, and your value to that sponsor.

This approach works hand-in-hand with the "punching above your weight" concept to make what you're offering look, feel, and operate for the sponsor like something much bigger than it really is (Figure 6.1).

Your Team

Developing offers is something that is very difficult to do on your own. It is basically a directed brainstorm and requires different perspectives to do it thoroughly and creatively.

Ideally, you will have several people involved in the process of offer development, but at the very least, ensure there are two of you. The people taking part don't specifically need to have a role in sponsorship. Some good roles to include are

Event
(event-controlled)

Event Experience
(audience-controlled)

Figure 6.1
*The event versus the
event experience*

- Marketing
- Membership or audience development
- Business development
- Communications
- Production
- Executive director

It may also be useful to include one or more board members in this process from time to time, as this will give them some insight into the process and amount of work that goes into selling sponsorship. They may be a little more realistic with their sponsorship targets once they understand what goes into it.

Offer Brainstorm Process

The offer brainstorm process is something originally developed to help sponsors leverage their investments. (If you've read Kim's book, *The Corporate Sponsorship Toolkit*, this will look familiar.) But with a few tweaks, this process

It is virtually
impossible
to develop a
strong offer on
your own.

works very well for finding the ideas that will underpin your offer and make your proposal stand out from almost every other proposal a sponsor will receive.

We recommend that you and your team throw yourselves into this process with some abandon. Let yourselves have the crazy ideas. You're not committing yourselves to anything, at this point, but it's only by allowing yourselves to get really creative that you'll allow yourselves to let go of "how it's always been done."

So, choose the sponsor for whom you're going to develop the offer, and let's get cracking!

Homework

Before you are ready to lead an offer development session, you need to do some homework. Spending 30 minutes using ABI/Inform Full-Text Online is a very strong option.

Once you've logged onto ABI/Inform Full-Text Online, do three searches:

- The sponsor's category of business and category of your property and "corporate sponsorship" (i.e., "insurance and hockey and corporate sponsorship")
- Category of your property and "corporate sponsorship" (i.e., "festival and corporate sponsorship")
- The sponsor's category of business and "corporate sponsorship" (i.e., "retailer and corporate sponsorship").

This will provide you with some leverage ideas and angles that you can drop into the brainstorm process to get people going and/or if the process starts to stagnate. Plus, there may be a number of ideas you can . . . how can we put this . . . borrow with pride.

Backgrounding

Before you are prepared to develop the actual leverage ideas, you need to figure out what raw materials you have to work with. So with your team, go through these steps. Capture what you do in a way that allows you to reference it easily later—butcher paper tacked to the wall is low-tech but very effective.

Background Step 1: Perceptions

Start off by asking your team to list people's perceptions of the property. Better yet, pull out your brand bullseye and have a quick review. Add anything your team thinks has been missed. Ensure that you also capture misconceptions, because people can have incorrect perceptions about what you do, and you need to take that into account.

Background Step 2: Best and Worst

- What are the best things about this property? What do people tell you they love? What do they want more of? What makes them attend, join, donate, or whatever?
- What are the worst things about this property? What is most frustrating or least convenient? What are the deterrents to attending, joining, donating, etc.?

The idea here is to be honest. Don't sugarcoat the bad stuff, as this knowledge could prove useful later on.

Event Experience Touch-Points

List all of the ways people interact with the property. Following is a sample list of some typical touch-points for an event. The touch-points for a charity or museum or team or association could be very different.

- Attending the event itself
- Caring about the event, team, cause, etc.
- Anticipation
- Ticket purchase (or other commitment)
- Buying merchandise
- National pride
- Proximity
- Experiencing the event itself via media (broadcast, online)
- Event coverage in media
- Online participation—websites, social media, e-newsletters, forums, reviews, etc.
- Gambling or tipping
- Attending event-themed parties
- Transportation, parking
- Weather
- (In)convenience
- Stories, memories, bragging rights

Brand Touch-Points

Now, think about the sponsor's brand. Similar to the above, list all of the ways their target markets interact with the brand. Following is a sample of some brand touch-points. Again, while these may be very different from one brand to another, these should provide a good starting point.

- Buying/using the brand
- Brand packaging
- Brand website
- Micro-site
- Social media activities—Twitter, Facebook, YouTube, etc.
- Customer service
- Retail or branch experience
- Advertising
- Promotions—media, retail, on- or in-pack, online, etc.
- Collateral materials

Case Studies: Adding Value

New Zealand cereal brand **Weet-Bix** used their small sponsorship of New Zealand's national rugby team, the All Blacks, to bring fans closer to the team. The many great leverage activities include Face2Face, where people upload their photos and are matched with the All Black they look most like and All Blacks trading cards in-pack.

Sharpie, autograph pen of choice, has created multiple ways to amplify fans' experiences at the games and events they sponsor. These include sign-making stations and virtual autograph stations, where fans can practice their autographs on balls (like the pros!) with digital Sharpies.

Hyundai sponsored the hit program *Walking Dead*. To highlight the safety features of their cars, they created an app allowing people to virtually customize a Hyundai "Zombie Survival Machine" and share it with their networks: www.walkingdeadchopshop.com.

The National Space Centre in the United Kingdom provided telecommunications giant **BT** with the opportunity for children to have their digital photo taken with ET. All of the photos were then posted to the BT website, driving traffic and providing an added-value experience for BT's target market of kids 10 to 13 and their families. In the first four months of operation, almost 70,000 children participated.

In Australia, **ANZ Bank** was the principal sponsor of the musical *Wicked*. They offered loads of exclusive content, and one lucky person won the chance for a walk-on role. They turned that into a win for many people through an open, shareable nomination process, and by creating and sharing lots of exclusive content around the experience of the winner. Official Bank of Oz, indeed!

- ATMs
- Loyalty marketing programs
- Statements/bills
- Cards
- In-flight materials
- Service, maintenance, warrantees
- Staff communications
- Staff training, team building
- Shareholder communications
- Retail or broker incentives
- Other sponsorships

The Offer

You're now ready to start brainstorming ideas, from which you can choose a few to form the basis of your offer.

Brainstorming Rules

From here on in, there are a few rules:

- There are no rules.
- You own the sponsor's company. This is a very important part of this process. It must be completed from the sponsor's point of view, and you may need to remind the team of that from time to time.
- You have unlimited funds.
- There are no political agendas.
- No one will say no to you.
- Anything is feasible.
- You can have any benefits you want from the sponsee (i.e., you).

Now that you have removed all barriers to creativity, you are ready to start!

Brainstorm Step 1: The Experience

Remembering that *you are the sponsor*, look at your list of the best and worst things about your property.

How can we amplify the best stuff about this property?

- Make it bigger and better?

> You will probably spend as much time building the background as brainstorming ideas.

- Make attendees, fans, or our customers more a part of the experience?
- Extend the time frame?
- Help the target markets achieve their own goals? (Think: Achieve a personal best in the marathon you're sponsoring.)
- Give them more input, a stronger voice?

How can we improve the bad stuff?

- Improve convenience or accessibility?
- Alleviate annoyances?
- Make it easier for them to be there?

The goal is to provide small, meaningful benefits for all or most of your (the sponsor's) target market. If someone suggests an idea where only one person wins, ask whether the idea represents a win for lots of people or just a few.

More Case Studies: Adding Value

In the lead-up to the 2010 Winter Olympics, Canadian brewer **Molson** undertook a range of activities created to share and amplify Canadians' national pride, including a "Made from Canada Rally Book" with thousands of fan messages that was presented to the Canadian Hockey Team before a crucial game, and the creation of a 370 square meter mural made up of fan photos submitted on their website and displayed on an outer wall of their Vancouver brewery.

As an official sponsor of Major League Soccer, **AT&T U-verse** provides a "game of the week" that avid fans can only view online to ensure that they are able to watch their team play: http://uverseonline.att.net/mls.

New **Bank of America** customers can sign up for Pink Ribbon checking accounts and credit cards, with a donation to Susan G Komen for the Cure every year plus a small percentage donation for every dollar spent through the account. Checks, cards, and statements feature Susan G Komen for the Cure branding.

As the official vehicle of the Deutsche Bank Championship, **BMW** offers owners free parking at the event. As title sponsor of the BMW Championship, BMW offers private parking for BMW owners, who also receive access into the BMW Owners Pavilion on the 16th Green.

In a similar vein, if you are a **State Farm Insurance** customer and show your card, you can get parking at Atlanta Falcons games for half price in the State Farm Lot.

People attend parades for the atmosphere, and **Santa.com** made the crowd an even bigger part of the atmosphere at the Santa.com Holiday Parade. They filled the streets with camera-wielding elves who snapped hundreds of digital photos of attendees, which were then shown on parade floats for everyone to see—instant holiday stardom!

Another approach is to suggest that it's just fine to have one big prize, as long as the process around it creates those small wins. Can people showcase their creativity? Vote or provide other input? Create something they can share? There are numerous options to ensure there are wins along the way, even if it's just one person that gets the big prize.

Brainstorm Step 2: Consumer-Generated Content

Creating opportunities for people to share related content is now a critical part of leveraging any sponsorship. It makes people feel like they are participating, not just spectating, and the sponsor is facilitating it. Ask: Can we provide ways for our target markets to create user-generated content?

- Before the event/season?
- During the event/season?

And Even More Case Studies: Adding Value

At the Deutsche Bank Championship, the **Wall Street Journal** offered a special golf-themed gift to anyone that signed up for a subscription.

MAC Cosmetics used their sponsorship of New Zealand Fashion Week to offer useful services, such as secure lockers, for the professional makeup artists and other VIPs.

Investment firm **Charles Schwab** leveraged their sponsorship of the PGA Tour with a microsite featuring a series of golfing tips with Tiger Woods's former swing coach, Hank Haney, Game Tracker, and the novel Mental Game Assessment.

In 2010, **American Express** sponsored a range of live concerts with popular artists including Arcade Fire and John Legend, and live streamed them on YouTube channels operated by label-owned music video site Vevo, with which it has a syndication partnership. American Express cardholders received ticket presale options, with a certain number of tickets reserved for American Express customers, and cardholders receive access to tickets normally one day before the general public.

All users could watch live on YouTube and on demand after the event and could select their own camera angles during the shows and in some cases collaborate with artists on-stage, creating a unique "behind the scenes" concert experience access to artists for American Express cardholders.

As an official sponsor of the NFL, **NetApp** has developed a proprietary team ranking system (NetApp NFL Protection Power Ranking) on a website for the sales team to use as a means of engagement for current and prospective customers. Fans can also participate in the weekly trivia challenge and test their NetApp NFL IQ: http://www.netappfootball.com/.

- After the event/season?

  What kinds of content can people create?

- Providing feedback or input?
- Submitting videos, photos, or artwork?
- Submitting stories?
- Participation in Q&As or debate?
- Reviews?
- Crowdsourcing?
- Voting? People's choice?

Brainstorm Step 3: Brand Experience

This step looks at the experiences people have with the sponsor's brand (the touch-points). You will probably be able to use aspects of the sponsorship to make the brand experience better.

Can you use any of the intellectual property to improve the brand experience?

- Sponsorship-driven offers for brand users?
- Expertise, blogs, behind-the-scenes information for your customers?

Can you take inspiration from the event to change or improve your products?

- Sponsorship-themed? Limited edition?
- More creative?

Case Studies: Consumer-Generated Content

Pepsi Max sponsored the halftime show of the Canadian Football League's Grey Cup, their championship game. They allowed fans to log on to a website to "create the playlist," voting for their favorites from halftime band Blue Rodeo, which were then played on the night.

For the 2009 NHL Playoffs, brewer **Molson** created the Molson Canadian Official Guide to Playoff Grooming, encouraging fans to upload photos of their funny and offbeat playoff grooming rituals to the Molson Facebook page.

Chick-fil-A created a microsite featuring a customizable "wave" for the U.S. college football season. People could upload photos of themselves and friends, customize the "wave" experience, and share in social media.

When **Gatorade** rolled out their immersive G Series Mobile Locker Room, part of the tour was to visit eight U.S. high schools. Schools were picked from photos and descriptions of their teams' locker room rituals, submitted to the Gatorade Facebook page. Schools with the most "likes" earned visits.

- Easier to use?
- "You told us, we listened"?

Can you use any aspects of the sponsorship to showcase your brand's alignment to target market priorities, concerns, or passions?

- What messages can you use?

Brainstorm Step 4: Achieving Objectives

You are now looking at how you can use the sponsorship to achieve brand needs and broader business needs. We've included a sample list below. Depending on the sponsor's category of business, or how the business is structured, you may want to customize it to suit.

How can we use this sponsorship to help us achieve our marketing and business objectives with external markets (end-users)?

- Information, trial, demonstration
- Build followers and/or databases
- Promotional offers
- Loyalty offers
- Endorsement
- "Inspired by" products and uses
- Demonstrate brand positioning

    With VIP customers?

- Creative hospitality
- Pass-through rights

Case Study: Target Market Alignment

Rather than going down the well-worn track of performance and glory, **P&G** used their sponsorship of the 2012 Olympic Games in an extraordinary way. Their platform was "Proud sponsor of mums," and with that they celebrated all that mums do to help their kids be all they can be.

Strongbow (alcoholic cider), sponsor of the 12-mile obstacle course series Tough Mudder in the UK, used the investment to underpin their "Earn it" positioning. How? Everyone who finishes gets a pint of Strongbow at a competitor bar at the end of the race.

With internal markets?

- Incentive programs
- Staff events
- Volunteerism
- Donations

With intermediary markets (retailers, brokers, resellers, agents)?

- Retail promotions
- Incentive programs
- Creative hospitality

Brainstorm Step 5: Integration

This step is all about ensuring the integration is thorough—across all appropriate marketing activities (Figure 6.2). This saves the sponsor a lot of money—as sponsorship is acting as a catalyst to make the money they're already spending work harder. Again, this is provided as a sample only, as your list may be very different.

Can we integrate this sponsorship across our existing activities?

- Brand marketing
- Positioning
- Competitive advantage
- Advertising
- Sales
- Website, other web and mobile activities
- Social media
- Loyalty/database marketing
- Public relations
- Promotions
- Sales
- Media
- Retail
- On/in-pack
- Online
- Retailers, resellers, or storefronts
- New product launch
- Human resources
- Shareholder management

Figure 6.2
Sponsorship
centralized

Brainstorm Step 6: Vetting

At this point, what you will be faced with is a whiteboard, or a lot of butcher paper, full of a huge array of ideas for your potential sponsor. Some of them will be standouts and others less so, and now you need to pick which ideas you're going to include in your proposal.

Ask your team to choose the best several ideas (you may amalgamate some ideas).

- Has the sponsor achieved each of their key objectives?
- Have they achieved win-win-win for each of their key target markets?
- Is there anything here that detracts from the event experience?
- Is there anything here that is bad for you?
- What benefits—outside of the normal, hygiene benefits of tickets, signage, hospitality, and endorsement—will you need to provide to the sponsor to make these happen?

And that's it. It's messy, but you've got the guts of your sponsorship offer. In the next chapter, we'll go over how to formalize that into a strong proposal and price it correctly.

Special Considerations

When developing offers, there are a few special circumstances that you can address.

Short Lead Time

As you may have ascertained, some of the leverage ideas you're going to provide to a sponsor could take months for them to implement. What you don't want is for them to look at your proposal, realize they don't have enough time to make a leverage plan happen, and tell you they want to talk to you about next year. Instead, you should realize that your lead time is a bit short and select the ideas you provide based on how quick and easy they are to implement.

What constitutes a short lead time? For a significant sponsorship, anything under six months is starting to get too close to plan and implement great leverage. By selecting your leverage ideas appropriately, you can potentially lengthen your sales window by a couple of months.

Creating Offers for Retailers

Retailers have an enviable position in sponsorship, and one that you can take advantage of if you know how.

When you walk around the grocery store, you need to realize that every brand that is on display or being sampled or featured in their weekly sales circular has paid for the privilege. A whole range of payments are made from vendors (the brands that are being sold in the store) to the retailer, but collectively, you can refer to them as vendor allowances.

If you can come up with ways for a retail sponsor to involve a few of their vendors in the sponsorship, they can charge those vendors for the privilege, lowering their functional cost of sponsoring you and making it easier for them to say yes. The activity they'll charge for generally centers around activity in-store and in media controlled by the retailer, not activity at your event.

Creating Offers for Vendors

The flip side of creating offers for retailers is creating offers for brands that sell through retailers or some other kind of middleman.

These brands pay to be featured by the retailer—it's that important—so if you can come up with leverage ideas that create value for one of their retail partners, they could get even more bang for their vendor allowance buck. This

Retailers love sponsorships where they can involve their vendors.

is often very simple: Look at your best ideas and ask whether there is any way to get one of their key retailers involved.

Creating Offers for Media

Media sponsors tend to want one or more of the following:

- Exclusive rights to the broadcast or other important IP, such as a newspaper distributing an official festival program.

Leverage All-Star: Volkswagen

Volkswagen is one of the bigger sponsors of Australian Rules Football team the Sydney Swans. Their target market is clearly family car buyers, and this very family-oriented fan base provided the perfect platform for nurturing their relationship with potential buyers and showcasing their (mainly) four-wheel-drives. In taking on this sponsorship, they have created one of the most consistently strong, win-win-win sponsorships we've ever seen. A few highlights:

- Like the other major sponsors, they have the right to show an ad on the big screen during a break in the game. Rather than show an ad for their cars, they showcase the fans. Before every home game, fans literally line up to sit in the backseat of one of their 4WDs, buckle in, and sing the team song on video with their friends. Those hundreds of videos are then culled and edited into a montage of fans singing the song, while the whole stadium sings along with them. Meanwhile, they're getting hundreds of people a week into their cars. (And what a lot of room there is back there!)
- They offer a series of skills games in front of the stadium, such as goal-kicking competitions, and one where contestants have

to hand-ball (yes, that's what it's called) an Aussie Rules ball through a spinning tire and into the back of a 4WD. (And what a big cargo area it has!)

- They offer multiple face-painting stations and airbrushed team logos for the kids . . . and a fair few adults!
- One home game a year, anyone driving a VW parks for free.
- In the lead-up to the finals season, they asked all of the players what their "Pump-Up Playlists" were and set up a website to showcase them. They also played music from one star player a week's Pump-Up Playlist during breaks in the game, showing an insight into the musical taste of some big sporting heroes. They also invited people to submit their own Pump-Up Playlists, creating an aggregate of the favorite pregame songs across all of the fans.

While they are clearly showcasing their cars, more than that, they are aligning with the fans and adding enormous value to the family fans' experience. Well done, Volkswagen.

Cheer, cheer the red and the white . . .

(Full disclosure: Kim is a Swans fan . . . and a mum.)

- Increased audience (viewership, readership, listenership). Their ad rates are based on CPM or cost-per-thousand, so if you can help them get bigger numbers, their existing ads are worth more.
- More advertising. Try to provide them with content that will either attract advertisers they don't normally get (like your other sponsors) or create a forum where their current advertisers can advertise more.
- Profiling specific personalities, shows, or features.

If you can tick one, or preferably more, of those boxes, you are much more likely to get a yes and the media you need from them.

CHAPTER 7

Proposals

We'll now go back to our kitchen analogy. You have an inventory of all of your ingredients, the **Sponsor Information Checklist** has provided you with a recipe, your offer has provided a firm vision of the finished meal, so now it's time to start cooking!

The Number One Job of a Proposal

Before you can start to structure a proposal that will sell, you need to understand and embrace the number one job it needs to do. That job is not to help you sell it to your contact—it's for that contact to sell it internally.

Sponsorship is now so heavily integrated into different areas of a sponsor's business that even if the brand manager is a huge fan and ready to say "yes," he or she will still need to present the business case to colleagues for their sign-off before he or she can be assured it will be a success.

What to Include in a Proposal

In order to give the sponsor enough information to make a decision, a proposal must contain the following points.

Overview

Paint the picture, tantalize the sponsor with both what your organization is about and how you can benefit them. Be absolutely sure to include details about why your property is meaningful to your target markets—the passion your fans have for what you do, and the larger relevance to target markets that will interest the sponsor.

> The number one job of your proposal is to help the brand manager sell it internally.

About [the Property]

This is really property FAQ, listing dates, times, locations, projected attendance, ticket costs, membership numbers, etc.—all the hard data. The information provided here could vary widely depending on the type of property. The idea is that you don't want your potential sponsor getting three-quarters of the way through the proposal and not knowing when the event happens, when it's launched, where you're located, or other key pieces of information.

Target Markets

If a sponsor is going to consider your event, one of the first things they need to know is who you are targeting. Showcase your target market segments, using both psychographic and demographic information. Ideally, you will be able to support this section with comprehensive market research information, but even if you don't have that (yet!), try to be as complete as you can be. You may want to consider including your "one person" target market descriptions (from Chapter 2). If they have helped you to understand your market segments, they may also help a potential sponsor.

You may want to keep the order of your segments flexible, so you can put the most important segments to your potential sponsor on top. Don't ever use phrases such as "lovers of art," "museum goers," or "general audience." These types of phrases are too general and indicate to sponsors that you know nothing about your audience.

You can address your target markets as a separate part of the proposal, or you can incorporate them in your marketing plan overview, outlined in the next section. We tend to favor keeping them separate.

Marketing Plan

This is an overview of the marketing plan you have already created. It outlines exactly how you will be marketing yourself to your target markets, the value, reach, and audience of all marketing components, which media you are using, and your publicity plan.

Creative Ideas for Leverage

This is where you get to strut your stuff and demonstrate your understanding of your potential sponsor's needs.

Start by outlining the sponsor's marketing objectives, as you understand them. Then, drop in the strongest ideas you and your team came up with in the offer brainstorm session, ensuring you mention how each of these ideas helps them achieve their objectives. There is nothing that will help sponsors say yes to a strong sponsorship opportunity more than that will.

There are some people who will say this is dangerous, that sponsors will steal your creative ideas and do them with someone else. Yes, that is a possibility, but it doesn't really happen that often. Use confidentiality wording (we've provided later in this chapter) and include the ideas. In many cases, creative ideas for leverage will be the difference between yes and no.

Comprehensive List of Benefits

This is where you list the benefits that you will provide as part of this offer. These should be taken from your inventory and reflect a comprehensive package, but should never include everything in your inventory. Tailoring the list is absolutely essential.

Use bullet points and, depending upon how long the list is, you may want to categorize the benefits as they are categorized on your inventory.

Investment

This should reflect the total investment, including:

- Cash
- Contra or in-kind investment
- Promotional support that directly benefits your organization

You should also include payment due dates and any performance incentives in this section.

Bonuses

Your case for investment will be a lot stronger if you can provide the potential sponsor with a precedent as to exactly how this has worked for other companies like them and/or a precedent as to exactly how your other sponsors have achieved a commercial return (in other words, used their sponsorship to change the perceptions and behavior of their target markets). If you have this information, put it in a section before the "Comprehensive list of benefits."

How Long Should It Be?

As a rough guideline, in order to get all of the information into the proposal that the sponsor will need, you are looking at a minimum of 7 to 10 pages. If you have a lot of leverage ideas, research, precedents, or a very comprehensive marketing plan, you could go up to about 12 pages or even a little more.

More important than size, however, is that it is easy and fast to read. This will be more a testament to your ability to format the proposal nicely and use concise wording than the actual amount of information included.

Deck Versus Document?

While there is a temptation to use the in-built features of PowerPoint to create a pretty presentation, a deck of slides just doesn't have the scope to convey the amount of information a sponsor will need to sell the opportunity internally and make a decision. You are only going to be able to give them that in a well-formatted full proposal, most likely formatted in a word processing program. So, if you're going to be sending the proposal, send them a full proposal, not a deck.

If you are going to do a stand-up presentation, create a great sponsorship proposal first—one that you will leave behind that is complete enough to make the whole business case without you being there. Then, using the full proposal as a guide, create a concise deck hitting the main points and talk to those points. Don't try to wedge all of your proposal content into a deck for presentation. If your preparation is strong, you'll be able to present with minimal wording on your presentation.

Once you're done with the presentation, hand your contact three copies of the full proposal and either include a USB drive with an electronic copy or e-mail one later. That makes it easy to distribute to key colleagues.

To Tease or Not to Tease?

This is a really good question and a matter of style.

One school of thought is that you should have a two-page teaser—a summary of the property, target markets, key marketing strategies, and ways you've identified you "fit" with the sponsor. This, of course, assumes that they will be interested and you'll get an opportunity to put your best foot forward with a full, and fully customized, proposal later.

Unfortunately, this isn't always the case, and in recent years, sponsors have become even pickier. We have shifted away from that approach, in most cases, to one that favors an orientation toward sponsor needs and full customization from the start. Do your homework, ask the right questions, and make the first sponsorship document you commit to writing your very best effort. Don't tease, wow.

Using the Sponsorship Proposal Template

We have included a **Sponsorship Proposal Template** later in this chapter for you to use as a guideline. Clearly, you will need to adapt this to your own property and style, but this should give you a good place to start. For best results, you may want to consider the following suggestions:

- You must include all of the information in the template in order for a sponsor to be able to make a decision.
- We prefer a proposal that starts each proposal section on its own page, keeping it easy and straightforward to read.
- Do not use an executive summary—your contact will tend to read that and not get to the meat of the proposal. Instead, use your cover letter to tell the contact very briefly what it is about and how it relates to them (see the **Proposal Cover Letter** in Chapter 8).
- If you already have other sponsors committed, highlight this in your cover letter. If at all possible, include existing audience research.
- A major selling point for sponsors is that research will be done during the course of the sponsorship and provided to the sponsor, including at least a couple of questions provided by the sponsor. The perceived value of this to the sponsor is much higher than it may cost you.
- Create a proposal with an eye for detail and presentation. The more professional it looks, the more credible you are. Use the magic that technology offers to its fullest potential—insert photos, maps, artwork, or whatever is appropriate into your proposal document and print it in color. Keep it professional and don't go overboard, but do use technology to help you build the atmosphere and personality of your event within the proposal document.

- You can provide such items as brochures and calendars of events for review by the sponsor, but do not make the sponsor search for pertinent information in these documents. You also need to keep in mind that anything extra won't tend to travel around to other sponsor stakeholders with the proposal. If it is important (such as key dates or locations), it must be included in the proposal itself, ideally in the event details section.
- In this day and age, many proposals are submitted in PDF form via email or an online submission mechanism. There is no reason you can't include supporting artwork or other documents—either as an attachment or to dress up the proposal itself (they can click on small artwork to see it bigger). If you are submitting it in hard copy, either comb bind your proposal or neatly staple it and enclose it in a presentation folder.
- Do not send a video or other multimedia with your proposal. It wastes money, and sponsors almost never look at them. If you are invited to make a presentation, you may have a video loaded into your laptop to show only if requested. If they don't request that, you could offer to email a link to it if they want it for further review. Our insider tip: most won't.

Confidentiality

Unfortunately, we have all heard of cases where a sponsee went to a company with a great idea for an event but was turned down, only to see their idea implemented directly by the company a few months or a year later. In truth this is uncommon, but is more common if you are asked to submit the proposal through an agency. In any case, it does make sense to protect your ideas.

If the proposal includes any of your creative ideas, it should include a legal statement that all concepts included are your property. A sample can be found below. This should be placed *before* the body of your proposal, such as at the bottom of your title page.

> © Copyright [*organization name*] 2015. This publication is copyrighted and remains the intellectual property of [*organization*]. No part of it may be reproduced by any means without the prior written permission of [*organization*].

Depending upon the confidentiality of it, you may also want to include this wording:

> The information contained in this proposal is confidential, and no part of it may be copied and/or disclosed to any person without the express permission of [*organization*].

Pricing

While developing your sponsorship proposal, you also need to address pricing. This is no doubt the most vexing area of creating a proposal, and, unfortunately, we cannot offer any hard-and-fast rules. We can, however, offer a few strategies that should help.

First and foremost, the total fee must be less expensive than if the sponsor were to run the event on their own. The overall package must represent value for money.

No matter what, never tell the potential sponsor how you are going to spend the money! This undermines your value and indicates your need rather than your worth. It also undermines the perception that you are a professional, viable organization whether they participate or not. It is not unusual for a sponsor to request a breakdown of marketing and promotional expenditure.

It used to be that you could use equivalent advertising costs as a benchmark, but the sophistication of most sponsors has grown to such a point that they identify that sponsorship is a unique marketing medium, offering a degree of relevance and connection with people that precludes any direct comparison of costs. Unfortunately, that just makes pricing more difficult. There are no hard-and-fast rules, but we do have some guidelines that should help you get there.

Calculating Your Baseline Fee

When calculating your price, you must firstly understand that a significant chunk of the sponsorship fee will go toward providing the promised benefits, as well as paying for the sale, servicing, and administration of the sponsorship. The difference between those costs and the fee is your profit—the amount that you will actually be able to put toward increasing your revenue base.

> Cost of providing benefits offered
>
> + Staff and administration costs
>
> + Sales costs
>
> + Servicing costs
> _____
>
> = Your total cost

Once you have calculated the total cost of providing the sponsorship, you need to add in your profit. Your profit is the money you get to use as income

> Never tell the potential sponsor how you are going to spend the money.

> Remember, your baseline fee is *only* a baseline, not your final price.

to underwrite an event or program, or simply to add to your bottom line. As a rough guideline, your baseline fee will be two to three times your total cost, for a profit of 100 to 200 percent against your costs.

Total cost to deliver the program × 3 = Baseline fee

Total cost to deliver the program × 2 = Red line fee

Once you know your baseline fee, you need to stack it up against market indicators. These indicators could show that you are in the right ballpark or, more likely, they could show that you are significantly under- or overpriced. If your baseline fee is overpriced against the market, you will have to readdress the benefits package and/or how it is delivered to ensure that it provides adequate income for your event. There is no use going to all the trouble to sell and service a sponsorship if it's not providing you with any benefit, or worse, if it costs you more to provide the sponsorship than you charge for the package.

No sponsorship should be valued solely on what you need.

Determining Market Price

Once you have determined your baseline fee, you need to adjust it to reflect the marketplace in which you operate. Ask yourself the following questions.

- What is the cost of similar sponsorship products on the market? Corporate sponsorship managers talk to each other and know the price of similar sponsorship packages. You need to have that same understanding.
- How does your product stand up? If similar events are offering the standard "tickets and logo exposure" package and you are offering a creative and multifaceted marketing opportunity, then you can promote your offer as having a much higher value.
- How does your sponsorship servicing measure up? If you are constantly willing to go the extra mile to make a sponsorship work, then you will be consistently adding value to the package and your current sponsors are likely to vouch for you.
- Are there any other variables that might affect your price? What if your team wins the national championships? What if you lose your star player?
- How much is your potential sponsor likely to invest? Precedent is not always a reliable indicator, but if you know a sponsor has never invested more than $20,000 in your organization and you are suddenly approaching them with a package valued at more than $100,000, you need to understand that you will probably encounter some resistance. You will

CHAPTER 7 / PROPOSALS

need to build a strong case for that level of investment, as well as possibly being prepared to negotiate for a lower level of benefits.

- No sponsorship proposal should be valued solely on what you need to make the project work.

These questions should get you pretty close to the market value of your event. In order to double-check yourself, you should do the following:

- Pay attention to the marketplace—read sponsorship publications, join a sponsorship or marketing association, extend your network.
- Use your network—we know people who won't send out a proposal without running it past three trusted colleagues first.

Multiyear Agreements

It is almost always better to go for a multiyear agreement than for a single year. It gives you some steady income and peace of mind, and it gives the sponsor time to really maximize their leverage and results.

When structuring a multiyear agreement, keep in mind the following things:

- If your event is new and will likely grow bigger and more valuable as time goes on, you should structure your fees to reflect larger payments in later years.
- If your event has a long track record of delivering the goods, you may elect a flat payment structure.
- If your event is new and you have one key sponsor who is the "perceived owner" of the event, you *may* be able to get a larger fee in the first year to assist in underwriting the infrastructure, but this will come at a dramatic cost in future years.

What If the Adjusted Fee Is Too Low?

If you've done all of your calculations and used your network and research to determine the fair market value, and the realistic fee is nearing your red-zone number (200 percent of costs), you have a number of options for structuring the fee to make it work for you.

Multiyear Discounts

You could offer them a multiyear deal. With costs of $10,000, a sponsorship fee of $22,000 may not look very appealing for one year, but if you can make it

$22,000 a year for a three-year contract, or $22,000, $24,000, $26,000 across a three-year contract, it may seem like a much better option.

Proactively Offer Incentive-Based Fees

We are strongly in favor of fee structures that incorporate a component that is performance based. This creates an incentive for the sponsee to deliver as promised—to go that extra mile—and sponsors see this as a refreshing departure from sponsees that take the money and run.

It also means that you could make more money on the sponsorship because you are lowering the risk to the sponsor (and let's face it, some sponsors still think sponsorship is a risk!). The key is to tie the performance-based component to specific, quantifiable, and desirable outcomes.

Instead of charging $10,000 cash for a sponsorship from a carmaker, you could do this:

- $8,000 up-front payment
- $2,000 if more than 60 attendees test drive their car
- $2,000 if they get more than 200 qualified prospects onto their database

This gives you a total of $12,000, reduces the perceived risk to the sponsor, and shows that you are absolutely confident that you will produce results. Of course, if you are not confident of producing results, do not do it. In fact, if you are not confident of producing results, get out of sponsorship!

One thing to note: When incentive-based fees are mentioned to sponsors, they will often immediately want to negotiate an incentive based upon sales. Whatever you do, don't agree to a sales-based incentive.

You can provide a lot of the ingredients to making a sale, including:

- Promoting the product
- Enhancing the product's image
- Providing opportunities for sales (e.g., on-site sales or sales to your members)
- Product demonstrations
- Relationship-building opportunities

What you can't deliver are actual sales, as these will be largely based upon the quality and value inherent in the product. For instance, a soft-drink manufacturer may be the exclusive vendor at your summer event, but if a malfunc-

Incentive-based fees lower the perceived risk to the sponsor.

Never agree to a sales-based fee.

tion occurs and the drinks are warm and flat, or if they price it above market value, they won't hit their sales projections no matter how many people you get through your gate. You should not be held accountable for that.

It is far better to negotiate an incentive based upon how many people come to your event and leave delivering the right product at the right price to your sponsor.

Contra Sponsorship

Contra sponsorship occurs when a sponsor pays for their sponsorship with products or services instead of cash. Also known as barter, trade, or in-kind sponsorship, contra sponsorship makes up at least a portion of a large number of sponsorships.

When negotiating for contra sponsorship, keep three things in mind.

1. Contra sponsorship is only of value to you if:
   a. You have budgeted for the specific item already. In that case, it is only worth as much as it is saving you in cash expenditure. For example, if a company offers to loan you $10,000 in new computer equipment when your planned expenditure was only $2,000 in lease payments, the offer is only worth $2,000 to you.
   b. It adds value to your other sponsorship packages. For instance, if you secure a radio sponsor, you could include airtime in your other sponsorship packages, making them more attractive for other potential sponsors.
2. If the contra sponsor is saving you cash, they are as valuable to you as a fully cash sponsor and they need to be serviced as a cash sponsor (see Part 3).
3. You still need money to run your event or property, so endeavor to negotiate sponsorships where contra sponsorship is only a component of the investment.

When you look at the contra option, don't unnecessarily limit yourself. Most people think only of a sponsored product such as an airline providing free travel, a high-technology company providing computers, etc.

The fact is that sponsors have access to dozens of opportunities and services that can save you a lot of money. What follows is a generic sponsor contra list. This is a great tool to use when negotiating with a sponsor, particularly one that is baulking at making the full investment in cash.

> Contra sponsorship is only of value if you have budgeted for that item already.

Promotion

- Media promotion
- Promotion of sponsee through retailers
- Promotion of property on pack
- Promotion in internal employee communication
- Promotion to customers (social media, mailings, magazine, newsletter, website, database, etc.)
- Property signage on sponsor building

Media

- Access to heavily discounted media rates through sponsor's media buyer
- Tags on existing advertising
- New advertisements profiling property
- Providing a limited media schedule (probably shared with sponsor)

Creativity

- Creative work for the property done by sponsor's advertising agency or in-house graphic department

People

- Provision of sponsor-contracted celebrity for property endorsement or appearances
- Donation of employee for fixed-term assignment (full- or part-time for set number of weeks/months)
- Employee volunteers to augment on-site staff
- Access to in-house experts and subcontractors (social media, public relations, printing, media planning, database development, web development, SEO, etc.)

Travel

- Access to discounted airline or hotel deals
- Contra travel or hotel (if sponsor is in the travel business)

Infrastructure

- Office space
- Office equipment or services
- Event equipment or services

Other Contra Products or Services

- For use as prizes, incentives, or giveaways
- To add value to other sponsorship packages

Equivalent Opportunity Cost

When calculating your price you also need to understand what you are competing against in terms of media—the "equivalent opportunity cost," as media buyers put it. This is particularly the case if you are approaching a brand manager, as they will likely have to reallocate money from some other media to your sponsorship if they commit.

If you are seeking money for a sponsorship, you need to understand how a sponsor *could* spend this money. You need to understand that you are not only competing with other sponsorship seekers but you are also competing with the main media, endorsements, and sales promotions.

Questions you need to ask to determine how else a sponsor could be spending their money include

- How many television commercials could they buy in peak viewing with that investment?
- How many black and white pages in metropolitan daily newspapers?
- How many color pages in mainstream or targeted magazines?
- How many weeks of 30-second spots, at a rate of 30 per week, on metropolitan radio?
- How many billboards?

You should be able to get these costs from your advertising agency or media placement company. If you don't have either of these, you will need to secure price lists (which can often be found online) from key media throughout your marketplace and make an educated estimate.

If your event or program is national in scope, get national figures. If it is limited to one city or region, then get figures specific to that region. And remember to use figures that are representative of the discounts given to large advertisers, not casual rates, which will be much higher.

In addition to giving you an understanding of your competitive position, knowing what a sponsor could get for their investment can really help you during the sales process, particularly if your event or program offers strong benefits over time.

Imagine being able to make a case for your highly targeted, strongly matched two-month event, offering a whole range of benefits to meet the sponsor's objectives versus them placing five advertisements during *60 Minutes*. Used judiciously, this can be a very powerful argument, but you must be absolutely confident in the value of your offer.

Proposal Issues

There are a number of issues that come up over and over again around the creation and presentation of sponsorship proposals. We have addressed some of the most common ones here.

Should We Offer Different Sponsorship Levels?

A lot of sponsorship seekers offer levels to their potential sponsors—gold, silver, and bronze levels are very popular (and overused to the point of being a cliché). The main problem with this approach is that, without realizing it, most sponsees formulate the packages so that all of the levels get access to the best benefits, with the main difference being that the lower levels get fewer of the same things.

Clearly, this is not an approach that is conducive to creating strong, high-level sponsorships. It undermines the true value of the relationship, creating instead a bargain hunter's paradise.

At the same time, some sponsors like options. So, if a sponsor specifically asks for options, the trick is working out how to offer sponsors a choice without undermining your value and potential revenue. We have identified two good ways around this: "The apple and orange approach" and "The up-selling approach."

The Apple and Orange Approach

This approach revolves around the strategy of offering two packages that are completely different from each other, each emphasizing a differing set of sponsor objectives. You don't want the potential sponsor to be able to compare them on a benefit-for-benefit basis, so you create an apple and an orange. Ideally, the packages should be priced similarly, but even if they aren't, this strategy can work very well.

This is very different from the "levels" strategy of offering three different-sized apples. If all the potential sponsor wants is an apple, they will almost certainly take the smallest, cheapest one.

The following is a very generalized example of two packages that a basketball team could offer to a potential confectionery sponsor—same sponsee, same sponsor, but very different outcomes.

Offer 1: Emphasis on VIP Hospitality
- Use of private box (seating 12) for eight featured games
- Autographed team merchandise for all sponsor guests

- Postgame player meet-and-greets in the box for each game (one or two players, as available), as well as team mascot
- VIP clinic with the team for kids and grandkids of the sponsor's key customers
- Inclusion of VIPs' children in halftime activities (as appropriate)
- Thirty pairs of premium tickets to other games
- VIP tickets and travel for six to an all-star game

Offer 2: Emphasis on New Product Launch
- Naming rights to a feature game
- Media launch for new product at the game
- Exit sampling of new product for all attendees of launch game
- Content for sponsor to create an app around the new product
- Exclusive content for use in the new product's social media activities
- Endorsement of new product
- Naming rights to team mascot
- Attendance at launch by coach and mascot
- Halftime on-court product launch stunt and interactive audience contest
- Use of hospitality room for VIP guests at featured game (seating 50)

The Up-Selling Approach

Another strategy that we favor is offering one highly tailored package, with an optional upgrade available at extra cost. Our experience is that, in a high percentage of cases, once the potential sponsor is sold on the concept of a partnership with a sponsee, they look at the upgrade as an opportunity to maximize the sponsorship and take it up.

Do remember to go through the pricing exercise for both the offer and the upgrade to ensure that you are covering all of your costs.

Following is an example of the offer and upgrade prepared by the same basketball team to the same confectionery company potential sponsor.

Sponsorship Offer
- Naming rights to a feature game
- Media launch for new product at the game
- Content for sponsor to create an app around the new product
- Exclusive content for use in the new product's social media activities
- Endorsement of new product
- Naming rights to team mascot

- Attendance at launch by coach and mascot
- Halftime on-court product launch stunt and audience contest
- Exit sampling of new product for all attendees of launch game
- Use of hospitality room for VIP guests at featured game (seating 50)
- Postgame player meet-and-greet in the hospitality room (one or two players, as available), as well as team mascot
- Consumer raffle boxes located around venue
- Twenty-four pairs of reserved seat tickets to future games for use in consumer raffles

Optional VIP Hospitality Upgrade
- Use of private box (seating 12) for six additional featured games
- Inclusion of VIPs' children in halftime activities (as appropriate)
- VIP clinic with the team for kids and grandkids of the sponsor's key customers
- VIP tickets and travel for six to an all-star game

How Do We Define Category Exclusivity?

The only rule of exclusivity is: the more exclusivity is granted, the more valuable it is.

There are three types of exclusivity:

- Sponsorship
- Signage (in cases where the venue may have existing, conflicting signage)
- Sales

Most exclusivity is granted on the basis of categories, which is often referred to in proposals and contracts as "category exclusivity." This usually refers to the category of business that a company is in, for example, airline, carbonated soft drink, ice cream, beer. You can make this exclusivity more valuable and attractive to your sponsor by extending across competitive categories.

An example of this would be to grant Pepsi sponsorship and sales exclusivity across categories such as carbonated soft drinks (their true category), noncarbonated soft drinks, sports drinks, fruit juices, fruit and iced-tea based drinks, flavored milk, and water.

When preparing an offer, you need to balance the degree of exclusivity you offer the sponsor with the financial impact on your organization. If you granted Pepsi the exclusivity outlined above, you will surely get more money from them for the sponsorship, but it also cuts out a lot of other potential sponsors and the revenue they could bring in.

On the other hand, if you are having a hard time selling a category, you could consider breaking it into smaller, more affordable chunks. For instance, you could divide the IT category into hardware, software, ISP, and peripheral categories. Way back in 1996, the Atlanta Olympics famously broke up the automotive category after being unsuccessful in selling it to one manufacturer, and sold separate sponsorships in categories including "official pickup truck" and "official luxury car." This can be effective, but it can also be confusing, so you will need to work closely with sponsors in similar categories to ensure that they either work together (as IT sponsors often do) or stay well out of each other's way.

Do We Need a Glossy Sales Brochure or Video?

Unfortunately, when it comes to selling sponsorship, a lot of sponsees rely on flash over substance. They produce glossy sales brochures outlining the sponsorship packages (often laid out in levels). While these brochures are often beautifully prepared, they lack what sponsors want most—customization.

Rather than going to the effort and expense of creating slick sales materials, put that effort into researching your potential sponsors and creating highly customized proposals. Every one of the sponsors we have polled has supported this contention. Your proposal should be neat and professional—do put it on letterhead and bind it or present it as a tidy PDF. That is all the sponsor expects from the presentation.

What is useful to sponsors is providing examples of some of your event promotional materials from previous years, if you have them. If not, you could include one or two mock-ups of the planned materials for the current event. This will showcase the style and degree of professionalism that your organization has, as well as add color to the presentation.

Do you need a video? In a word, no. Sponsors never watch them, and if you bring one along with you to your meeting, you are burning your short window with the sponsor showing them something that is inherently uncustomized, and they know full well it has been edited to show you in the most flattering possible light. A well-planned and enthusiastic verbal presentation will give you a lot more mileage.

Photographs and diagrams are a different story. If your event is extremely visual, such as an art exhibition, photographs are a must. If your event is an

> Do not rely on flash to sell a proposal.

expo of some type, a map or other diagram will give the sponsor an opportunity to understand your vision and their place in it. Include these things right in your proposal document.

Should We Go to One Company at a Time, or Can We Go to Several?

In a perfect world, you would only go to one company in any given product category at a time. But, as you have already gathered from reading this book, creating relationships takes time. You are highly unlikely to have enough lead time before your event to research, approach, and negotiate your sponsorships using this approach.

In reality, it is perfectly all right to have several offers out at one time. If you have done your background research, this should not exceed 10 or 12 companies, and the offers will most likely be very different from each other, reflecting the different needs of the various companies.

How Much Lead Time Does a Potential Sponsor Need?

Most sponsors set their larger sponsorship expenditures as part of their marketing budget, 12 to 18 months before the events. They will often have an additional amount of money set aside for opportunistic spending if something else comes up. This amount is usually, but not always, fairly limited and will not accommodate major sponsorships. Only if something really extraordinary comes along will they breach this plan.

In addition, companies need time to maximize sponsorships. Usually, the more product lines, customer types, distribution channels, and so on they have, the longer it will take them to make the most of their sponsorships. This should be as important to you as it is to them because a happy sponsor is a good sponsor.

It is imperative that you ask the question about lead times when doing your background research on potential sponsors. Only then will you know for sure what their policy is. As a very rough guideline, we have found the following time frames to be common across a lot of companies.

12–24 months
- Major sponsorships of mega events
- Multinational sponsorships requiring buy-in from across an organization
- Multiyear events

9–12 months
- Most sponsorships come under this time frame.

6–9 months
- If you go below 9 months, you should still have some success at creating major sponsorship relationships, but you need to ensure that the leverage ideas included in your offer can be implemented between their yes and your launch.

4–6 months
- In this territory, you may have some success mainly with medium to smaller sponsors. You will probably start having to undercut the value of the sponsorship because the sponsor won't have time to maximize the program fully. You will also start running into budget problems and may have to get creative with pricing and payments.
- If you are looking for a smaller investment (under $100,000 or so), you can often have success without undercutting your value right down to four months.
- If you have missed the budgeting time frame, you will probably be accessing a limited pool of opportunistic funds. This is another reason going to the brand manager—who holds that type of budget and authority—is much better than approaching a sponsorship manager.

Under 4 months
- These investments are reserved for surprise or unanticipated events.
- Unanticipated events are events such as a major sporting team winning the championship. Around that one unanticipated event, a wide range of other sponsorable events could crop up. These are the only type of events that we recommend sponsors should consider with less than four months' lead time.
- If you are trying to sell sponsorship for a planned event with less than four months' lead time, you are extremely unlikely to be successful. Not only do you hit obstacles such as the sponsor not having enough time to maximize the sponsorship or the budget already being set, but it also smacks of desperation and could undermine your credibility as a strong and highly sponsorable organization for years.

When Is the Best Time to Approach Sponsors?

The answer to this is tied to the amount of sponsorship you're seeking. If you are looking for a moderate amount of sponsorship—a maximum of $100,000 to $250,000, depending on the size of their overall marketing budget—you can seek sponsorship anytime, as they probably have enough "play" in their budget to accommodate a great idea like yours.

If you're looking for more money, the best time to approach a potential sponsor is before they have set the marketing budget for the year in which your event or organization is seeking sponsorship. It is as simple as that. Again, you need to ask the question of the potential sponsor when you are doing your preliminary research—well before providing them with a proposal.

There is one timing long shot that you can try, however. If you have a smaller sponsorship on offer, you may want to approach a potential sponsor within six to eight weeks of the end of the financial year. If they have any unspent funds in their sponsorship budget for that year, you may be able to access them. Extra funds are usually a result of the above-mentioned opportunistic budget not being fully utilized over the course of the year.

Sponsorship Proposal Template

1

Great North Airways
and
The Toronto International
Fishing Expo

Date

Use your own judgment when doing the title page, but do show the sponsor name and your name together using the word "and." If you are selling the naming rights or presenting sponsorship (e.g., The Toronto International Fishing Expo presented by Great North Airways), show the name of the event as it would be if they took up the sponsorship.

Always date your proposal, and always put it on a professional letterhead.

2

"The worst day fishing
is better than
the best day working"

Anonymous

Use this page to set the stage. You can use a relevant quote—funny, inspirational, or something that just says it all. Your challenge is to really get to the core of what your property is about—the beauty of flowers, the spirit of competition, the dignity of the underprivileged. There are lots of good quote sites on the Internet.

Another option is one arresting statistic. Or if your event is very visual, an image of something relatively simple—one flower, a pair of dancers—can be very powerful on its own or with a quote or statistic.

3

Overview

In November 2015, Toronto's Exhibition Place will throw open its doors and welcome 85,000 enthusiastic fishermen and women to the Toronto International Fishing Expo.

They will be treated to more than 100 demonstrations and activities for all types and levels of experience. They will enjoy more than 450 exhibitors from Canada and the United States and will have the opportunity to try out their gear on the largest indoor trout lake in the world. And as high consumers of fishing tourism, they will flock to our brand-new Fishing Adventures area and can even book their trips on site.

The Expo marks the only event on the Toronto event calendar that is specifically designed for fishing enthusiasts, and is a destination event for fishermen and women across the region. Nearby hotels fill up with groups of friends travelling into Toronto to attend the Expo and take in all that Toronto has to offer.

Approximately 40 percent of Canadian men fish at least once a year, with a quarter of them fishing at least once a month. These men and women love their sport, and they make sure that they are equipped for it to be as successful and enjoyable as possible. On average, these fishermen and women spend more than $260 each at the Expo on fishing equipment alone, with many exhibitors tracking extensive online sales for months after the event. And although in 2014 we only had very limited on-site travel booking available, over 250 fishing trips were booked.

Even if they can't attend, for some reason, fishing enthusiasts love the Toronto International Fishing Expo. We have over 140,000 followers on Twitter and Facebook, and a strong content share rate on both. Combined with an average of 18,000 downloads of our Virtual Expo exhibitor offer book, and exceptionally high open and click rate on emails to our database of 88,000 fishing enthusiasts, our virtual audience is strong, engaged, and active.

Where does Great North fit in? Based upon our visitor survey last year, more than 65 percent of fishermen fly to a fishing destination at least once every two years, with the average size of their group being 4–6. This represents about 75 percent Canadian destination and the remainder mainly in the United States, Mexico, and the Caribbean, allowing Great North to showcase not only international destinations, but your extensive regional network as well.

As a major sponsor of the Toronto International Fishing Expo and naming rights sponsor to our new travel area, Great North Fishing Adventures, complete with exclusive on-site booking facilities, Great North will enjoy a major profile with this lucrative market. You will also have the platform to create meaningful leverage activities, cementing your relationship with these consumers, tourist boards, adventure travel specialists, and travel agents.

Give a good overview of what your property is about and how being involved will benefit the sponsor. At this point in the proposal, your appeal is basically emotional. You want your target to be able to visualize the event and how its involvement will look and feel. Use emotional wording—a lot of strong adjectives (use a thesaurus).

Also very important is to describe what your property means to your target markets—why they care, the depth of their passion. Sponsors know that it is more powerful to connect with fewer passionate fans than to be in front of millions of disinterested onlookers.

As a general rule, two-thirds of this page should be devoted to visualizing the event, and the remainder to visualizing the sponsorship.

4

Fast Facts

Dates and times	Friday, 23 October 2015, 1:00 a.m.–10:00 p.m. Saturday, 24 October 2015, 10:00 a.m.–8:00 p.m. Sunday, 25 October 2015, 10:00 a.m.–6:00 p.m.
Location	Exhibition Place, Toronto
Attendees	We are expecting 85,000 attendees over the three-day show. This is a projected 7 percent increase on 2014. Attendance has increased by an average of 5–10 percent over each of the past five years.
Virtual attendees	In the six weeks leading up to and through the Expo, we anticipate close to 23,000 downloads of the Virtual Expo exhibitor offer book. This is consistent with the 25 percent per annum growth in virtual attendance we've seen over the past four years.
Cost	$22 adults, $10 for children under 12, children under 5 are free. Family tickets (for up to two adults and two children over 5) can be purchased for $50.
History	The Toronto International Fishing Expo has been going for 27 years and has never grown by less than 4% in attendance in any year.
Parking and transportation	There is ample under-cover parking in the Exhibition Place parking ramp, as well as in other ramps located in the precinct. Exhibition Place is well serviced by bus, streetcar, and train.

This is where you list the hard information about your property. Be straightforward and completely unemotional. This will not only answer a lot of questions your target sponsor may have, but is also your opportunity to show how organized you are.

5

Target Markets

Based upon audience research (attached), our media and promotional campaign is aimed directly at the following demographic and psychographic groups.

Fishing Adventurers

These tend to be upscale males, 28–45, who generally take one major fishing trip per year, generally travelling in groups of 4–6. They are low consumers of fishing products, high consumers of fishing tourism. These people make up 24 percent of our audience and average $4,500 per year expenditure each on fishing tourism.

Flashy Fishermen

This is a small, but big-spending market. Tend to be successful business owners and/or people who have recently had a windfall. Want a boat and want the best of everything. These people make up approximately 10 percent of our audience, but outstrip all others in average spend, with over $1,000 each in product sales. In addition to spending up on equipment, they love expensive, high adventure trips—anything where they get a big story to tell!

Fishing Enthusiasts

This group includes people from all walks of life who fish more than 20 times per year. Tend to be boat owners and trade their boats in every 5–7 years. Based on audience research, these people make up 46 percent of our audience, and accounted for 57 percent of all product sales in 2013. Take regular short fishing breaks and major, fly-in trips every 4–6 years (but would like to do it more often).

Social Fishermen

These are occasional to regular fishermen. They tend to fish in groups of family or friends and see fishing as a quality time activity for families, and in particular, to bond with their children or grandchildren. View the Fishing Expo in the same manner—as an opportunity to spend time with the kids. Heavily into participation aspects of the Expo, particularly ones that are kid-friendly. Particularly high consumers of "starter" equipment for kids and grandkids, as well as small upgrades for their older boats or other equipment. Make up approximately 20 percent of the audience.

As with the previous five years, we will be embarking upon comprehensive market research again in 2015. We are happy to include up to four travel-related questions on Great North's behalf and will provide Great North with the full results of the research.

If the sponsor's primary target market is your secondary or tertiary target market, be sure to emphasize the marketplace(s) that are most relevant to them.

This is where you list the hard information about the event. Be straightforward and completely unemotional. This will not only answer a lot of questions your target sponsor may have, but is also your opportunity to show how organized you are.

6

Marketing Plan

Based upon target market research, we have created a marketing plan that will generate interest in and drive attendance to and interaction with the Expo, while specifically targeting our key markets.

Main Media

Our total budget for paid and promotional media is $150,000, and with that we have been able to negotiate $450,000 in media value. A full media schedule and an audience profile are attached in the Appendix.

Television

Our comprehensive television campaign focuses on two main areas—people who are into fishing and people who are into fishing (or other adventure) travel—with separate promotions and advertisements targeting each of them.

- Two four-week media promotions, run in conjunction with CTV Sport 1 programs "Lon Davies' Fishing World" and CTV Adventure's "Great Vacations." "Fishing World" reaches 100,000 avid fishermen and women in the greater Toronto area every week. "Great Vacations," CTV Adventure's new vacation program, reaches 350,000 people, mainly active travelers, each week.
- Paid media schedule on both channels, supported by tactical advertising on the news and breakfast programming. These schedules will run for four weeks prior to and through the Toronto International Fishing Expo. Placement will determine which of the two ads will run at any given time.

Radio

We have negotiated a three-week drive-time promotional schedule on Q107 (classic rock) running prior to and through the Expo. The schedule is anchored by a major fishing vacation promotion. This station matches our core audience profiles almost exactly.

This schedule will be augmented by two-week limited schedules on Boom 97.3 and The Fan 590, reinforcing the messages on the other two stations most listened to by our Greater Toronto audience and ensuring that we get the most complete coverage of our key markets in the lead-up to the Expo.

Newspaper

The Toronto International Fishing Expo is sponsored by the *Toronto Mirror*. As part of that partnership, we have negotiated a series of five advertisements per week, including 1/6th page ads in the Friday What's On section and page-dominant ads in the Saturday Travel section.

Magazines

We are embarking upon a limited magazine campaign, with placements in *Travel and Leisure* and *Fish Lover* magazines.

Overview your marketing plan, emphasizing the most important elements. Be sure to note what is and is not confirmed. Do not mislead your sponsors.

6

Marketing Plan (continued)

Website

We have a year-round website—www.fishextoronto.ca—generating 1,480,000 hits annually, with 37 percent of those hits in the month prior to the Expo. The website includes a wide variety of information about the show, its sponsors, and exhibitors and is featured on all appropriate media promotion and publicity.

After huge success in 2013 with creating a little bit of how-to content and comedy on the website in the lead-up to the Expo, we are pulling out all the stops and will be creating content including:

- Downloadable Expo app
- How-to articles × 3 by Lon Davies
- Humorous how-to articles x 3 by sports comic Steve Sando (example: "How to get a girly-girl to go fishing")
- Recommended plan of attack for finding what you're after at the Expo, depending on your interests

Database

Our opt-in email database numbers more than 88,000 interested fishermen and women. We will be sending them a prelaunch announcement of dates, including a code to preorder their Expo tickets at a significant discount from Ticketmaster.

Social Media

We engage with our 122,000 Facebook "likers" and almost 18,000 Twitter followers all year, but efforts will intensify across the three months in the lead-up to the Expo. Our strategy is still in development, but will include planned, tactical, and ad hoc activities. Our planned activities include

- Promotion of exclusive content available on the Expo website
- Promotion of sponsor leverage activities and offers—particularly those that add value to the participant experience
- Best fishing joke contest
- Encouraging followers to post and share their best fishing stories (with prizes)
- Call for extras for our new 2015 ads

Search Marketing

We will be using Google AdWords for search advertising. We are preparing a range of short ads that will appear to people in Greater Toronto who search for terms such as "fishing equipment," "fishing trips," "fishing boat," "fishing rod," etc. Ads will run for three weeks prior to the start of the Expo.

Publicity

We have engaged the services of one of the country's top publicists, [insert publicist or company name], who has/have designed a campaign targeting both general and niche media. This campaign will kick off with a fishing-themed media launch (complete with rods) on a boat near the Toronto Waterfront on September 13 and will continue through the Expo.

We will be providing media access to top experts and celebrities, including Lon Davies and the cast of "Great Vacations" for interviews, photos, and expert commentary.

As this is the first year for the Great North Fishing Adventures area, we will be concentrating a large portion of our publicity effort on the promotion of this part of the Expo. Great North will benefit greatly from the promotion of travel destinations and packages, a key part of this strategy. We are also very happy to assist Great North in developing a publicity plan that targets your specific consumer and intermediary markets.

7

Leverage Ideas

Based on our research and a subsequent phone meeting with Great North, we understand your key objectives in the upcoming year are as follows:

- Increasing revenue, particularly for higher profit products
- Promote high-quality (high-profit) holiday travel to frequent business travelers and groups
- Extend the success of your endorsed gourmet tourism packages into other areas
- Provide added value to higher-level frequent flyers
- Showcase new services and packages to online travel sites, travel aggregators, and key travel agents
- Fly the flag to grassroots Canadians in the face of increasing foreign airline competition
- Showcase your new business class service

Using the tools and benefits provided by The Toronto International Fishing Expo, we have come up with a number of ways that Great North Airways can achieve these objectives.

Travel Packages

Lon Davies and the cast of "Great Vacations" have committed to nominating their favorite fishing destinations in Australia and overseas. Great North will have exclusive access to these lists, which can be used to develop "endorsed" fishing travel packages for sale at the Expo, on your website and through your travel agent network.

On-Site Sales

As naming rights sponsor to the Great North Fishing Adventures area, you will be located in a large, central area, themed to resemble a fishing cabin. Arrangements have been made to provide this area with power and other cabling necessary to run a Great North reservations area on-site. Great North will be the sole air travel company represented at the Expo.

As this is the first year for the Great North Fishing Adventures area, there is little direct precedent, but similar areas at the Great Adventure Sports Expo and Waterfront Golf Show have resulted in on-site bookings valued at between $12 and $14 per attendee. At a projected 85,000 attendees, this equates to on-site sales valued at between $1 million and $1.2 million.

To ensure the greatest possible opportunity for Great North to develop travel packages with our other travel exhibitors, we will provide Great North with an exhibitor list and contact details no later than eight weeks prior to the Expo.

If hospitality is a major factor in the package, outline all hospitality opportunities here. If it is a minor factor, move this back toward the benefits section.

If on-site sales, preferred vending status, or product demonstration is a big factor, you will also want to include a section on sales, vending, and display in this area of your proposal.

7

Leverage Ideas (continued)

Travel Industry Hospitality

On Saturday night, 24 October, we will be throwing a travel agents, websites, and travel aggregators–only cocktail party in the Great North Fishing Adventures area. Great North will be promoted as the host of this party, and you are welcome to invite up to 100 guests on top of the 250 core adventure travel specialists identified by the Expo.

A number of our celebrities and demonstrators will be on hand to discuss these destinations with agents. A feature will be a fishing "tournament" where guests will compete for a number of travel prizes by casting their line into the trout lake (which borders the Great North Fishing Adventures area). To keep it light, prizes will be awarded for biggest fish, smallest fish, prettiest fish, most stylish cast, etc.

You are welcome to showcase your newly designed business class seats and other amenities at the cocktail party and throughout the Expo. You may also want to promote the new business class as the ideal option for discerning leisure and adventure travelers.

Social Media

We have a number of social media concepts for you.

The Ultimate Fishing Adventure

You can ask your social media followers to nominate the ultimate fishing adventure—either one they've done or the one they want to do more than anything. There can be voting to find the most "ultimate," which can then be offered as a prize for people visiting the Great North Fishing Adventures area.

What's the Farthest You've Travelled to Fish?

You can ask your Facebook "likers" to tell you where is the farthest away or most unusual place they've ever fished (bonus if they have a photo). You can give a pair of Expo passes to the best/furthest answers, and could even interview some of the most interesting to feature in-flight or on an interactive map, along with how people can get there flying Great North and partners.

The One Thing I Can't Live Without on a Fishing Adventure

Ask your followers to nominate the one thing they can't live without—or one fishing thing and one non-fishing thing—on a fishing adventure. You can feature the funniest/best answers online and in-flight, alongside a professional fisherman or woman's recommended packing list.

Great North Fishing Adventures App

Any or all of the above ideas could be turned into an Great North Fishing Adventures app, featuring your best and most unusual fishing destinations, packing lists, best times, an interactive quiz resulting in individualized recommended fishing destinations, and a range of "ultimate fishing adventures" at different price points.

Great North Lounge

We will provide a space in the Fishing Adventures area for Great North to create a fishing lodge–styled, private lounge for your higher-level frequent fliers and Great North Club members. This lounge could also feature a bag check service.

We would encourage you to also dress part of your Toronto lounges like a fishing lodge, extending your sponsorship and allowing an in-lounge promotional platform for your luxury fishing and adventure destinations.

7

Leverage Ideas (continued)

Frequent Flyers

We are happy to offer preticketing and a ticket discount to your frequent flyers. We will provide you with artwork and the Ticketmaster code, and you can forward that by email to the appropriate customers.

In-Flight

You could turn the favorite fishing destinations lists from Lon Davies and the "Great Vacations" crew into an in-flight video and/or magazine feature. This is included in our partnership agreement with them, as it also promotes their shows. The producers of each show have indicated that they will assist however they can, but if you need their on-air personalities for a video, that would be a separate contract.

We strongly suggest that you utilize this sponsorship across your range of customer publications, including Great North Club's frequent flyer newsletter and your in-flight publication, *Go Great North*. These could feature a range of subjects, including:

- Fishing destination profiles
- Fishing tips from our experts
- How to pack your fishing gear for air travel

We will provide all required assistance to develop content for these publications and have a number of exhibitors who are already interested in advertising and/or developing co-promotions with you.

You may also want to consider contracting Steve Sando to do a humorous, fishing-themed segment for your in-flight programming. Note that Steve has indicated that he is open to this, but again, would need to be contracted separately.

Great North Club Promotion

We suggest that you run a simple enter-to-win promotion for your highest-value customers, members of the Great North Club. As these members are generally in the higher socioeconomic bracket, it would be important to ensure that entry is easy and the perceived value of the prizes is high.

- The grand prize winner would receive a group fishing package for six to an exotic international location. The Cook Islands Tourist Board has expressed interest in providing hotel accommodation and daily top-level fishing trips (both deep sea and inland), if you think this destination is appropriate for your core customers.
- A second place winner would receive a group fishing package for four to one of Australia's top regional fishing destinations. Again, the Yukon Tourism Council has agreed to provide lodge accommodation, meals, and fishing trips, including a full day at a destination so remote it can only be reached by helicopter. If you would prefer to feature another destination, we are happy to work with you to arrange the ground portion of the package.
- 2,500 third prize winners will receive a complimentary double pass to the Toronto International Fishing Expo (provided as part of your sponsorship package).

Entry will be in Great North Club lounges, and could be as simple as swiping their club membership cards (as you did last year for the Indy Car promotion).

8

Benefits

As a major sponsor of the Toronto International Fishing Expo and naming rights sponsor of the Great North Fishing Adventures area, you will receive the following comprehensive package of benefits:

Sponsorship

- Naming rights sponsorship of the Great North Fishing Adventures area, incorporating the Great North logo in all signage and promotional material
- Major sponsorship of the Toronto International Fishing Expo (we are limited to three major sponsors)
- Official airline partner status
- Sponsorship and sales exclusivity in the category of air travel
- Endorsement on Great North Fishing Adventures app

On-Site

- 10 m × 10 m site in prime, central location in the Fishing Adventures area. This site has a themed "fishing cabin" structure on it and is fully cabled for computers and electricity access
- Additional 10m x 10m site in the Fishing Adventures area, adjacent to your main site, for use as the exclusive Great North Lounge
- Opportunity to book air travel and packages on-site
- Logo acknowledgment on all "Toronto International Fishing Expo" signage

Hospitality and Networking

- Host status for Saturday evening travel agent cocktail party
- Ability to invite up to 100 additional travel agents (on top of the 250 adventure travel specialists we have already identified)
- Introduction to all Fishing Adventures exhibitors a minimum of eight weeks prior to the Expo
- Facilitation of travel cross-promotions and packages with other exhibitors

Access to Intellectual Property

- Exclusive use of "favorite fishing destinations" lists developed and endorsed by Lon Davies and the cast of "Great Vacations" for in-flight and club magazines, in-flight entertainment, web, and social media leverage activities
- Exclusive license to create and sell travel packages based on the "favorite fishing destinations" lists

We have only provided a sampling of the benefits that might go along with this package—ideally, this list should be at least a couple of pages long. Use your inventory and create a comprehensive list of real benefits. Depending upon how long the list is, you may want to categorize the benefits (like the inventory).

A hint to all of you—logo exposure is only a small fraction of a good benefits package.

This package must, must, must be customized to your sponsor's needs.

8

Benefits (continued)

Social Media
- Promotion of Great North's sponsorship to Expo social media networks
- Heavy social media promotion of Great North leverage activities that add value to the event experience
- Heavy social media promotion of Great North Fishing Adventures app

Media Profile
- Use of Great North as an intrinsic part of all travel-oriented publicity activities (promoting travel packages, destinations, on-site booking, etc.)
- Logo/name inclusion in all paid and promotional media and publicity
- Assistance with developing and implementing a publicity plan for Great North's key marketplaces

Tickets
- 25 VIP passes to the Expo
- 8 VIP car parking spaces
- 2,500 adult double passes to the Expo, for use in promoting the Expo to your business travel customers

9

Investment

Your investment for this comprehensive sponsorship relationship will be:

- $160,000 cash
- $15,000 domestic air travel for use by event staff (to be used by December 31, 2015)
- Provision of return air travel for two to the Cook Islands, for use as a drawing prize facilitating our audience research (full credit for the prize will be given to Great North)
- Provision of return air travel for two to Whitehorse, for use as the major prize for our promotion on Q107 (full credit for the prize will be given to Great North)
- Commitment to strongly promote the Toronto International Fishing Expo to your Great North Club members and frequent flyers, as well as in *Go Great North* magazine

   Half of the cash component will be due upon signing a contract, with the remainder due on August 1, 2015. The entire domestic air travel fund should be made available to the Toronto International Fishing Expo upon signing the contract.

Outline how much this is going to cost in cash and contra. Be sure to include a proposed payment schedule. We also like to include a minimum promotional commitment, ensuring that they embark upon at least some activities to maximize the sponsorship and that they are activities that will benefit you, the sponsorship seeker, as well.

One note on pricing; if your country has a goods and services tax or VAT, you need to indicate if that is included in the price or needs to be added on. Generally, sponsorship fees are quoted without GST or VAT.

CHAPTER 8

Sales Process

Sales Checklist

You have done your research, the sponsor is interested, and there's no spinach in your teeth—it must be time for a meeting!

Prepare, Prepare, Prepare

It has been suggested that the sales process is 75 percent preparation, 10 percent sales pitch, and 15 percent follow-up. If you have the opportunity to meet the sponsor in person, ensure that you know everything you can possibly find out about their company before you walk through the door. You need to know what matters to your potential sponsors and how they measure success. Are they after sales opportunities, launching a new product, preparing for a share issue, or embarking on any of a myriad of other marketing activities? Get your **Sponsor Information Checklist** filled out as much as you can before you meet, and you will have a much more fruitful discussion.

Make Contact with the Right Person

Companies are full of people who can say no but can't say yes. You want to ensure that the person you meet with is not in that category.

Good Contacts

The best contact you can have is the brand manager or group brand manager (overseeing a whole group of related brands in categories such as "cereal" or "broadband"). These are the people who can say yes, who do have budget control and flexibility, and most sponsorship seekers don't target them, so you are more likely to get their attention.

In smaller companies, the marketing manager is a good option. No marketing manager? Try the general manager.

If you have a geographically targeted opportunity for a national or global brand, you may want to contact the regional marketing manager or general manager. Often, they have their own budgets, but even if they don't—or if your offer outstrips what they can approve—a regional manager can advocate for you with the head office.

Worse Contacts

Sponsorship managers are not generally your friend. One of their primary jobs is as gatekeeper—keeping you away from the real decision makers. And because they have the word *sponsorship* in their job titles, most sponsorship seekers assume that's the right place to make an approach, so there is a lot of competition for their attention. Your offer may be amazing, but the chances of them addressing it and shifting it to the decision maker efficiently are probably slim.

Another bad option is the CEO or other senior executive. They won't say yes, but they don't want to say no either, so your proposal will get handed down the chain until it gets to the sponsorship manager, who will then deal with it as above.

Avoid at All Costs

Brands often work with a number of agencies—advertising, PR, social media, event production, etc.—and these agencies often play the role of gatekeeper, whether it's been assigned to them or not. And while many have seen the light on full integration of their clients' marketing plans, others play to their comfort zones and will see your offer as a threat. A handful of them will even steal your creative ideas, give you the flick, and present them to the client as their own (rare, but it happens). Don't submit proposals to agencies. It's volunteering to put an external third party between you and the decision maker, and that's never wise.

If agencies are a no-go, online sponsorship submission forms are even more so. This is nothing but automated gatekeeping. Ignore them completely and speak with the brand manager.

What If You're Referred Away from the Brand Manager?

If you've done the right thing and approached the brand manager (or marketing manager/GM), and they've then referred you to the sponsorship manager, there is about a 99 percent probability they've told you no and they just want the professional gatekeeper to do it for them. You can do what they ask, but it's a long shot.

If they refer you to their online form or an agency, that really is a for-sure no. Don't continue to waste your time and energy. Just move on to a more receptive prospect.

With any of these, there are exceptions, but it's much better to play by the rules than to count on you being that exception.

Determine What You Want to Achieve from This Meeting

Ideally, your initial meeting should be about gathering and confirming information. Both you and the potential sponsor want information. You want to create a customized proposal that addresses your sponsor's specific marketing objectives, and you need to expand on what you know in order to connect them with an appropriate offer. On the other side, your potential sponsor wants to know about you and your event. Your counterpart will be asking you a few key questions:

- Who are you, and why should I do business with you?
- What's unique about this property, and is it meaningful to my brand's target markets?
- Why will people attend or participate?
- What's in it for me?
- How much is it going to cost me?

It will increase your credibility exponentially if you can answer all of these questions before the sponsor asks them. You should be able to sum up your event, your expertise, and your enthusiasm concisely, providing the key information to your potential sponsor, so that you can then get on with your own information gathering.

Check Your Vocabulary

It is important in sales meetings to speak the corporate language. This reminds your corporate contacts that you think like they do—in business terms. Start substituting corporate terms for terms that are often used by smaller sponsees and nonprofit organizations (see the following table for some examples).

Instead of . . .	Use
"Awareness," "exposure," "branding," or "profile"	"Opportunity to connect with your target market" or "opportunity to build relevance and relationships"
"Small audience" or "small audience of . . ."	"Highly targeted," "pure demographic," "enthusiasts," or "niche market"
"Support," "help," or "assist"	"Invest"
"Cost" or "fee"	"Investment"
"Donation" or "gift"	"Investment"
"Donor," "funder," or "supporter"	"Investor," "sponsor," or "partner"
"Reaching a small audience"	"Narrowcasting" (the opposite of broadcasting)
"Surplus" (extra funds)	"Profit"
"Marketing dollars"	"Sponsorship" or "investment"

Opportunity
to connect
with your
target market.

Mind Your Manners

Be on time and keep the meeting on track and on schedule. Speak with confidence, smile, and shake hands firmly. Speak clearly and remember you are there to gather and check information. Remember, you have two ears and one mouth for a reason—you need to listen twice as much as you speak. Whatever you do, don't go into hyper sales mode. And be sure to follow up the meeting with a personal thank-you note (see sample later in this chapter).

Don't Act Needy

If you are a nonprofit organization, make it clear that you are not looking for a donation. Ensure that your contact knows that you are not asking for a donation because this will often be their assumption. It will be even more imperative for you to be very businesslike, using business vocabulary and discussing the project in terms of it being an investment.

Always Focus on the Sponsor's Needs

Remember as you talk that these people are not interested in meeting your needs but in achieving their own business objectives.

On a related note, don't talk in depth about the connection between your organization and the sponsor. They are much less interested in your organization than they are in making a connection with target markets that interest them. Position your organization as a conduit for building those relationships.

Don't Discuss Price

Don't talk about the price until after you have excited them about the idea. Avoid setting your price until after the initial meeting. It is acceptable to discuss a price range or an indicative amount but always follow that with the caveat that it is only an indication and that the fee will be set based upon the benefits package offered as a result of the meeting.

Be Enthusiastic

Your enthusiasm is your greatest selling tool. Following the meeting, send a thank-you letter outlining what you have discussed, answering any questions, and indicating when they will receive your formal proposal.

Using a Broker

No one can sell your organization or its products the way you can. However, if your organization lacks the skills, experience, or resources to sell your sponsorship property, hire a broker.

What to Look for in a Broker or an Agent

Experience

Ensure that your broker or agent supplies you with a list of clients (including the specific events or properties he or she has acted as a broker for), amounts raised for each, how long the sales processes took, and references. If you are working with a larger sales agency, be sure to get references on both the agency and the specific person or team handling your event.

Understanding of the Product

Does your broker understand and empathize with your project? Has he or she worked with similar properties?

Value Added

Determine exactly what your broker will and will not do. A good broker will work with you to ensure that the property, marketing plan, and offer work for potential sponsors.

Professional Affiliations

Is the broker a member of at least one recognized sponsorship or marketing association?

Exclusivity

No sponsorship brokers worth their salt will handle a property unless they have exclusive selling rights. Tag teams are bad for them and bad for you. Have they insisted on exclusivity? For how long? It is not uncommon for a broker to request a period of three to twelve months for the securing of sponsorship.

Hunger

How hungry is your sponsorship broker? A good broker is hungry for the project. Is yours?

Presentation

How does your broker present himself or herself? Is the broker professional? What are his or her meeting and presentation skills like?

How S/he Works

Ask how the broker sells properties. What is the broker's strategy and philosophy? If the broker takes an uncustomized, shotgun approach to sales, don't use him or her.

Marketing and Business Knowledge

Many brokers specialize in particular areas—sports, events, arts, community. Find out the areas of specialization. Who are the broker's contacts? What are his or her networks?

Follow-up and Reporting

At the beginning of the contract period, establish how frequently you want the broker to report back, what information you need, and in what format.

Fees and Payments

Brokers work on a commission basis with the fees ranging anywhere from 10 to 30 percent or even more. Brokers are paid this commission only if they successfully negotiate the sponsorship on your behalf. Brokers are responsible for producing their own sales material. However, if you want flash brochures, videos, and whiz-bang presentation materials, you will be expected to cover production and printing costs. Also, you need to be clear on whether the commission is to be paid from the total amount sought or added to it. For example, if the broker is raising $100,000, are you paying $20,000 of the $100,000 the broker raises, or does the broker have to raise $120,000 to cover his or her own commission? The latter is becoming much more common and is usually more desirable for you.

Contracts and Letters of Agreement

Ensure you have a contract or letter of agreement. The contract should include commission payable, reporting deadlines, clearances and sign-offs, exclusions, time frame, and amount sought. Also, include whether the commission is to be added to the total amount sought or paid from it.

Consulting Assistance

If you need assistance determining the nature of the property, pricing, and packaging or assistance in managing the sponsorship, the broker will charge an hourly fee or a project fee for these services. Fees range from $150 to $300 per hour.

Where to Find Brokers

There are a number of ways you can find a broker.

- **Personal referrals.** Use your network and find out who's good.
- **LinkedIn.** Use your best, most practical, least spammy LinkedIn groups to get referrals to good brokers that specialize in your category.
- **Sponsorship association.** Call your local sponsorship association and ask for a referral. We have a list of sponsorship associations in Appendix 2.
- **Power Sponsorship.** PowerSponsorship.com has a broker registry with contact details for brokers around the world.

Other Ways of Selling

While we are big advocates of contacting a sponsor directly and tailoring an offer to their needs, this is not the only way to get your opportunities in front of the right people. Here we outline a number of other channels through which you can introduce your organization and/or sell sponsorship.

Agencies

Although we're not fans of submitting sponsorship proposals to agencies, that doesn't mean you shouldn't introduce yourself and your property to them. The purpose is not hard sell and not about any specific client, but rather to show agencies how you can help them add value to their clientele.

Share Our Strength, a small U.S.-based antihunger organization, introduced itself and its sponsorship opportunities to a range of PR agencies that represented major food manufacturers and producers. Eighteen months after these initial introductions, Gollan Harris Chicago invited Share Our Strength to pitch a sponsorship proposal to one of its largest clients, Tyson Foods. The pitch resulted in a multimillion-dollar partnership.

Matchmaking Services

There are several websites offering sponsorship seekers the opportunity to list their opportunities on a database. The idea is that sponsors will search based on their needs and find a good opportunity. This approach is easy and cheap and would seem to be a good idea. Unfortunately, there are also some downsides.

It is difficult to know how many sponsors will be searching the database during your window of opportunity, much less the number that will be appropriate to you. Our experience is that you will hear from far more companies trying to sell something to you than sponsors who want to discuss investing in your event. Finally, if you do have a strong partnership orientation, it will be very difficult to showcase that in this type of forum. The upshot is that if it is free or very inexpensive, give it a go, but expect to be inundated with junk mail.

Directories

A number of event directories operate in much the same way as the matchmaking services—dividing events mainly by type, time of year, and region. The main difference is that these directories tend to be annual, established, and have a wide, reliable readership of corporate sponsors. Sponsors often use these directories as a starting point to understand what sponsorships are out there. If they are interested, they then contact the property directly to discuss the opportunity and develop a partnership.

We recommend listing in established directories, particularly those published by sponsorship associations and publications (see Appendix 2). Note, you will still get junk mail, but the potential of your listing contributing to a sponsorship deal is most likely a lot higher than with online matchmaking services.

Internet Auctions

We are starting to see sponsorship being sold via Internet auction sites, such as eBay, with some packages being sold for well above the normal asking price. While this approach does get the sponsorship in front of a lot of potential buyers, the lack of discussion and customization and the abbreviated decision time frame tend to create short-term transactions rather than long-term, marketing-oriented partnerships.

If you want to try this out, we recommend using it only for sponsorships offering a very limited array of benefits, such as hospitality packages or exclusive vending rights.

⬇ Preliminary Letter

June 26, 2015

Mr. Andrew Tofte
Managing Director
ARN Australia Pty Limited
Unit A, 108 McEvoy St
Waterloo NSW 2017

Dear Mr. Tofte:

As you requested, I am writing to introduce the School Administrators Federation (SAF), to tell you about its services, and to invite you to consider a sponsorship proposal.

When decisions affecting education and school administration are made, it is the SAF's business to understand all the issues involved. The Federation has unrivalled access to all aspects of Australia's school administration system, bringing together the interests of those who manage schools, those who work in them, those who design and build them, and those who supply them with goods and services.

SAF is a nonprofit national industry association of school administrators. Founded in 1989, SAF works to enhance the quality of school administration for public and private schools across the nation.

The Federation is recognized by governments, educational professionals, and the teaching community as a national leader in the school administration industry and is well placed to give you access to all the important networks relevant to your marketing needs.

Our regular activities include

- **Annual Conference of School Administrators**—Our national conference brings together teachers, administrators, policy makers, purchasing officers, and suppliers. The 2015 conference is to be held at the Adelaide Convention Exhibition Centre from Friday, November 14, to Tuesday, November 18.
- **Seminars**—Administration workshops, as well as financial management and purchasing seminars are held throughout the year and enjoy sellout attendance with over 15,000 participants annually. Our webinar programs are newer, attracting an average of 90 administrators for each session.
- **Publications**—SAF produces a newsletter, Schools Administrator Today, and an education administrator paper, Head of the Class, every quarter. Circulation for our publications is over 120,000.
- **Awards**—SAF recognizes and encourages innovation and excellence in school administration with the National School Administrator of the Year awards.
- **Industry information**—SAF has access to a wide range of up-to-date national and international school administrator information and can assist suppliers, policy makers, and educational professionals with industry research requests. We maintain an active database of over 25,000 purchasing officers and school administrators.

At SAF, we are committed to creating and maintaining win-win partnerships with industry suppliers. We have a number of sponsorship opportunities ranging from sales and exhibition properties to exclusive conference packages.

I have included a brochure on SAF for your interest.

I will ring your offices on Tuesday morning to discuss your specific marketing and sponsorship objectives and how we might tailor a proposal for you.

Sincerely,

Ernie Shedder
Marketing Manager

Proposal Cover Letter

January 15, 2015

Miranda Morgan
Managing Director
Fresh Milk of Minnesota
3333 University Avenue SE
Minneapolis MN 55414

Dear Miranda:

Thank you for inviting me to discuss your sponsorship marketing objectives. I enjoyed our meeting and feel confident that we have developed a sponsorship proposal to meet both your immediate and long-term needs.

Your Situation
[*A brief overview of where they are and what they want.*]

Your Objectives
As a result of our meeting, I have assessed that the specific sponsorship marketing objectives for your organization are to: [*Briefly list specific objectives in bullet points.*]

The Project/Event [*Provide a brief overview of the project.*]
Marketing and promotional benefits [*Provide a very brief overview of the type and value of benefits.*]

Investment
Your investment in [*event*] will be repaid many times over as a result of your organization's improved ability to identify and cultivate [*clients, customers, sales*].

The Next Step
I have attached a detailed proposal for [*event*]. Included in this document are the media advertising strategy and the public relations and promotional strategies.

　　Thank you once again for the chance to submit this proposal. We look forward to exploring a partnership with you and hope that we will have the opportunity to contribute to the success of your organization over the long term.

Sincerely,

Davina Kruger
Sponsorship Director

⬇ Meeting Thank-You Letter

August 26, 2015

Kerry Gemmell
Sponsorship Manager
Positively Vodka Importers
17–23 Longbridge Street
London Southbank SE1 0AA

Dear Kerry:

Thank you for taking time from your busy schedule to meet with me today to discuss your marketing objectives and your sponsorship guidelines.

The Ratcatcher Theatre Company is committed to producing contemporary theatre productions that reflect our audiences' expectations. We are a contemporary, cutting-edge company producing British theatre for British audiences. Like Positively Vodka, we are committed to building new audiences through carefully targeted sampling programs.

I am confident that a partnership with the Ratcatcher Theatre Company will benefit both our organizations. Our upcoming subscription campaign targeting younger executives and opinion leaders provides a great opportunity for Positively Vodka to promote its newest range of flavored vodkas.

I will forward a formal proposal to you on Friday. Thank you again for taking the time to meet with me today.

Sincerely,

Gretchen Larson
Marketing Manager

Rejection Thank-You Letter

February 24, 2015

Olivia Charles
Marketing Director
Acme Toy Company
17 Smith Street
Bryanston 2021
South Africa

Dear Olivia:

I appreciate your having taken the time to review our proposal.

As you might expect, I am disappointed that Acme Toys cannot sponsor our School Bike Safety Project. As we discussed, our project provides unique marketing and promotional opportunities and access to your target markets in a cost-effective and creative manner. However, we recognize that it is impossible for you to invest in every potential sponsorship proposal.

I would very much like to keep in touch with you. We are currently developing a range of educational projects that are specifically targeting young families, and I feel confident that your marketing objectives can be addressed with one of our upcoming projects.

Thank you again for your considering our proposal.

Sincerely,

Mia Alexander
General Manager

CHAPTER 9

Special Considerations for Nonprofit Organizations

We added this chapter in the third edition of this book, and when we contemplated including it, we wondered if it was really necessary. In reality, sponsorship is sponsorship, and the approach and process for doing it well is exactly the same whether you are a European children's charity or an American university bowl game.

In the end, we realized that nonprofit organizations do face a number of additional challenges and have some unique opportunities, so we decided to include this chapter to address those special considerations.

Rumor and Innuendo

You may find yourself facing a lot of preconceived notions about what sponsorship of a nonprofit organization is about. You need to accept that, no matter how proactive and partnership oriented your organization is, many others with less enlightened outlooks have gone before you, burning bridges as they went.

In this chapter we have outlined some of the more common attitudes held by sponsors, and a few techniques that can break you out of that pigeonhole.

You are Looking for a Handout

Corporate sponsorship of nonprofits has not been around to any great degree for very long. In fact, when it all started, many nonprofits simply changed the wording—asking for a donation to asking for sponsorship—without changing any of the underlying structure. Sponsors would invest marketing money, be treated like donors, get no return, and learn to be very skeptical of nonprofits looking for sponsorship.

To counteract this, there are a few things you can and should do:

- Ensure you don't focus on your organization's need, particularly in early conversations. Give them a thumbnail sketch and then move on.
- Use those early conversations to gain information from the sponsor on their overall marketing objectives and target markets, and how they see these changing in the future. Although they may have a nonprofit strategy in place, asking those very objective-oriented questions, rather than asking them what they support, will position you as a potential commercial partner.
- Do not ever let your personal passion for your organization's mission blind you to commercial realities. Your organization may do amazing things, but that doesn't make you the perfect partner for every sponsor out there. Concentrate on finding the right fit, and you will end up with a portfolio of fantastic partners that bring money, promotion, expertise, and more to the relationship.
- Clearly acknowledge to the sponsor that while you are a nonprofit organization and clearly have funding needs and a social agenda, you understand that they need to be able to justify their investments and make a meaningful return.
- Do your very best to speak with a brand manager, if you can. The brand manager is the caretaker of brand health and often hasn't had the experience of being burned by nonprofits in the past. If you approach the partnership strategically, they could very well be receptive.
- If you do all of the above and the sponsor still refers you to their (often underfunded and fully committed) foundation, they really aren't seeing a lot of potential for the partnership. Keep in contact, as future projects may be a better fit, but it's probably better to just move on.

You Don't Know How to Be a Real Partner

A number of times, we've asked nonprofit audiences to define their "dream sponsor." Inevitably, someone will say, "someone who gives us a lot of money and doesn't make us work hard for it." Invariably, this comment is met by a roomful of nods of agreement. Again, this may not be your approach (and we hope it isn't), but there are a lot of nonprofits out there defining the perfect sponsor as a virtual silent partner.

Managing this perception is about managing their fear, just like the "handout" perception. We suggest that you do all of the above, and add a couple more:

- If you have current sponsors who are achieving a commercial return—that is, changing people's perceptions and/or behaviors—by all means, use them as case studies. The best way to prove you can be a real partner is to showcase the fact that you are one already.
- Ask your sponsors (current and any former sponsors with whom you parted on amicable terms) for references. In particular, ask them to outline some of the objectives they've met through the sponsorship. You get bonus points if they invite potential sponsors to contact them.

They Won't Be Able to Achieve "Real" Objectives Using Cause Sponsorship

This perception has more to do with a sponsor's own lack of vision and leverage, but it is certainly something you will have to counteract at one time or another. Again, all of the above strategies will be helpful, but we would add one more.

If you have a potential sponsor that refers to nonprofit sponsorship as "good corporate citizenship," "giving back to the community," "warm fuzzies," or some other related euphemism, you need to dig deeper. These are not real objectives; they are camouflaging the real objectives—for you and for the sponsor. Ask them, "If you are successful at being a good corporate citizen, what does that mean to your staff? Customers? How would it change what they think of you? How they interact with you?" That's not a hard thing to ask, but the result is that they should tell you about the results they want to achieve—their real objectives.

"Good corporate citizenship" and "giving back" are euphemisms, not objectives.

It Will Be Difficult to End the Relationship
If the Sponsor's Needs Change

From time to time, a sponsor's needs will change and it will be time to drop a sponsorship and do something else. Nonprofit sponsorships get dropped, too, but they can be so ungraceful about it that it's scary to contemplate.

We know of nonprofits who have tried to pull rank—going to the chief executive, or even a government minister, to complain about being abandoned by a sponsor—as well as many who threaten to go to the media. A few even do go to the media, which can get really ugly.

Now, what kind of partnership is it when the nonprofit organization is ready to resort to threats of blackmail to continue getting the money? We'll tell you: one that is going to scare every other sponsor away for a good long time.

We're sure you would never do something so dastardly to a sponsor you have spent years valuing, but to be sure they know it, we suggest the following:

- From the very start, you need to tell the sponsor—and back it up with actions—that you will do everything you can to assist them in achieving their goals, but that you understand that it needs to meet their strategic needs, and if those needs change, you will understand.
- Ensure you are servicing your sponsors really well. In addition to staying abreast of their sponsorship plans, you should be asking about their forward planning and if any changes will affect the relevance of your organization to their brand. That way, you should know as early as possible if a renewal isn't on the cards.
- If the sponsorship has high visibility, you should offer to issue a joint media release that positions the split as amicable, based on a change in strategy, and setting you up as a great partner to other sponsors.
- If their exit is really going to hurt, don't try to convince them to stay—that decision has been made. Instead, ask them to ease the transition. They could pay for you to attend a workshop, secure a consultant to assist you in fine-tuning your offering, or sponsor you for one additional year at a much lower level. Assuming they left because of a change in strategy, they may also be able to provide you with referrals to other sponsors who may be more appropriate.

Never threaten a sponsor into renewing.

Your Real Competition and Your Real Edge

With the huge range of nonprofits out there—from local to global, children to aged, education to environment, health to homelessness—it would be very easy to think that sponsors are choosing first to sponsor one or more nonprofits, and then deciding which ones.

Not so! As sponsorship decisions are increasingly driven by brand management teams, you need to understand that they make their decisions based primarily on two things:

1. **Brand fit.** Does it underpin any of the brand's values or attributes? Can it achieve a range of objectives?
2. **Target market fit.** Is it relevant to at least one of the brand's target markets? Is there scope to provide the target market with a functional or emotional benefit?

What this means is that you are not competing against other nonprofits, but against anything that brand could sponsor, plus advertising, sales and media promotions, online activities, endorsements, and anything else they might do to market the brand.

Before you freak out about the huge amount of largely well-resourced competition, take a deep breath and hear this: there are some things on that list that a nonprofit organization will be able to do better than anyone else.

Nonprofits tend to inspire deeply held passion and admiration in their supporters. The potential for providing a sponsor with an emotional added-value benefit for their customers is outstanding.

One of the major factors for success that we've seen over the years is that the more individualized and real you can make the investment, the more relevant it will be—even to people who may not be fervent supporters:

- "Every dollar donated will vaccinate X children from all major childhood diseases."
- "In 2014, our staff planted over 20,000 native trees with their own hands and donated enough to plant 55,000 more. That's almost 500 acres and three times as many trees as there are in Central Park!"
- "A $20 donation could pay for the doorknob this family turns every time they walk into their first real home."

- "We didn't see a doctor to minimize scarring, we saw Green Plan. They showed us how we can cost-effectively rejuvenate retired mine sites, creating new habitats and dramatically reducing the long-term impact on Australia."

The biggest thing to keep in mind, however, is that nonprofits—and no one else—can provide a sponsor with an opportunity to make their customers and staff the heroes. Say that to them. It's very powerful.

Get the Right Advice

We would never say a bad word about fundraisers—a passionate, resourceful bunch working in a highly competitive field. What we will say is that there are not a lot of fundraising workshops, conferences, publications, or other resources that are 100 percent up to date with best-practice sponsorship. It's a highly specialized, highly changeable industry and just not their core capability.

With that in mind, you need to be careful about where you get your information on corporate sponsorship. You need to be sure to get the information from organizations who do corporate sponsorship—not fundraising—as their core job.

- **Workshops.** Attend workshops aimed at both for-profits and nonprofits. You need to understand and practice the process, and it's the same for everyone. Better yet, balance your training between the sponsee side and the sponsor side. It can be very enlightening to understand what sponsors are after from the sponsors' own mouths.
- **Conferences.** A nonprofit conference with one session on sponsorship is unlikely to be your best source of cutting-edge information. Go to a conference serving the entire sponsorship industry and attend a range of sessions. You can learn as much from an astute motor racing team as you can from a successful nonprofit organization.
- **Associations and publications.** Read sponsorship industry publications, subscribe to industry websites and newsletters, and join industry associations. To get you started, a huge range of sponsorship resources are listed in Appendix 2.
- **Consultants.** If you decide you need strategic or brokering assistance from a consultant, again, try to secure a consultant that works across the range of sponsorship seekers, including nonprofits.

There is nothing stopping you from being a member of fundraising associations or going to nonprofit conferences, as you probably need a range of skills in your job. Just understand that you will probably need to augment those resources with some that are specialized for sponsorship.

Partnership Options

Nonprofits have more options for partnering with sponsors than any other type of sponsee. The most common structures are outlined below, but the key is that any of these can and should be leveraged by the sponsor as if it were a standard sponsorship.

- **Cause sponsorship.** This is the standard sponsorship structure. A sponsor makes an investment of cash, goods, or services in a nonprofit organization and receives a range of leverageable benefits in return.
- **Cause-related marketing (CRM).** The sponsor creates a sales promotion whereby it makes a donation every time a customer makes a purchase. For instance, you might buy recycled paper towels, and every time you buy that brand, it donates 10 cents to the Wildlife Conservation Society. There is often, but not always, a flat sponsorship or licensing fee paid to the nonprofit organization, and the total cause-related donation is almost always capped.
- **Donation facilitation.** This is where a sponsor creates an easy "funnel" for donations, such as Qantas collecting loose change from passengers, in any currency, and donating it to UNICEF, to the tune of millions of dollars.
- **Donation matching.** This is similar to the above, but the sponsor agrees to match all donations made, often to a capped amount.

The CSR Trap

As corporations move toward corporate social responsibility (CSR), two things have happened:

1. Some corporations have elected not to become more socially responsible in their environmental, workplace, or other practices and instead have elected to write checks to nonprofits.
2. Some nonprofits have positioned writing that check as ticking the CSR "box," further enabling this flawed take on CSR.

Nonprofit
sponsorship
and corporate
social
responsibility
are *not* the
same thing.

CSR is a measure of how responsible a company is in the manner in which it carries out business and makes money, as well as the sustainability of those measures.

CSR is not a measure of how much money a company spends sponsoring or donating to nonprofits. Sponsoring nonprofits can be very powerful and, if authentic, a big statement about the values of a company and its brands, but it doesn't work if it's not authentic. Sponsoring environmental organizations does not undo continuing and unaddressed environmental damage. Sponsoring World Vision does not undo using subcontractors who engage child labor.

If there is an authentic match between a company's CSR initiatives and what your organization does, they can certainly use the sponsorship to underpin those values. By the same token, if your organization can provide meaningful assistance to them in achieving CSR targets—providing expertise, infrastructure, or other means—then you can connect CSR and sponsorship.

However you look at it, always remember, running a business in an ethical manner and sponsoring your organization are not the same thing. Writing you a check is not CSR.

CHAPTER 10

Negotiation

The object of the negotiation process is to create a win-win-win deal; that is, the sponsee wins, the sponsor wins, and the target markets win. In order to achieve this level of partnership, both parties must be completely open about their objectives. This should be a fairly straightforward task if the development of the offer is done in a fully collaborative manner, as recommended throughout this book.

Rules for Negotiating

Either way, there are a number of rules that will make negotiating sponsorship a lot easier for you.

Negotiate Peer-to-Peer

Be sure you carry out the negotiation with someone who has the authority to negotiate and the ability to approve the expenditure. You will find that, in many companies, different levels of marketing executives will have different levels of financial authority.

Know Your Bottom Line

In the heat of a meeting, it is easy to get caught up in the process and make a deal that you realize later does not achieve your financial objectives.

Before you go into any negotiation, be sure to do your homework. Go back to your pricing exercises and set yourself a bottom limit that you will under no circumstances fall below (e.g., 225 percent of your cost to deliver the program). You may also want to set yourself a limit as to how much of the fee you will accept in contra.

Keep the Target Markets in the Picture

If the target markets—your audience, their customers, etc.—don't win, it's not going to work for anyone. Some sponsors get this and some don't. Even if you are negotiating with a sponsor who doesn't get it, it's in everyone's best interest if you keep talking about how various aspects of the sponsorship will impact (or not impact) on the target markets.

Have Something up Your Sleeve

When you create an offer for a sponsor, always keep a couple of nice benefits up your sleeve to use during the negotiation process. If you plan from the start to negotiate by offering them more, rather than settling for less money (and calculate your costs accordingly), you will end up far better off in the end.

Don't Be Bullied

Some sponsors routinely offer 20 to 25 percent less than your asking price, assuming that if you are hungry enough, you will be grateful for anything. Don't fall for this ploy.

You need to approach the negotiation from a position of confidence—you are holding a negotiation, not a fire sale. You've done your research and know your value. If they have a problem with the price point, then you need to adjust your package accordingly. Do not ever simply accept a discounted offer. A sponsor worth working with will respect your need to protect the value of your property.

If you have approached the sponsorship process in a fully professional manner and taken all of the above negotiation advice, and the potential sponsor is still treating you like a second-class organization, walk away because the relationship will never get any better.

Stay Composed No Matter What

Negotiations can be difficult, no question about it. Even if you have created a strong offer and followed the guidelines set out here, sometimes you will work with a sponsor who is an old-style negotiator, approaching the process as adversarial rather than collaborative.

If things start heating up, call for time out. Tell the potential sponsor that it is clear you both need to give this relationship a fresh look. Tell them that you

The goal in any sponsorship negotiation is win-win-win.

You are holding a negotiation, not a fire sale.

will rework the offer, taking into account their concerns, and that you will get back to them in a couple of days. Then do it. Put any defensiveness or acrimony aside and find a way. Put the new offer in writing, which allows you to think it out fully, and remember to stay focused on a solution.

Also note, there may be times when a sponsorship negotiation will turn sour even when both sides are working together. This could be as the result of an international directive, a change in business climate, or because of an internal change at the company. Don't hold this against the potential sponsor as it is out of their control. Just stay composed and stay in touch, and when everything settles back down for them, resume discussions.

Be Prepared to Walk Away

Don't ever walk into a negotiation with the mindset that you need to close the deal. This puts you at a distinct disadvantage and will result in your giving up more than you need to cement the relationship. You might as well have a "kick me" sign on your back!

If at some point during the negotiation you determine that the relationship is unlikely to end up a win-win-win situation, then it is time to thank your counterpart and graciously walk away. This is an infinitely more positive outcome than creating a bad relationship. Sponsorship is notoriously incestuous—if you burn a bridge, it stays burned.

Payment Arrangements

Sometimes the payment arrangements will be as important to a sponsor as the amount of money committed, so you need to be prepared to work with them. We have already covered a number of payment structures in the Pricing section (Chapter 7). You use those same techniques in your negotiations, and we've outlined a couple more here.

Spreading Payments Across Time

Oftentimes, a sponsor will want to spread payments over time. There are several reasons for this, but the two overriding reasons are:

1. **Comfort level.** They want some assurance that the event is actually going ahead and that the benefits promised are being delivered. Often, once you

have gone through the first year of a sponsorship, the sponsor will be more comfortable paying the entire fee up front.

2. **Budgeting.** If they have already budgeted for that time period, they may need to access quarterly marketing funds or some other kind of time-bound budgets.

Whatever the reason, you need to be prepared to work with the sponsor. You should endeavor to secure a substantial proportion of the fee up front, both as a measure of good faith and to assist you in your cash flow in the lead-up to your event.

It is reasonable that fees above a given amount ($15,000 to $20,000) be paid in installments. One common way of doing this is to request one-third upon signing of the agreement, another third three months later, and the final installment two weeks before the event starts.

Ongoing contracts, such as sponsorships of cultural organizations or sporting teams, may be paid annually, semiannually, or quarterly.

Also keep in mind that if you are negotiating a small sponsorship with a company that has a major sponsorship budget, it may be more convenient for them to pay the entire amount at once. The only way to know which payment option they prefer is to ask.

Spreading Payments Across Budgeting Cycles

It may be necessary to spread payments across financial years, particularly for larger sponsorships or investments made after the current period has been budgeted. This can often make finding the money for your opportunity easier for the sponsor.

Companies' financial years vary widely, with multinationals often mirroring the financial year in their home country. Some companies have their own fiscal year. You should have found out what financial year they operate under

---

Case Studies: Payment Structures

Recruitment company **Manpower** won the Swedish Sponsor of the Year Award with their sponsorship of various causes. Manpower's main investment is expertise, providing skills such as management, consulting, and bookkeeping to causes for a minimum of three months. They have provided many thousands of hours so far, and have successfully demonstrated their service not only to the causes themselves, but to their other sponsors, board members, and associated organizations.

during your initial research but, as a general guideline, here are a few typical periods:

- United States: 1 January–31 December
- Japan: 1 April—31 March
- Australia/New Zealand: 1 July—30 June
- United Kingdom: 1 April—31 March

Contracts

When entering into a sponsorship agreement, the hope is always that the sponsorship will go perfectly and the terms of the contract will never be called into play. Unfortunately, this is not always the case, so it is important to understand the issues.

Types of Agreements

Always have some sort of written agreement in force. The more formal the agreement, the more likely it will be complete and legally binding. In order of desirability, these are the types of agreements you could have:

1. A legal contract drawn up by a lawyer and bearing signatures and company seals of both organizations
2. A legal contract adapted from a template drawn up by a lawyer (we have included a comprehensive pro forma that has been created for this book by Gadens Lawyers, Australia), bearing signatures and company seals of both organizations
3. A letter of agreement outlining all points of agreement, including benefits, communication, and payment dates, and signed by both organizations
4. A confirmation letter from the sponsee outlining the benefits and payment dates (this is not desirable and should be avoided)

Determine at what level you need a letter of agreement or a contract. Often a letter of agreement, signed by both parties, will be used for sponsorships valued at under a certain amount, anywhere from $5,000 to $20,000 (and we've seen as high as $100,000). Above that amount, a full contract will be required.

If you have a good **Sponsorship Agreement Pro Forma** (see Appendix 3), it will make your job much easier when it comes to developing an appropriate agreement. This is a very useful tool that can be utilized in several ways:

- As the basis for your agreement
- As your "first pass" at a legal contract that will then be given to a lawyer for fine-tuning (saving you a considerable amount in legal fees)
- As a reference, so that you are aware of possible issues and legal considerations

We do not recommend using the pro forma as the basis for your agreement unless you have a lawyer check the agreement prior to entering into it.

Who Should Provide the Contract?

It is nearly always quicker and more straightforward for the sponsee to develop the contract, as corporate legal departments are notoriously bureaucratic and often develop contracts that are difficult to read and less than win-win.

Resolving Disputes

When structuring an agreement, always try to work in a series of steps for resolving any conflicts that might arise. You only move on to the next step when what you have already tried has not worked. The four basic steps are, in order:

1. **Discussion.** This means having a meeting with the express purpose of coming to a resolution that is agreeable to both parties.
2. **Mediation.** This involves getting an independent arbiter to mediate a discussion between the parties, ensuring that they stay on track and open to solutions.
3. **Arbitration.** This is similar to mediation, except that the parties agree that the arbiter will hear both sides and make a decision. Beware, this could be almost as expensive as litigation.
4. **Litigation.** A long and usually expensive foray into the legal system, which is to be avoided if at all possible.

Exclusivity

There are three types of exclusivity:

1. Sponsorship
2. Signage (in cases where the venue may have existing conflicting signage)
3. Sales

You can grant exclusivity across any or all of these areas, and the more you grant, the more valuable it is to the sponsor. For more on this, see "How Do We Define Category Exclusivity?" in Chapter 7.

Exclusive sales provisions could contravene trade practices or antitrust laws. This is another reason why it is important for a lawyer to prepare or check your agreement.

Sponsorship Agreement Pro Forma

Included in Appendix 3 is a **Sponsorship Agreement Pro Forma** that was developed specifically for us by Lionel Hogg, Partner of Gadens Lawyers. The full agreement can also be found in your downloadable tools.

This sample agreement may be a useful starting point for a sponsorship agreement. However, it is very general because it is impossible to draft a document that accounts for all situations or for legal differences in all countries.

Ideally, it should be used as a template that is completed by the sponsee and sponsor and then given to a lawyer to check the drafting, change it to suit the law of the relevant place, and better outline the rights of the parties. This will ensure that the agreement process is collaborative and will probably cost you far less than securing a lawyer to draft an agreement from scratch.

Warning

The **Sponsorship Agreement Pro Forma** document is provided as a sample only and is not a substitute for legal advice. You should seek the advice of a suitably qualified and experienced lawyer before using this document.

In particular, you or your lawyer should:

- **Check the law in your jurisdiction.** Make sure this agreement is appropriate wherever you are located.
- **Check for changes to the law.** Law and practice may have altered since this document was drafted or you last checked the situation.
- **Modify wherever necessary.** Review this document critically and never use it without first amending it to suit your needs. Remember, each sponsorship is different, and the parties may agree to allocate risks and responsibilities differently from this template.
- **Beware of the limits of expertise.** If you are not legally qualified, or are not familiar with this area of the law, do not use this document without first obtaining qualified legal advice about it.

This warning is governed by the laws of New South Wales, Australia.

How This Agreement Works

The Agreement assumes that there are standard clauses that should be in every agreement and special clauses needed for your sponsorship. The standard clauses that should apply all of the time are called the "Standard Conditions." The parts that relate to your specific sponsorship are the "Schedules" and the "Special Conditions."

The Schedules and Special Conditions have precedence over the Standard Conditions. In other words, what you insert is more important than what is already written. This is why it is vital to use a lawyer or know what you are doing.

Read the Agreement

Before doing anything, read the Agreement and see how it might apply to your situation. There may be Standard Conditions that are unsuitable. There may be new conditions that you need to add. Do not assume that the Agreement is right for you.

The sample agreement is for an *exclusive* sponsorship in the relevant sponsorship category.

Complete the Schedules

You should complete each Schedule following the guidance notes in that Schedule.

For example, Schedule 23 is called "Sponsor's Termination Events." The guidance note tells you to see clause 9.2. You should read clause 9.2 and understand the circumstances in which the sponsor has a right to terminate the agreement. You then insert into Schedule 23 *any other circumstances* peculiar to your sponsorship. For instance, you might want to terminate the agreement if the team being sponsored loses its license to play in the major league or if the contracted lead performers for the musical withdraw their services.

Add Special Conditions

The Special Conditions (at the end of the Schedules) enable you to insert other conditions that are not dealt with by this sample agreement.

Changing Standard Conditions

You should *not* change the Standard Conditions without consulting a lawyer. The Agreement is drafted as a package, and changing the Standard Conditions might have an unintended domino effect on other terms.

If you have to change the Standard Conditions, do so by adding a Special Condition, such as "clause 18 of the Standard Conditions does not apply."

Sign the Agreement

The parties sign and date the document on the last page. Make sure that the person with whom you do the deal is authorized to sign.

Finding a Lawyer

You should consult a lawyer practicing in your jurisdiction and experienced in sponsorship matters. If you don't have a good sponsorship lawyer, there are a number of sports law organizations around the world that can provide a referral, or you can contact Gadens Lawyers in Australia.

Although you may not be a sporting organization, these associations will be a great source for referrals, as sponsorship law skills are quite transferable across sponsorship genres.

Full contact details for a number of these organizations can be found in Appendix 2.

If You Have Questions About the Pro Forma Agreement

If you or your lawyer have questions about the **Sponsorship Agreement Pro Forma**, you are welcome to contact its author:

Lionel Hogg
Partner
Gadens Lawyers
GPO Box 129
Brisbane QLD 4001 Australia
Phone: +61 7 3231 1518
email: lhogg@qld.gadens.com.au

Part **3**

Servicing

CHAPTER 11

Sponsorship Planning and Management

Sourcing and acquiring new sponsors is not the hardest part of a sponsorship manager's job. Servicing your sponsor is when the real work begins. Sponsorship is all about building and maintaining long-term relationships. The primary responsibility of organizations receiving sponsorship is to build positive relationships with their sponsors by ensuring that all agreed benefits are provided within the negotiated time frame.

It is equally important that organizations are committed to ensuring that their sponsors are provided with information, feedback, and quantitative and qualitative research results that will assist their sponsors in determining if their objectives have been met. Simply providing the sponsor with the contracted benefits and a media report at the end of the event means you are only doing half the job.

Sponsors require and deserve total commitment from their sponsees. Evaluation is perhaps one of the most overlooked areas of sponsorship servicing today. The most successful sponsorship managers provide complete sponsorship service, which includes in-depth ongoing summary evaluation and assessment.

There is no secret on how to manage your sponsorships effectively. Once you have acquired your sponsorship, it comes down to three simple steps:

1. **Develop** a sponsorship plan
2. **Implement** the sponsorship plan
3. **Evaluate** the sponsorship plan.

Develop the Sponsorship Implementation Plan

Once you have found a sponsor for your event, you must firstly develop a sponsorship plan. The sponsorship plan defines what you and the sponsor want to achieve and how you are going to manage the sponsorship. Every sponsorship, regardless of its size or value, requires its own plan.

Every sponsorship plan should include

- An executive summary
- A situation analysis
- A list of objectives
- Strategies to meet those objectives
- Performance indicators that will be used to measure the success of those strategies
- Target audiences
- An action list/timeline/accountability list
- A budget
- An evaluation strategy

A sponsorship plan states what you want to achieve, how you are going to achieve it and how you will know when you have achieved it. A **Sponsorship Implementation Plan** template can be found later in this chapter.

In terms of quantifying returns on a sponsorship investment, a sponsorship plan provides you with two critical strategies for measuring returns—performance indicators and evaluation. If it is in your plan, you will not forget it. You will also have agreement from within your organization and from the sponsor as to what you are trying to achieve and how you will measure the results.

Implement the Sponsorship Plan

Sponsorship is about creating an effective relationship between your organization and the sponsor. Managing the sponsorship or implementing a well-thought-out sponsorship plan is about building and maintaining that relationship.

Evaluate the Sponsorship Plan

If you have followed your sponsorship plan, you will have identified performance indicators and ways of measuring or evaluating whether the sponsor has

> Every sponsorship, regardless of its size, requires a sponsorship implementation plan.

successfully met their sponsorship objectives. The best sponsorship implementation and evaluation plans are drawn up in consultation with your sponsors.

Your evaluation plan should include the following, some of which you will provide and some the sponsor will carry out:

- Pre- and post-sponsorship surveys
- Sales or visitation figures at your event
- Qualitative research results
- Media assessment

Sponsorship Implementation Plan

You should create a sponsorship implementation plan for each of your sponsors. This should be comprehensive, providing a blueprint for the execution of the program.

Introduction

Include details on the overall aims and objectives of the sponsorship plan. Briefly outline the strategies that you will undertake to assist the sponsor in meeting the objectives.

Situational Analysis

Give a brief overview of the state of the sponsorship, who the key contacts are, and any major issues that might affect the sponsorship.

If the sponsorship is ongoing, outline the history of the sponsorship, recommendations for enhancement, and tactics that will be undertaken to refocus the sponsorship.

Sponsor Objectives

In bullet points, detail the objectives of the sponsorship. Remember, objectives must always be SMART—specific, measurable, achievable, results oriented, and time bound.

Each objective should be followed by a list of quantification mechanisms relevant to the objective. For example, one of the sponsor's objectives is to create a contact database of 5,000 exhibition attendees intending to purchase a luxury car within the next 12 months, and they want to achieve that by the fourth week. Your quantification mechanisms may be:

- Number of names on the database
- Quality of information on the database

- Timeliness of capturing the information
- Timeliness of forwarding the completed database to the sponsor

Target Markets

Who are the target markets? Who else might this program affect? Your list may include staff, audiences, senior management, media, and ticket holders.

Sponsorship Benefits

Include a list of all benefits that have been included in the sponsorship contract as well as a list of any other benefits that may have been agreed to. A detailed list will assist both the sponsors and the sponsee in keeping tabs on the marketing opportunities available.

Evaluation

You should work with your sponsor to determine how they will measure the success of the sponsorship program. Detail how the sponsorship will be evaluated through key performance indicators.

Action List

Detail every marketing activity, event, media launch, report, meeting, and every aspect of the provision of benefits and information you have promised the sponsor. Next to the item, indicate the time frame and person responsible.

Double-Check Your Costs

When calculating costs, be sure to look at every benefit promised and every objective to be met. These costs will vary widely depending upon the type of event and benefits offered. Listed here are some of the more common costs encountered to get you started:

- VIP hospitality—tickets, invitations, catering, parking, gifts, security, travel/transport and accommodation
- Signage—production, maintenance, construction, storage, backdrops, transport
- Advertising—design, production, media time/space, agency advice

- Endorsement or appearance fees
- Promotional material—design, printing, shipping
- Prize money, competition prizes
- Product samples and discounts
- Legal fees
- Media/public relations support—media kits (design and production), media training, photographers, launch venue
- Evaluation—research fees, compilation of data
- Servicing costs—staff costs (remember to calculate the real cost of employment), consultants, travel

---

Budget
Detail all costs that are required to make this sponsorship plan happen. Ensure that you have accurately costed support and management of the sponsorship. Use your organization's formula for calculating real staff and administration costs of employment (including overheads). See "Calculating Overheads" in Chapter 2 for more information.

Managing the Sponsor

Although sponsors are generally becoming much more professional in the way that they do business, as a major stakeholder you will probably still find yourself managing the process at one time or another. The following information should help.

Sponsee Information Kit

In your first meeting with the sponsor once the contract is signed, we suggest providing the sponsor with an information kit that contains the following items:

- Details and an overview of responsibilities for all key contacts on your side
- A copy of your sponsorship plan (minus the budget)
- Media/marketing matrix, showing dates for all marketing activities, preferably including the promotional activities of all sponsors as well
- Key dates and deadlines
- Logos, artwork, photos, or other IP, including any guidelines, PMS colors, etc. in a range of electronic formats
- Approval process (for sponsor using your logo or other IP)
- Report template, showing what you intend to provide to the sponsor on a monthly or bi-monthly basis (a template is provided later in this chapter)
- Any other information or materials that will streamline the sponsorship process.

Providing an information kit will start the relationship on the right foot.

Sponsor Information Kit

At that same meeting, we suggest you also request an information kit from your sponsor that contains the following items:

- Details and an overview of responsibilities for all key contacts on the sponsor's side
- A restatement of their objectives for this sponsorship, your target markets, core brand values, etc.

- How the sponsorship will be measured and sponsee performance will be evaluated (key performance indicators)
- Logos and other IP, including any guidelines, in a variety of formats
- Any other information or materials that will streamline the sponsorship process

Regular Meetings

No, having a beer with them in the skybox does not count. You need to hold regular meetings with the sponsor from inception of the contract right through to the conclusion. This will ensure that you are aware of their situation and goals at all times and will ensure that you keep on top of all developments, opportunities, and potential trouble spots.

As for timing, we find biweekly meetings to be very beneficial. Under no circumstances should you go longer than a month between meetings.

Written Updates

If you only have time to meet monthly, then you should definitely be providing a midmonth written update to your sponsor. This only needs to be a concise report of where the sponsorship is, noting anything that is currently outstanding. Ask the sponsor from the outset what information they will need so there is no confusion. The following short reporting template should be very useful in gathering this information.

 # Reporting Template

[SPONSORSHIP NAME]

Report date:

Report period:

Report prepared by:

Contracted benefits provided to [sponsor] during the month of [previous month]:

Added-value benefits provided to [sponsor] during the month of [previous month]:

Overview of activities to be undertaken by [sponsee] during the month of [next month]:

Cash payments or contra to be provided during the month of [*next month*]:

Key dates, meetings, and activities for upcoming month(s):

Opportunities/issues to address:

Put Everything in Writing

It is important to put everything in writing. This way, you have some recourse if something does not get done, addressed, or checked. Every time you meet, someone needs to take notes and confirm all action items, including responsibilities and timelines, in writing.

Also, if something needs doing between meetings (and it always does), be sure to put that in writing as well. It does not need to be formal, just a quick email will be sufficient.

A great option is to use an online project management website, which both parties can log onto at any time. New action items, deadlines, meetings, changes and more can be documented at any time, with reminders sent. You can upload and share documents, make comments, create to-do lists, and more. There are a number of companies that offer this service. Our two favorites are Trello (www.trello.com) and Basecamp (www.basecamphq.com). Chances are, once you start using tools like these for sponsor management, you'll end up using them for a whole range of management tracking applications.

CHAPTER 12

Leverage

Although we've already addressed the importance of leverage to a sponsor when we talked about creating an offer, your job isn't finished. Once a sponsor is on board, it's critical to their success (and your renewal) that they actually leverage their sponsorship.

As a quick review, leverage is what a sponsor does with the sponsorship. You are selling opportunity; it is the leverage activities they undertake around it that provide them with the results they need for their brand and their company.

You may be thinking to yourself, "What does this have to do with me? I've already sold the sponsorship!," and to an extent, you'd be right. It's not your responsibility to leverage, but understanding some of the options for leveraging a sponsorship will allow you to gently educate your sponsors and encourage them to make the most of their sponsorship. We all know that a happy sponsor is a good sponsor, so helping them to achieve their goals is always in your best interest:

- They will achieve measurable objectives (and be more inclined to renew).
- They will see you putting effort into helping them achieve those objectives (and be more inclined to renew).
- Their leverage activities will augment your marketing plan.
- Their leverage activities will add value to your audience's event experience.
- Their leverage activities may introduce your property to new markets.
- They will advocate you to other potential sponsors.
- They will be more likely to renew easily and at a higher level.

You are probably also wondering what to do with that 10 to 15 percent of the sponsorship fee that we have told you to hold aside for servicing the sponsor. Again, that money is not to be used for taking them to lunch or for

> Although leveraging is not your responsibility, encouraging it is always in your best interests.

providing benefits that you have already promised in your agreement. It is for providing additional benefits that will assist your sponsor in achieving their objectives—*leveraging their sponsorship*.

When to Talk Leverage

The most important time to talk leverage with a sponsor is during the sales phase, and the most powerful thing you can do during that phase is to incorporate creative ideas for leverage into your proposal. This not only provides them with some strategic ideas and shortens their planning phase, but it sets the stage for them to really use the sponsorship, and does that from an early point in the relationship.

For your existing sponsors, the best time to start talking leverage is now. Sponsorship is, by its very nature, time-limited, and every day that goes by with a sponsorship unleveraged is a day they'll never get back. As soon as practical, schedule some time to speak with your sponsors about how they're going to leverage the sponsorship.

Encouraging Leverage

There are a number of strategies you can undertake to encourage your sponsors to effectively leverage their sponsorships.

Feed Them Leverage Ideas

We've gone through the whole process of finding big ideas for a sponsor leverage program back in Chapter 6: "Creating the Offer." You should definitely be using that process to feed the sponsor ideas and create a vision for what the sponsorship can accomplish both during the initial sale and during renewal. But don't stop there. If you've got a sponsor in the middle of a contract and they're just not leveraging, one of your options is to go through that process on their behalf and present the ideas to them.

A good way to approach this would be to say something like:

> "We have recently taken a new and more sophisticated approach to sponsorship. That has given us a broader vision for what can be accomplished by sponsoring our property, and in the process, we've come up with some creative ideas that may help you get even more out of your investment."

The best time to talk leverage is now.

Run a Leverage Brainstorm Session

Even better than feeding them your ideas is to run a leverage brainstorm session with them. Tell them that you've got a new approach to helping sponsors leverage their investments and would they like to get together a group of stakeholders—people from departments that could potentially benefit from the sponsorship—for a leverage planning session, which you would be happy to facilitate.

Sponsors usually love the suggestion, as you're basically volunteering to help them with both the planning and the internal sell-in in one fell swoop.

Once they've said yes, you should encourage them to invite a whole range of people, such as:

- Marketing management
- Brand management (one or a variety of brands)
- Sales
- Social media
- Website management
- Loyalty marketing/customer retention
- Advertising (in-house or agency)
- PR (in-house or agency)
- Major customer management
- New product development
- Retail liaison
- Human resources

These may all be different people or teams, there could be some crossover, or your sponsor could identify other roles to participate. Just consider this a starting place.

When they're all in the same room with you and a big whiteboard or some butcher paper, take them through the same brainstorm process we taught you in Chapter 6. Remember, however, that you are facilitating a brainstorm, and that's all about the possibilities. They have to keep an open mind, and so do you. They could come up with a fantastic idea that is good for them, you, and the fans, but requires swapping around some benefits. As long as they are willing to give up some less appropriate benefits, you should be willing to be flexible for a great idea.

Be willing to
be flexible for a
great idea.

Educate Them

Another option that's becoming popular with sponsorship seekers is to host a sponsor education session. You could run the workshop yourself, but it is often a stronger statement about your commitment to the sponsors and their results if you hire a good, well-credentialed sponsorship educator to lead the day. You can make it a straightforward workshop about theory, case studies, and maybe some group exercises, which would be typical.

Another option that we've increasingly seen (and done) is to hold a session where the facilitator introduces the theory of best-practice sponsorship and then takes the participants through the development of their leverage programs right there in the workshop. If you go with this option, encourage your sponsors to bring as many of their team as they can, as the process is based on a series of creative brainstorms and it's faster and more effective if they work as a team. The bonus for the sponsors is that you're basically increasing the overall skill level of their staff, and they'll love you for it!

Encourage Sponsor Case Studies

Sponsors love to hear how other sponsors are doing, and if you've got some really creative, win-win-win sponsors, you should ask if you can share their case study with the other sponsors. You can do this in an email, a sponsor newsletter, or you can hold a sponsor function and ask a couple of sponsors to stand up and do 10-minute case studies.

What you will find is that you'll have at least a couple of stalwart, old-school sponsors who will realize that all of that best-practice stuff you've been advocating isn't just hoo-ha—it actually works! This can be one of your most effective options to get those sponsors turned around and using the sponsorship well.

Share Case Studies and Good Resources

If you're taking our advice, you'll be regularly reading blogs and publications, as well as searching ABI/Inform Full-Text Online. You'll no doubt come across some case studies of sponsors doing great things with properties like yours. Share those case studies with relevant sponsors. You could say, "I was doing some research and came across a case study where an insurance company in Hong Kong took a really creative approach to their festival sponsorship. I thought you'd be interested, and if you'd like to talk about doing something similar, just let me know."

You should also share good sponsorship resources when you find them. There might be a fantastic blog or online tutorial or white paper that will help your sponsors, and they will appreciate that you're thinking about them all of the time.

Help the Sponsor to Integrate

This type of integration leverages the sponsor's program by marrying the power of sponsorship to the myriad marketing vehicles that they already have in place. Although there are still costs associated with integration, the cost is generally lower than creating separate supporting programs from scratch.

The basic idea is that sponsorship is no longer supported by big, incremental leverage budgets. There was a "rule" that was routinely espoused—the one-to-one rule—that said for every dollar a sponsor spends on the sponsorship fee, they should spend another dollar leveraging. As sponsorship became more cluttered, that became the two-to-one rule, but common sense has prevailed.

Great sponsors have identified that sponsorship is a great way to make marketing money they're already spending work harder. They use sponsorship as a catalyst to add relevance and meaning and passion to their existing marketing, making it more powerful and substantially reducing the amount they need to spend to leverage it. The best sponsors in the world only spend 10 to 25 percent of the sponsorship fee, incrementally, to leverage most of their sponsorships, and the starting place for that is integration.

The good news for you as the sponsee is that every time the sponsor promotes the sponsorship through their various marketing channels, they are also promoting your property. Encouraging this type of integration can greatly extend your marketing reach and has real commercial value to your organization.

Holding a leverage planning session, as outlined earlier, is an ideal way to facilitate integration. But, if you can't convince the sponsor of the value of getting together for a leverage planning session, you can still help your sponsor get buy-in from their various business units. Work with your key contact to engender their participation through any or all of the following methods:

- Meet with business unit decision makers to determine their sponsorship needs and discuss how your organization can help them achieve those objectives.
- Provide decision makers with a written overview of the sponsorship benefits, target markets reached, and some ideas as to how they could leverage the sponsorship.

Integration has real commercial value to *your organization.*

- Provide a couple of case studies of how other sponsors of your property (or even similar properties in other markets) have achieved tangible results in each of their areas of operation.
- Invite decision makers to your event so they get a feel for it and so you can start building a relationship.
- As business units do start using the sponsorship, keep other decision makers informed about how it's going.

This can be done in a subtle or straightforward manner. You will need to work with your key contact to determine which method will get the best response within their company (Figure 12.1).

Leverage All-Star: Orange

Orange, one of the UK's major mobile phone carriers, has been sponsoring the Glastonbury Festival for over a decade. Rather than letting it get stale, they have stayed focused and continued to evolve their leverage activities, which span a range of best-practice leverage approaches. Recent activities included:

- **Microsite.** Orange's Festival microsite provides an epicenter for all of their Glastonbury-related activities. It is a top destination for music fans all year round and really worth a look: web.orange.co.uk/p/glastonbury.
- **Chill 'n' Charge Tent.** Now infamous, the Chill 'n' Charge tent provides customers with a place to recharge their mobiles at this multiday festival (where most people stay in tents). There are 600 chargers and more than 30 broadband points in the tent, as well as live music by top artists.
- **GlastoNav.** An interactive, constantly updated festival planner for mobile phones.

- **Free music.** Orange customers who text a special number receive full tracks, ringtones, and more for their mobile.
- **Power Pump.** Extending their commitment to green innovations, Orange has created a foot-powered phone charger for Festival-goers. This follows on the heels (so to speak) of previous years' Dance Charger and Recharge Pod.
- **Exclusive content.** The Festival microsite features interviews and video blogs with the stars, behind-the-scenes information and photos, highlights, and a massive photo gallery of Festival life.
- **Communal blogging.** Customers are encouraged to send photos and stories from the festival to a special Festival number, creating a massive communal blog.
- **Festival Survival Guide.** A practical online guide to surviving the Festival, including such gems as "change your socks every day."

Figure 12.1
Sponsorship
centralized

Leverage Options and Issues

We've provided a good road map to create leverage ideas, but there are a few leverage options that you and the sponsor may not think of, and some that need to be handled with particular care.

- Media promotion
- Sponsor cross-promotion
- Non-sponsor cross-promotion
- Retail promotion
- Internal promotion

The different types of promotions are defined below.

Media Promotion

Media promotion is when a sponsor develops a cross-promotion with one or more media organizations. This is very common and can be extremely powerful—the more creative the execution the better.

Sponsor Cross-Promotion

This is when two or more sponsors work together to create a promotion that achieves objectives for each of them.

As sponsors of the same property, they already have something in common. They are also probably interested in the same marketplace (or at least segments of the same marketplace). It makes perfect sense that sponsors can get together to create cross-promotions that support both sponsorships—saving both parties money while doubling the communication base.

Some sponsees go to great lengths to keep their sponsors apart, afraid that they will compare notes on benefits and costs. We do not recommend this strategy and, instead, recommend that you facilitate sponsor cooperation. After all, if your sponsorships work better, you are more likely to have happy, productive sponsors that you will retain year after year. Plus, if they wanted to talk, they don't need your permission to do it.

Non-Sponsor Cross-Promotions

Cross-promoting with non-sponsors can provide a lot of freedom in selecting cross-promotional partners and, hence, excellent results can be gained. You must, however, be aware of some potential areas for conflict.

Cross-promotions can be used by non-sponsors as a means for ambushing their competition; for example, if the event sponsor, Gatorade, created a promotion with non-sponsor Reebok, when Nike is among the other event sponsors. The deal may be great and their intentions may be honorable, but you could be caught up in controversy. If you want to be seen as protecting your

> You should be proactive in getting your sponsors together.

Case Study: Media Promotion

This case study is definitely vintage, but is still a great example of win-win-win with a media partner.

Totino's pizza was a sponsor of the Minnesota Twins baseball team. They decided to stand out from the crowd of mainly visibility-oriented sponsors by creating a promotion with one of the top radio stations in town, with dozens of winners attending spring training with the team in Florida, all expenses paid. The hook—contestants had to rewrite the words to the classic baseball anthem, "Take Me Out to the Ballgame," using Totino's name and pleading its case as to why they should be chosen. Entries, along with proofs of purchase of its pizzas, were sent to the radio station, with the best entries chosen to sing their songs on air. The morning drive-time team flew down to spring training and did their show live from the stadium for a week and had lots of on-air interaction with the team.

sponsors from ambush, you must ensure that no promotional partners are seen as competing, directly or indirectly, with your current sponsors.

Even if there isn't a potential conflict involved, sponsees need to be careful about cross-promotions with non-sponsors. If you are not careful about limiting the benefits provided (through the sponsor) to their partner, you may end up with a situation where the non-sponsor is getting the benefits of sponsorship without paying a fee. Do two things: ensure your contract employs ample controls for passing on benefits to a partner; and be sure that the benefits delivered to your own organization through the cross-promotion are greater than the perceived loss. Media can also be a problem. If an event has an official media partner and one of your sponsors does a media promotion with a competitor, there are likely to be some noses out of joint, although that rarely stops it from happening.

Retail Cross-Promotion

Retail cross-promotion involves the sponsor's retailers and/or distribution system and is often a key element in fully leveraged sponsorship programs. Retail cross-promotion can add weight to other sales promotional activities and can serve to communicate the marketing message powerfully at the point of purchase.

Although the above example deals with a very targeted customer group, retail sponsorship can work just as well with a wide variety of retail outlets, such as grocery stores, specialty retailers, or petrol stations.

On the side of the retailer, a powerful cross-promotion can serve to increase store traffic and sales, as well as to create a point of difference from the competition. In order to achieve this for the retailer, the sponsor must be willing to share perceived ownership of all or part of their sponsorship of your organization.

> Warning: Non-sponsor cross-promotions can be very problematic.

Case Study: Sponsor Cross-Promotion

Avon, an international beauty and personal care company that has strong ties to empowering women as small business starters, adopted the breast cancer awareness cause. Since 1992, the company has raised more than $780 million, and in 2001 created their own signature event, the Avon Walk for Breast Cancer. Reebok has partnered with Avon to support the breast cancer cause through its line of Pink Ribbon footwear where they will donate a minimum of $300,000 and up to $750,000 to the Avon Breast Cancer Crusade through the sale of its Pink Ribbon clothing line.

> We strongly
> recommend
> retail cross-
> promotions.

As the sponsee, a major retail promotion driven by one of your sponsors can be an extraordinarily effective way to communicate your marketing message. So if it is not conflicting with other paying sponsors, we wholeheartedly recommend that you are proactive on this point.

Staff Programs

As powerful as sponsorship can be for communicating with a sponsor's customers, it can be just as powerful for communicating with their employees and shareholders. It can help them to increase their knowledge base, boost morale, increase productivity, or simply give something back to the people who make their company what it is.

Within a larger sponsorship portfolio, it is not above the realm of possibility that a sponsor could select a sponsorship specifically to achieve employee-based objectives.

When looking at promoting sponsorships internally, be sure to think about what is important to the sponsor's employees. There are no hard-and-fast rules, but here are some suggestions:

- Merchandising, usually done to employees or shareholders at cost
- Employee perks (merchandise, tickets, celebrity appearances, etc.)
- Product knowledge programs
- Incentive programs
- Volunteer programs, creating fun ways for the sponsor's employees to become materially involved in the sponsorship
- Contests for an employee to travel to a major event to be the company "representative'
- "Family day at . . ." where employees and their families go for free.

Case Study: Retail Cross-Promotions

Yorkshire Tea, 2013 sponsor of the most prestigious series in international cricket, The Ashes, used their sponsorship to deepen their ties with key UK retailer **Asda**. They rolled out an interactive, outdoor cricket center to the Asda stores closest to the grounds where the matches were played. People could choose to relax and have a cup of tea or test their bowling speed. This activity resulted in a 50 percent rise in sales in those Asda stores.

VIP Hospitality

Many sponsors have realized that standard VIP hospitality programs—sky-boxes, tickets to the opera, etc.—are no longer cutting it. Their customers were receiving too many invitations from too many companies, and they were all virtually identical. Many sponsees have responded by developing much more creative hospitality opportunities that allow their sponsors to stand apart from the crowd and appeal to their customers in a far more personal way.

Work with your sponsors to determine who their key customers are and what will appeal to them. If they are family oriented, create something that lets them spend quality time with their kids. If they are young and sporty, create something that appeals to their sense of competition or adventure. If they are status oriented, create something that stands out as an exclusive, must-attend event. Whatever you do, try to encourage the sponsor to think outside the square and do something that has real meaning to their key customers.

Ambush Protection

No other aspect of sponsorship has received as much attention in recent years as ambush marketing. Ambush marketing is, very simply, when a non-sponsor undertakes activities that do one or both of the following:

- Create confusion in the marketplace as to who the rightful sponsor is. This is often accomplished through the creation of promotions that have the look and feel of the event, or use similar or leading words, without actually

---

Case Study: Employee Programs

Northern Ireland had the highest incidence of breast cancer in the developed world, and there was a crying need for both education and fundraising. Action Cancer worked with the Nambarrie Tea Company to create an award-winning cause-related marketing program that accomplished both. The key to their success was staff involvement. Nambarrie actually shut down production for a day so that staff could create boxes of "Breast Cancer Awareness" ribbons instead, which Nambarrie's route drivers then delivered to stores around Northern Ireland. Not only were the staff involved in the creation of an on-pack promotion that raised over £200 000 for the charity, they also helped educate the community about breast cancer, and calls to Action Cancer's help line increased dramatically.

saying they are a sponsor. The result is that the non-sponsor receives much of the benefit of being a sponsor without paying the fee.

• Undermine a rightful sponsor. Even if a company does not engage in the more obvious type of ambush outlined above, they can still cause problems for a rightful sponsor. A classic example is the major football event that was sponsored by a brewer. A rival brewer paid a stripper a few hundred dollars to streak across the field at an appropriate moment. The result was that virtually every newspaper in the country ran a photo of the streaker instead of the game on the front page of the sports section.

There are two ways for a sponsor to be protected against ambush, and even then it can happen.

Case Studies: Hospitality

As a Corporate Champion of the NCAA, **AT&T** receives tickets and other various assets to the Men's Basketball Final Four and National Championship. AT&T creates a fun-filled weekend around the Final Four that includes propriety events with NBA Legends, VIP access to NCAA-sponsored events, dinners, brunch, and game tickets. They are able to spend valuable time outside the office with key customers and clients and expose them to sales and marketing people at AT&T.

Habitat for Humanity encourages their sponsors to invite their key customers to build days, and sponsors are seeing big uptake. They are finding that the idea of picking up a hammer to help build a house for an underprivileged family has a lot of appeal to key customers, and the demonstration of shared values creates bonds on a whole different level.

Several Ryder Cup golf matches feature high-tech business centers created by telecommunications company **Sprint**. They allow businesspeople attending the all-day event to keep in touch with the office by email, phone, and even videoconferencing, showcasing Sprint's products while providing a truly valuable service to clients and potential clients alike.

ABN AMRO found their hospitality package at the symphony was losing its appeal to clients. The symphony worked closely with the bank to create a series of exclusive, top quality, one-of-a-kind events, often in offbeat locations. The clients loved it from the start, and it quickly became the place to be for major decision makers and an unbeatable relationship-building opportunity.

Many sponsees are starting to cater for family hospitality by creating events for the children and grandchildren of VIPs, such as sports clinics, behind-the-scenes tours, and family days in hospitality suites (often complete with personalized merchandise and autograph sessions). Some sponsees even use children of VIPs in or around the event itself, often as extras in event advertising and public relations.

Legal

The main problem with preventing ambush marketing is that most of the time it is perfectly legal. The only time that it is not legal is if the ambushing company falsely represents that it is a sponsor, claims endorsement by the sponsee, or blatantly misleads the public into believing these things to be true.

The best way to protect your sponsors through legal channels is to ensure that ambush protection is written into the contract. This will demonstrate that you will not under any circumstances sell sponsorship, vending rights, or signage to any of the sponsor's competitors and will compel you to protect their rights within the scope of any media or subcontractor deals. But this is still only a partial measure because most ambushes have nothing directly to do with the sponsee.

Strategic

The best ambush protection a sponsor can possibly have is to leverage their sponsorship fully. If they have created a strong program of support for their investment, any activities mounted by their competition will look weak and stupid by comparison.

If you want to assist the sponsor in checking their vulnerability, work closely with them to assess potential risk areas and assist in any way you can to minimize those risks.

CHAPTER 13

Sponsorship Measurement

With the massive increase in sponsor sophistication in the past few years, sponsorship measurement has become a huge challenge for sponsors and sponsorship seekers alike, so we decided to devote an entire chapter to it in this fourth edition.

Measuring sponsorship accurately isn't difficult, but it does require a specific mindset and a degree of getting real on both sides of the equation.

Who Does the Measuring?

The short answer is, "the sponsor." They are the only ones who can do it accurately. You simply can't.

When you sell the sponsorship, you are selling opportunity. It is the sponsor's leverage program that turns that opportunity into a result against the sponsor's marketing and business objectives. How could you possibly be in a better position than they are to measure their activity against their objectives?

The longer answer is, "the sponsor, but it is totally in your best interests to steer them in the right direction."

Like leverage, measurement is another one of those areas that is totally the sponsor's responsibility, but some sponsors are terrible at measurement. Some measure mechanisms like exposure and awareness that have nothing to do with changing perceptions or behaviors around their brand. Some try to change every sponsorship gain into a dollar figure, with some of them being ludicrously arbitrary. Some sponsors think you should do the measurement for them, even though it's their leverage programs that are creating the results against their objectives. And if your sponsor is not thinking in terms of measurement at all, that's really bad and you may need to do some gentle education.

In any case, even if you can't measure the sponsorship for them (and you really can't), if you can assist the sponsor to understand the full value of their investment in terms of objective-based outcomes, you will already have made your case for renewal of sponsorship.

ROI Versus ROO

Measuring sponsorship purely in terms of dollars doesn't work.

ROI, or return on investment, has turned into a monster in our industry. Somehow, many sponsors have adopted the view that every return can and should be turned into a dollar figure so that the final returns can be compared with the costs in a ratio. They then crossed their fingers that this figure came up to something more than what was paid. If their estimates fell short, the sponsorship manager would often whack some arbitrarily large dollar amount on the bottom and call it "good corporate citizenship." There is no question that many sponsorship managers have covered their behinds with that old gem.

The other argument against measuring sponsorship in terms of dollars is that this creates an unnatural preoccupation on the sponsor's part with "getting their money's worth." If we equate this with above-the-line advertising, it would be like a sponsorship manager patting himself or herself on the back and calling it a day because he or she paid $200,000 and got $280,000 worth of television advertising. Whether the advertisements actually achieved anything has not been quantified at all. It is exactly the same with measuring sponsorship. Whichever way you look at it, if a sponsor is measuring an entire sponsorship program in terms of dollars, they are measuring the process, not the results, and that's just plain silly.

The Shift to ROO

ROO, or return on objectives, takes back the idea that sponsorship measurement is multifaceted and based on overall marketing and business objectives. Good sponsorship practitioners have come to realize that, although there are some objectives that can be quantified in dollars, it is impossible to put an accurate dollar figure on many of the most important returns sponsorship can achieve, including:

- Shifts in consumer perception of the brand
- Increasing the loyalty or advocacy of key target markets
- Deepening of relationships with consumers
- Deepening of relationships with major clients
- Shifts in consumer behaviour
- Consumer understanding and alignment with core brand values and attributes
- Consumer understanding and alignment with key messages (e.g., "if you drink and drive, you're a bloody idiot" or "just do it')
- Introduction to new potential clients
- Launch, demonstration, or trial of a new product
- Networking with corporate and/or government decision makers
- Increased retail support or preference by a brand's intermediary market

That doesn't mean these (and many other) objectives aren't measurable, it simply means that they each have valid measures and benchmarks, and that to measure something as multifaceted as sponsorship, the measurement mechanisms will be multifaceted, as well.

Return on objectives brings the results of sponsorship right back to what the sponsor is trying to achieve in their marketing program. It also puts the responsibility in the right place. Sponsors set the objectives, will leverage the sponsorship to meet those objectives, and have the experts on staff who measure all of these areas and many more every day. On the following pages, we have a list of many of the objectives that a sponsor can measure.

Helping Your Sponsors Understand Their Results

Before helping a sponsor develop or improve their measurement mechanisms, you must keep in mind the following rules:

- Benchmarking is a must. A sponsor can't know what the sponsorship achieved if they don't know where they started.
- The objectives to be measured and how they'll be measured should be planned from the outset, right alongside leverage planning.
- Sponsorship is multifaceted, and the measurement needs to be, as well.

Helping your
sponsor
understand
how to
measure real
results is always
in your best
interest.

The basis of this type of measurement is that it's all about objectives, and if objectives are SMART, they should be measurable.

Each objective should be made as clear and specific as possible. Generalizations and ambiguity virtually guarantee that a sponsorship will be unmeasurable. Even if your organization has given a stellar performance on the sponsorship, the sponsor will have no idea whether the sponsorship has delivered on the objectives. And we hate to break it to you but, as a sponsorship seeker, the assumption by sponsors is that if they can't show that the sponsorship performed against objectives, then it didn't perform—and they'll blame it on you.

Sponsors are getting far more sophisticated, but we still occasionally see sponsors specify their objectives in a series of two-word phrases, such as "increase sales." While this is certainly a worthwhile pursuit, neither you nor the sponsor will be able to determine the extent to which this objective has been met because it is too vague. When faced with vague objectives such as this, you need to keep asking questions until you have agreed upon a SMART objective.

For example, if you have developed an initial objective of "increasing sales," you could ask the following types of questions:

Beware of
two-word
objectives.

- What type of sales (new customer, incremental, loyalty, or up-selling)?
- Through what distribution channel (retail, catalog, hotline, etc.)?
- To which target market(s)?
- During what time frame?
- From what benchmark?
- Determined how?

What Are All Those Kinds of Sales?

Just as there are different kinds of customers, there are also different kinds of sales. To demonstrate the differences between the four main types of sales, let's think about them in terms of a fast-food chain:

- **New customer.** Someone who has never been to the fast-food chain comes in for the first time.
- **Loyalty.** An existing customer starts coming in for lunch more often or starts coming in for other meals as well.

- **Incremental sales.** "Do you want fries with that?" In other words, when customers buy more items of food than they were planning (or than they usually do) on any given visit.
- **Up-selling.** "For just 50 cents you can upgrade to a Great Big Meal." In other words, buying an item that is bigger or more expensive than originally planned.

If you ask these questions, your sponsor will also most likely realize that they need to get their own sales department involved to define, benchmark, and measure this aspect of the sponsorship. That realization is a big win for a sponsee.

The following table provides some examples of typical short, snappy (but nonquantifiable) objectives and how they might be turned into SMART objectives.

Not	Instead
Increase sales	Create incremental sales of 10 percent over the benchmark of $240,000 per week during the six-week promotional period as determined by retailer case commitments in the Tri-State region.
Develop database	Develop a database of no fewer than 2,500 qualified prospects, as determined by salary level, age range, professional and family status, investment risk profile, and current insurance products owned. A profile of acceptable ranges is attached.
Gain publicity	Raise the understanding of the legal blood alcohol limit for drivers from 64 percent to 85 percent, and raise the proportion of our target market that "strongly agrees" with the statement, "I would never consider drinking and driving," from 34 percent to 55 percent over the 12-month sponsorship term.
Demonstrate "good corporate citizenship"	Increase positive responses within our target market about our firm's professionalism (from 45 percent to 64 percent), commitment to representing New Zealand positively overseas (from 12 percent to 35 percent), and intention to expand their business with us (from 42 percent to 66 percent) over the six-month promotional period, as determined by responses to our annual client survey. A profile of the target markets is attached.

Once the objectives have been fully developed, the big question for the sponsor is "If these objectives are achieved, will you consider this sponsorship to have been a success?" If the answer is no, then the objectives need to be developed or extended further. If the answer is yes, you know exactly what you are working toward.

Measurement Options

The most vexing part of creating SMART objectives is the "M" part, that is, making them measurable. Do not despair, however, as there are many more ways to measure sponsorship results than you realize.

Depending upon what objectives the sponsor is trying to achieve, you can work with them to ensure that one or more mechanisms are in place for each objective. If you've worked with their team on their leverage program, that is a great forum for determining measurement strategies with the stakeholders involved in those measures.

Some suggestions on measurement mechanisms for different categories of objectives can be found below.

Measurable in Dollars

- Incremental sales
- Profit on incremental sales
- Wholesale commitments
- Direct sales to your partner
- On-site sales
- New or promotional product orders (total or average)
- New or promotional product reorders (total or average)
- Profit on up-selling to existing customers
- New customer acquisitions
- Average spend of a target market
- Profitability of a target market

Measurable in Percentages

- Changes in brand perceptions
- Changes in purchase intent
- Changes in advocacy
- Retail promotional penetration/participation
- Increase in wholesale orders
- Increase in retail sales
- Sales promotion participation (as a percent of sales)
- Profitability
- Store traffic
- Employee participation in activities/offers
- Churn/loyalty

In addition, you can add all the dollar measures (above) and sheer number measures (below), as long as they can be reflected in a percentage change against benchmarks. For example, Canucks fans buy an average of $24 a month of our product, which is a 35 percent increase on our customer average.

Measurable in Sheer Numbers

- Promotional participation—sales, media, online, on-/in-pack, etc.
- Social media promotion participation
- User-generated content posted to social media and/or website
- Facebook likes, comments, post likes, shares, virality
- Twitter follows, responses, retweets, virality
- (Repeat for other social media)
- Visits and/or repeat visits to sponsorship-driven web page or microsite
- Sponsorship-driven newsletter sign-ups
- Downloads
- Coupon or merchandise redemption
- Employee participation or volunteering

Measured Subjectively

There are a few objectives that are very important to sponsors but can't be objectively measured against benchmarks. To be credible, any reports on the impact of a sponsorship on these areas should be done by the people who manage those relationships.

- VIP relationship building
- Media relations
- Government/regulator relations

Measuring Media

If you have ever been guilty of handing a sponsor a stack of media clippings at the end of an event, whether they have anything to do with the sponsorship or not (and most of us have at one time or another!), now is the time to clean up your act.

That approach to measuring media is called media monitoring—literally providing copies of all media clippings, television and radio interview transcripts, and tapes without any analysis of their value. Unfortunately, a folder of articles and clippings provides the sponsor with no insight on what they have achieved at all.

We're not fans of trying to put a value on public relations coverage, as that gets back into the territory of measuring outputs, not outcomes. That said, some companies still use this as a component of their measurement process, and you may need to assist if they ask.

Rather than trying to put arbitrary dollar figures on any coverage they may get through your property, we suggest you simply email links or scans of any meaningful coverage to their PR team, along with a short explanation to explain context, such as:

> "The local NBC affiliate was specifically interested in advice to parents to get their kids to eat well. We provided your "Healthy Families" kit, which precipitated your involvement in the linked news grab."

If you are gathering readership/viewership numbers and audience profiles for your own files, you can also pass along that information to the sponsor.

By taking this approach, you are assisting them as much as is appropriate, and their team can apply any figures or weights to the coverage that they see fit.

CHAPTER 14

Renewals and Exits

All good things must come to an end, and sponsorship is no exception. Whether the sponsorship has been short or long term, the time will eventually come when it will either be renewed or exited.

This scenario causes a lot of angst among some sponsorship seekers, particularly those who think themselves lucky for having signed up a sponsor in the first place, but it really doesn't need to. Like death and taxes, it is just part of the process.

Renewals

It is usually far easier to renew an existing sponsor than it is to find a new one, so taking the right approach to renewals will save you a lot of time, money, and angst.

Start Early

Many contracts have a specific time by which the renewal process will start, but our advice is to ignore it. Start the renewal process as early as you can, making it essentially an extension of your servicing activities. Throughout the sponsorship, you should be working with the sponsor to understand and meet their needs. As you get closer to the end of the contract, your vocabulary should shift from focusing on the coming year to a focus on the bigger picture and how you can continue to develop your relationship through coming years and events.

If you have been servicing your sponsor well, there will be no surprises.

The timing of when you will want to start discussing renewal in earnest will vary from one event to another, but you will need to keep the following well in mind:

- It takes most sponsors at least four to six months to create and implement a leverage program for a sponsorship. If their needs, and the benefits package you are offering to meet them, have changed significantly, you need to give them enough time to get a new leverage program together.
- Give yourself enough leeway so that, just in case the sponsor doesn't renew, you have plenty of time to resell the sponsorship.

Start Fresh

Many sponsorship seekers make the mistake of offering a sponsor the same benefits package again at renewal. This may be easy, but you will be missing out on a great opportunity to improve your relationship and their results.

The beginning of the renewal process is the ideal time to sit down with your sponsor to discuss their current needs, objectives, target markets and any new initiatives so that a new package can be developed that really does the job for them.

- Go through the same information-gathering process that you would if they were a new sponsor. You may even want to use the **Sponsor Information Checklist** as a guide.
- Speak with decision makers across the sponsor's business units. You may be able to create a package that meets more of their needs.
- Be open with the sponsor regarding your organization's marketing needs and challenges. This is a golden opportunity to re-create a relationship that achieves *mutual* marketing objectives.
- Suggest a leverage planning session with their team before you make a new offer, allowing you to reinvent the sponsorship and then to reinvigorate their buy-in.
- Don't be constrained by set benefits packages. Be flexible and creative in your response to the sponsor's needs. Use your inventory!

Exits

When a sponsor doesn't renew, it can be very stressful on an entire organization, and it can be very tempting to start apportioning blame. This is always

If your sponsor doesn't renew, don't lose your cool.

counterproductive. Most sponsorships are exited for strategic reasons, not because your organization has done anything wrong or because the sponsor is being unfair or arbitrary.

There are a number of reasons why a sponsor may want to exit a sponsorship, including:

- A major shift in objectives or target markets
- The sponsorship was entered into for the wrong reasons or it wasn't a good match from the start
- Lack of interest, and therefore integration, across the business units
- Consolidation of the sponsorship portfolio into fewer, larger investments
- A new sponsorship or brand manager who wants to overhaul the sponsorship portfolio whether it needs it or not
- Budget cutbacks
- A global directive to concentrate on a specific sponsorship or type of sponsorship (e.g., the Olympics)
- A corporate merger resulting in the duplication of some sponsorship investments, a major change in the type of event, and/or its audience (e.g., your organization has shifted from presenting a consumer travel show to a travel trade show).

Then again, the sponsorship may have simply passed its prime, and it's just time to do something else. It is widely accepted that the lifespan of a fully leveraged sponsorship averages around seven years. Even if the sponsorship has been livened up every year, at some point the returns gained by the sponsor are going to start diminishing and it will be time to move on.

Again, if you have been doing a good job at servicing your sponsor, the fact that they don't plan to renew should not come as any surprise. In most cases, you should know far enough ahead of time to find another sponsor to take their place.

Even if it does come as a surprise, try to take it in your stride. There have been many cases where sponsorship seekers have thrown the equivalent of a tantrum—going to the media, badmouthing the sponsor—and all they ever accomplished was looking like a bunch of idiots and scaring off potential new sponsors. After all, what sponsor would want to work with a sponsee who may try to damage the brand if the relationship doesn't go on forever?

Next Steps

As soon as you find out that your sponsor is not renewing, there are a few things you need to do:

1. Debrief the sponsor so you can understand exactly why they aren't renewing.
2. If your organization is at fault in any way, accept responsibility and go about fixing the problem. You should also discuss the problem with your other sponsors to let them know it is being addressed.
3. If your organization wasn't at fault, ask the sponsor for referrals to other sponsors who may be a better fit. You should also ask the sponsor if you can use them as a reference.
4. Ask your other sponsors for referrals.
5. Look at the benefits package you have been providing the sponsor. Is there an opportunity to use those benefits to increase your other existing sponsorships?
6. Take the opportunity to update your inventory and proposal template.
7. Get out there and find another sponsor.

What If It's Your Organization That Doesn't Want to Renew?

It happens. Sometimes a sponsor is unresponsive. Sometimes they are painful to work with. Sometimes they just don't fit well with your image or audience. Sometimes there is a better, more profitable, more active, and more partnership-oriented sponsor waiting in the wings. (If that is the case, count yourself lucky.)

Before you write off a sponsor, be sure you have done everything you can to get the relationship on track. If it's just not happening, try to afford the sponsor the same courtesy you would expect from them. Give them plenty of notice that you are not intending to go forward with the sponsorship and, without vilifying them, tell them why.

Conclusion

You've made it to the end of *The Sponsorship Seeker's Toolkit, Fourth Edition.* We're guessing that you're experiencing some combination of being overwhelmed with the amount of effort that goes into seeking sponsorship and excited by the possibilities.

Don't worry; that's all normal. And the first time you build a sponsorship proposal, it's going to feel like a herculean task. All we can say is that once you've done one best-practice proposal, it gets a lot easier. You will look at your work and see how it all flows and fits together and suddenly, the prospect of putting it in front of a sponsor will seem much less daunting. And we guarantee, the first time you get positive feedback from a prospective sponsor about the quality and professionalism of your offer, you'll know it's all been worth it.

We have developed and refined our approach over our combined 50-odd years in sponsorship. The results enjoyed by the thousands of participants in our workshops, keynotes, and webinars and by readers of previous editions who have raved nonstop since the book was first published in 1999 prove without a shadow of doubt that this approach works exceedingly well across a wide range of sponsorship seekers—from sport to culture to government, large organizations to small, beginners to seasoned professionals.

We understand that asking for money is never easy. What we have provided you with are the theory, tools, and inspiring examples so that you can create successful partnerships and you can do it with confidence. Our premise is simple and based on three key principles:

1. Understanding your brand, your target markets, and what you have to offer are the foundation stones of outstanding sponsorship.
2. Great sponsorship offers are anchored in great leverage ideas. Do your homework, get creative, and tell the sponsors how they can use the oppor-

tunity they're considering to achieve the brand and business objectives they need.

3. Sponsorship must be win-win-win throughout the relationship, or nobody wins.

There is no magic wand for sponsorship. Success revolves around good research and hard work. Consider the sales process as 75 percent preparation, 10 percent sales, and 15 percent follow through, and you will be pretty close to the mark. Most organizations barely prepare, approach sales as a simple transaction, and don't follow up at all. It's no wonder that most sponsorship efforts fail.

No one can guarantee that every proposal you create will be successful. What we can guarantee you is that if you follow the process we've outlined in this book, your offers will have a much greater rate of success.

It is important that all of us as practitioners recognize that sponsorship marketing is a rapidly evolving marketing tool. We need to work together—sharing ideas, evaluation techniques, and case studies—if we are to continue to succeed in creating win-win-win partnerships. Use the networks you have and that social media has created for us. Share case studies, advice, and insights whenever you can. Remember, what goes around comes around.

In the same vein, we would love to hear how this approach to sponsorship works for you and welcome your feedback. Our contact details can be found at the back of the book.

It has been our pleasure to bring you this Fourth Edition. The wealth of new case studies we've had to choose from is testament to the huge strides our industry has made since the last edition. It's an exciting time for all of us, and we wish you all the best with your sponsorship program!

Kim and Anne-Marie

Part 4

Appendices

APPENDIX 1

Glossary

Above-the-line advertising Traditional advertising venues—television, radio, newspaper, magazine, and outdoor advertising. Also known as *main media*.

Activation The sponsor-generated activities that take place around a sponsorship and deliver most of the value of a sponsorship investment. Also called *leverage*.

Added value The provision of an unexpected, meaningful benefit to a customer or sponsor, primarily done to strengthen the relationship with them.

Advertising Placing a commercial message in above-the-line media.

Advertorial When a company purchases the right to place favorable editorial material or editorial material with a distinctly commercial slant in a publication or on a program for a fee. Generally, it must carry wording that clearly states that it is a paid advertisement.

Agent An individual or organization that sells sponsorship properties on a commission or fee basis. Also known as a *broker*.

Ambush marketing	An organization creating the perception that they are a sponsor of a property, or somehow involved with the event experience, when they have not purchased the rights to that property.
Below-the-line advertising	Nontraditional advertising avenues (anything that is not "above the line"), such as sponsorship, publicity, sales promotion, online activities, relationship or loyalty marketing, coupons, database marketing, direct response, and retail promotions.
Brand marketing	Marketing activities with the primary goal of communicating the positioning, personality, and nonfunctional attributes of a brand.
Broker	An individual or organization that sells sponsorship properties on a commission or fee basis. Also known as an *agent*.
Cause-related marketing	Cause-related marketing is an investment that strategically links a product, service, or company with a cause or an issue and yields a return for the corporate partner, the nonprofit organization, and the community. Cause-related marketing may include licensing, sponsorship, joint ventures, underwriting, and sales promotion.
Clutter	A term used to describe an overload of sponsor messages around one event. It is also used more generally to describe the massive amount of advertising and other marketing messages ever present in developed society today.
Contra	Term to describe products or services that are provided in lieu of cash in exchange for sponsorship rights. Also known as *in-kind*.
Coverage	Media term referring to the proportion of the target market that has the opportunity to see

	or hear any one advertisement. It is expressed as a percentage of the total target market. Also known as *reach*.
Critical success factor	This refers to something you or your sponsor must do right for the sponsorship or event to be a success. Often there are a number of critical success factors for any given activity.
CRM	Customer relationship management. The area that controls and manages loyalty and database marketing activity. CRM can also stand for *cause-related marketing*.
Cross-promotion	When two or more organizations create promotional opportunities that benefit all partners.
Donation	An offering of product or cash that is given by a company without any anticipated commercial return.
Early adopter(s)	A person or group of people who tend to try new things earlier than others and spread opinions about them. These people are very important to new products and brands and often attract a large percentage of early marketing budgets. Also known as *trend setters* or *opinion leaders*.
Exclusivity	Exclusive rights to sponsorship or on-site sales. Typically defined by the sponsor's category of business (e.g., "exclusive automobile sponsor" or "exclusive beer vendor").
Fit	The degree to which a sponsorship opportunity matches a brand's objectives, attributes, and target markets.
Frequency	Media term referring to the average number of times each member of your target audience receives an advertising message over the course of the advertising campaign.

Gamification	The creation of social games around an event or property, with the goal being to deepen the connection with the target market. Can be created by the property or a sponsor.
Grant	The provision of funds or material for a specific project generally not linked to a company's core business. The grant must usually be acknowledged by the recipient and generally must be accounted for. A grant is given on the basis of the need for the project rather than the promotional and marketing opportunities it may provide.
Image transfer	The process by which a sponsor associates itself with the core values and attributes of a sponsee, with the goal being to authentically introduce or reinforce those attributes within their company or product.
In-kind	Term to describe products or services that are provided in lieu of cash in exchange for sponsorship rights. Also known as *contra*.
In-pack	The promotion of a sponsorship in the sponsor's actual product packaging. Often done in conjunction with "on-pack" promotion.
Launch	A public unveiling or announcement of the details of an event, program, or sponsorship that is specifically designed to gain publicity. The launch often marks the start of the marketing program.
Leverage	The sponsor-generated activities that take place around a sponsorship and deliver most of the value of a sponsorship investment. Also called *maximization* or *activation*.
Main media	Traditional advertising venues—television, radio, newspaper, magazine, and outdoor advertising. Also known as *above-the-line advertising*.

Marketing message	The key message that an organization wants to convey about their product or service through a sponsorship.
Marketing mix	A company's entire marketing program, made up of a mix of marketing activities.
Measurement	Evaluation of the results of the sponsorship program. Also called *quantification*.
Media sponsorship	An advertising package generally consisting of paid and/or contra advertising, unpaid promotion and/or editorial support, and exclusivity.
Merchandising	The creation of promotional items around an event that will then be sold or given away. Merchandise can be produced and distributed by either the event, the sponsor, or both.
Naming rights sponsorship	This is basically the same as a principal sponsorship with the added benefit of the sponsor having their name added to the event name (e.g., the Blockbuster Bowl or the Emirates Melbourne Cup). Also known as *title sponsorship*.
Narrowcasting	This is the opposite of broadcasting, that is, marketing to a tightly defined group. Also known as *niche marketing*.
Niche marketing	Targeting a group of people with a very tightly defined set of demographic and/or psychographic characteristics. Also known as *narrowcasting*.
Offer	The proposal offered to a potential sponsor. Also known as the *package*.
Official supplier	A (usually) low-level sponsorship in which the sponsor provides either a product or services to the event free or at a substantial discount, often not paying any additional sponsorship fee; or

pays a sponsorship fee to secure a guarantee from the sponsee that they will purchase the sponsor's product or service exclusively.

On-pack

The promotion of a sponsorship on the sponsor's actual product packaging. Often done in conjunction with "in-pack" promotion.

On-selling

A sponsor reselling portions of the purchased sponsor benefits to one or more other companies. This is usually done with the full knowledge and approval of the sponsee.

Opt-in

A database is said to be opt-in if everyone on it has explicitly requested to be contacted. Best practice is "double opt-in," where they opt-in to the database and that is confirmed with a follow up email, where they then have to click a link before their addition to the database.

Outdoor

Above-the-line advertising that takes place outdoors, such as billboards, posters, and taxi or bus signage. Also known as *out-of-home*.

Out-of-home

Above-the-line advertising that takes place outdoors, such as billboards, posters, and taxi or bus signage. Also known as *outdoor*.

Package

The proposal offered to a potential sponsor. Also known as the *offer*.

Packaging

Structuring the sponsoring benefits and their relationship to the event and the sponsee.

Pass-through rights

The right for a sponsor to on-sell or give some of the sponsorship benefits to another company.

Perimeter signage

Banners and/or signs that are located near an event but not inside the boundaries of the event itself.

Philanthropy	The voluntary giving of funds by foundations, trusts, bequests, corporations, or individuals to support human welfare in its broadest sense.
Point of difference (POD)	An attribute that differentiates a product from its competitors. Sponsorship can often be a powerful point of difference.
Point of sale (POS) material	A display, signage, or a promotional item produced for display with a product in the store and designed to create excitement and differentiate the product from its competitors.
Positioning	The personality of a brand, company, or event. Strong brand marketing is often focused on positioning.
Principal sponsor	This is the preeminent sponsor of any event or property, receiving the highest level of benefits and promotion.
Promoter	An individual or company who takes on some of the financial risk as well as responsibility for the marketing and promotion of the event in exchange for a portion of the profits.
Property	This term is used as a generic term for sponsee. Also known as *sponsorship seeker* or *rightsholder*.
Proposal	The sponsorship offer in written form.
Public relations	The process of gaining editorial media coverage (i.e., newspaper and magazine articles, television and radio coverage), generally in news, current affairs, or lifestyle programming. Also known as *publicity*.
Publicist	A specialist in gaining editorial media coverage.
Publicity	Editorial media coverage (i.e., newspaper and magazine articles, television and radio cov-

237

erage), generally in news, current affairs, or lifestyle programming. Also known as *public relations*.

Quantification

Evaluation of the results of the sponsorship program. Also known as *measurement*.

Reach

Media term referring to the proportion of the target market that has the opportunity to see or hear any one advertisement. It is expressed as a percentage of the total target market. Also known as *coverage*.

Reporting

The ongoing process of providing a sponsor with information regarding the performance of their sponsorship against agreed marketing objectives.

Rightsholder

This term is used as a generic term for *sponsee*. Also known as *sponsorship seeker* or *property*.

Sales promotion

Activities employed to encourage customers to buy a product or differentiate a product from the competition at the point of sale.

Sales sponsorship

A sponsorship that is entered into primarily to gain direct sales (e.g., a brewer sponsoring a festival in order to secure exclusive pouring rights or a hotel chain sponsoring a touring stage show to guarantee all of those room bookings).

Segmentation

Defining different segments of a marketplace based upon demographics, psychographics, perceptions, and buying patterns.

Servicing

The process of providing benefits to a sponsor, both what is agreed on and additional benefits to assist them in achieving their objectives. Servicing also encompasses strong two-way communication between the sponsor and sponsee, as well as reporting.

Signage	Signs that are specific to an event, such as banners, A-frames, scoreboards, etc. These can feature the marketing message of the sponsor, the event, or both.
Sponsee	The recipient of the sponsor's primary sponsorship investment (the fee). Typically, sponsees will fall into the categories of arts, cause, education, community service, event, individual, Internet site, sport, or venue.
Sponsor	The organization that buys sponsorship rights, packaged and granted by the sponsee.
Sponsorship	An investment in sport, community or government activities, the arts, a cause, individual, or broadcast that yields a commercial return for the sponsor. The investment can be made in financial, material, or human terms.
Sponsorship audit	The assessment of each component of a sponsor's sponsorship portfolio against stringent selection criteria, usually leading to a readjustment of the portfolio.
Sponsorship guidelines	A document produced by sponsors that provides potential sponsees with information on the objectives, target markets, parameters, scope, and categories of sponsorship investments made by a company.
Sponsorship plan	A detailed plan that documents how a sponsorship will be serviced and implemented by the sponsee.
Sponsorship policy	A document that indicates an organization's philosophy and approach to sponsorship, including why they are involved, key influences on the sponsorship process, and any sponsorship exclusions or limitations.

Sponsorship strategy	A formal document produced by a company or organization that outlines the target markets, objectives for sponsorship, and specific strategies to achieve these goals. This document is usually closely linked to an organization's marketing and/or revenue raising strategies. Generally, both sponsors and sponsees will have sponsorship strategies in place.
Sticky marketing	A marketing activity that "sticks," creating lasting changes in a market's perceptions or behavior.
Target audience	The most appropriate audience for a particular product, service, or event. The audience can be made up of one or several target markets, which can sometimes be quite diverse.
Target market	A group of people who are likely purchasers of a product or service, or who are strong candidates for attending an event, and who share a similar demographic and/or psychographic profile.
TARP (Target Audience Rating Point)	Media term referring to the percentage of the target market reached over the course of an advertising campaign. It is a gross measure, taking into account both reach (the number of people that your message reaches) and frequency.
Title sponsor	This is basically the same as a principal sponsorship with the added benefit of the sponsor having their name added to the event name (e.g., the Blockbuster Bowl or the Emirates Melbourne Cup). Also known as *naming rights sponsor*.
USP	Unique selling point. The unique attribute(s) of a product or brand that often forms the basis of marketing activities.

Vendor   An organization or company that sells a product or service at an event. This term is also used to describe a company that supplies a product to a retailer to sell (e.g., Kmart's vendors would include Black & Decker, Unilever, Coca-Cola, etc.).

Resources

We have put together this list of resources to assist you with skill building, research, and developing your networks. This is by no means an exhaustive list but should provide a strong base to get you started. Please note, we have not accepted any fees or special consideration from any of these organizations, nor are we responsible for their content. There are some cases where we are not familiar with an organization and have simply included their contact details.

Blogs

We recommend several blogs to follow for a constant feed of inspiration and ideas.

Kim Skildum-Reid's Sponsorship Blog
www.powersponsorship.com

Partnership Activation Blog by Brian Gainor
www.partnershipactivation.com

Sponsorship Blog by Linda Antoniadis
www.sponsorshipblog.com

The Business of Sports Blog by Russell Scibetti
www.thebusinessofsports.com

Culture Scout Blog by Patricia Martin
blog.patricia-martin.com

Chris Reed on Partnership Marketing
chrisreed.brandrepublic.com

SponsorPark's blog
www.sponsorpark.com/blog

Social Media

Twitter

Our best advice is to follow the hashtags #sponsorship, #sportsbiz, #eventprofs, and #fundraising. Within those, you will find some very astute content creators and curators to follow.

Sponsorship Insights LinkedIn Group

Search for the "Sponsorship Insights" group. Sponsorship Insights has a very good and substantial LinkedIn networking group that we highly recommend. The discussions are pertinent and lively, and it is refreshingly free of spam. For details, see www.linkedin.com.

Associations

This is a mix of sponsorship associations and some more general marketing, nonprofit, or sports business associations. Some of these more general organizations do currently offer sponsorship education and/or resources. If your country's associations don't, we have found most are open to suggestions from members with regard to topics and good resources. Ask for the support you need if you're not getting it.

International

International Festivals & Events Association (IFEA)

The IFEA is aimed at events and festival organizers, although it does have some good resources for sponsors of these types of events. There are chapters in 36 countries. For details, see www.ifea.com.

North America

Sponsorship Marketing Council of Canada

This Council was formed by the Canadian Association of Advertisers and supports primarily corporate sponsors, but has events open to all sponsorship professionals. For details, see www.sponsorshipmarketing.ca.

American Marketing Association

This large association has a wide variety of publications, conferences, workshops, and symposiums available across the United States, although sponsorship does not feature heavily in its education program at present. For more information, see the AMA website at www.marketingpower.com or contact the chapter in your area. A full list is available on the site.

Association of Canadian Advertisers

This association provides a lot of resources, primarily for corporate sponsors. They also host a well-regarded industry conference and Canada's premier sponsorship awards. For details, see www.acaweb.ca.

Canadian Institute of Marketing

This association is well respected across Canada, with chapters and activities in major cities. Its quarterly publication, *The Marketing Challenge*, regularly covers sponsorship. Current and back issues are available free of charge to both members and nonmembers on this website. For details, see www.professional marketer.ca.

Society for Nonprofit Organizations

With more than 6,000 members in the United States, this association provides a wealth of information, training, and other resources to the sector. For more information, see www.snpo.org.

Europe

European Sponsorship Association

This is the only pan-European sponsorship association, with awards, a major conference, and a new diploma course. For details, contact www.sponsorship .org.

Swedish Sponsorship Association

This very active sponsorship association has many great activities and resources, as well as holding the annual Scandinavian Sponsorship conference in Stockholm. For details, see www.sefs.se.

German Sponsorship Association

This is a big, active sponsorship association, hosting an annual sponsorship summit and awards, as well as providing other good resources to industry professionals. For more information, see www.faspo.de.

Norwegian Sponsor & Event Association

With many educational events and resources, this association is a big part of the sophisticated Scandinavian sponsorship industry. For more information, see www.sponsorforeningen.no.

Chartered Institute of Marketing (UK)

The Chartered Institute of Marketing is the largest marketing association in the world, with branches across the United Kingdom and the Republic of Ireland. It holds events internationally, not just in the United Kingdom. Sponsorship resources are limited, but general marketing resources and networking opportunities are outstanding. For more information, see www.cim.co.uk.

The Marketing Society Ltd (UK)

This association holds numerous events around the country, as well as a star-studded annual conference. Members also get free access to the magazines *Market Leader* and *Marketing Magazine*. For details, see www.marketing society.org.uk.

Marketing Institute of Ireland

The MII offers lots of marketing resources and networking. It also offers free subscriptions online to its biweekly marketing e-zine M@rketPlace to both members and nonmembers. For details, see www.mii.ie.

Asia

Hong Kong Institute of Marketing

This is Hong Kong's preeminent marketing organization, with a full complement of educational and networking activities. It also publishes *Asian Marketing Review*. For details, see www.hkim.org.hk.

Marketing Institute of Singapore

The MIS is Singapore's key marketing body, with a membership of around 4,500 professionals. For details, see www.mis.edu.sg.

Japan Marketing Association
The JMA has chapters in Kansai, Kyushu, and Hokkaido. For details, see www
.jma2-jp.org.

Institute of Marketing Malaysia
For details, see www.imm.org.my.

Indonesia Marketing Association
For details, see www.ima.or.id.

Institute of Marketing and Management (India)
For details, see www.immindia.com.

Korea Marketing Association
For details, see www.kma.re.kr.

Marketing Association of Thailand
For details, see www.marketingthai.or.th.

Australia/New Zealand

Australian Marketing Institute
The AMI regularly holds sponsorship-oriented functions and workshops and
is a good source of general marketing information. For details, see www.ami
.org.au.

New Zealand Marketing Council
For details, see www.marketing.org.nz.

Africa

Institute of Marketing Management (South Africa)
The IMM is a very active association, with many events and training sessions
around South Africa. For details, see www.imm.co.za.

Periodicals

Global

Brand Republic

Brand Republic is not one industry mag but a whole collection of marketing and media publications from Europe and Asia, all rolled into one mega website. The articles are great and searchable, and they have a fantastic set of bloggers. For details, see www.brandrepublic.com.

North America

The Sponsorship Report

This is Canada's own sponsorship publication. They also host a major annual sponsorship conference. For details, see www.sponsorship.ca.

Adweek

Brand marketing publication *Brandweek* has recently been folded into its sister publication, *Adweek*. You'll still find a big emphasis on below-the-line marketing activities, including sponsorship. For details, see www.adweek.com.

Marketing Magazine (Canada)

This is a well-respected marketing publication with strong marketing information for both Canadians and others. For details, see www.marketingmag.ca.

Sales & Marketing Management

This publication doesn't touch on sponsorship every time, but over the course of a year, it does have some excellent articles on the subject. For details, see www.salesandmarketing.com.

Advertising Age

AdAge is very advertising oriented but very complete in this regard. It has an excellent website with full articles available for free. For details, see www.adage.com.

SportsBusiness Daily

This is probably the preeminent North American publication on the business of sports. The coverage of sponsorship news is plentiful, and it will point you in the right direction to get more in-depth information. It is available online at www.sportsbusinessdaily.com.

Marketing News

This is the magazine of the American Marketing Association. Content runs the gamut, but does include sponsorship. See www.marketingpower.com.

Europe

SportBusiness

This is a very good resource with strong international coverage. For details, see www.sportbusiness.com.

Sponsor Tribune (Netherlands)

This sponsorship publication is well respected for its depth of content. For details, see www.sponsoronline.nl.

Marketing (UK)

This is one of the United Kingdom's preeminent marketing publications. It comes out weekly and has a money-back guarantee. Its website is excellent and very complete. For details, see www.marketinguk.co.uk.

Marketing Week (UK)

This is another top publication in the UK market. It is very comprehensive and covers sponsorship well. It has an excellent website. For details, see www .marketingweek.co.uk.

Marketing Ireland

This monthly consists mainly of snippets of news from around the region. While you are unlikely to get any in-depth coverage of sponsorship issues, it is certainly a good resource to keep you on top of the Irish marketing industry. For details, see www.marketing.ie.

IMJ (Irish Marketing Journal)

Somewhat more comprehensive than Ireland's *Marketing* magazine, there seems to be more of a balance between coverage of above- and below-the-line activities. They have a great website. For details, see www.irishmarketing journal.ie.

Asia

Asia Sponsorship News

This is Asia's only purely sponsorship publication. It is mostly about sponsorship news (not skills), but members get access to a deals and contacts database and they hold educational events. For details, see www.asiasponsorshipnews.com.

Campaign Asia-Pacific

This is the top cross-Asia marketing publication. For details, see www.campaignbrief.co.nz.

Australia/New Zealand

Australian Sponsorship News

This is Australia's only sponsorship publication and a good source of industry news and events. For more information, see www.sponsorshipnews.com.au.

Stop Press

This is New Zealand's top marketing magazine with an excellent website. For more information, see www.stoppress.co.nz.

AdNews

AdNews is a bit of a misnomer because this Australian biweekly has a much broader and more comprehensive view on marketing. It also incorporates some excellent sponsorship-oriented features. For more information, see www.adnews.com.au.

B&T/Professional Marketing

B&T is a weekly, advertising-oriented publication, although it does cover marketing in a larger sense as well. For more information, see www.bandt.com.au.

Campaign Brief

This is the preeminent marketing and advertising periodical in New Zealand. For more information, see www.campaignbrief.com/nz.

Other Useful Websites

Many of the above-listed resources have great websites, but there are a few other sites that we thought were worth a mention.

Advertising/Marketing/Sponsorship

Adworld
This site bills itself as "The No. 1 online information resource for the Irish marketing, advertising, and media business." It delivers. See www.adworld.ie.

Brand Republic
Brand Republic brings together the best of a variety of marketing and related publications and is a wealth of information and inspiration. Check them out on www.brandrepublic.com.

Power Sponsorship
Headed by Kim Skildum-Reid (coauthor of this book), Power Sponsorship provides in-house training, public workshops, webinars, and workshops tailored for government and industry groups, and expert sponsorship coaching. For more information, see www.powersponsorship.com.

PR Newswire
This website provides up-to-the-minute news releases from major U.S. corporations and events. It allows you to search all press releases, by company, for the last several years. (Our hint, add the word "sponsorship" to your search.) For more, see www.prnewswire.com.

Arts and Nonprofit
Although most of these sites are specific to one country or another, don't limit yourself geographically. Many of them feature good advice and links that will be useful to a wide range of cultural and nonprofit organizations.

Arts Management Network
This is a very complete site, with articles, links, books, and more for the cultural and broader nonprofit sector. For more, visit www.artsmanagement.net.

ArtsMarketing.org
This is a very interesting and very complete site run by the Arts & Business Council. It includes a lot of information on programs, education, and policy and has some excellent links. For more, see www.artsmarketing.org.

ArtsUSA
Run by Americans for the Arts, this is an excellent resource for arts marketing information, as well as broader resources for the arts community. For more, visit www.artsusa.org.

Cause Marketing Forum
This very comprehensive site offers great resources, educational events, and distance learning. For more, see www.causemarketingforum.com.

The NonProfit Times
In the online version of a real-life magazine out of the United States, we found some interesting articles, a good online directory, and some very useful links. For more, see www.nptimes.com.

NYFA Interactive
This is a site put up by the New York Foundation for the Arts. It is a service specifically for cultural institutions and includes *Current*, a good online publication, as well as terrific cultural links. For more, visit www.nyfa.org.

OurCommunity.com.au
This extremely complete website is a goldmine of information for community groups trying to establish and grow their capabilities. For more, visit www.ourcommunity.com.au.

Sponsorship Law

Although members of these associations are specifically specialized in sports or entertainment law, they will likely be well versed in sponsorship law and will be able to assist any sponsorship seeker that needs expert advice.

International Association of Entertainment Lawyers
This site features a searchable list of members.
www.iael.org

Sports Lawyer Association Inc. (USA)
www.sportslaw.org

Black Entertainment and Sports Lawyers Association (USA)
www.besla.org

British Association for Sport and Law
www.britishsportslaw.org

Australian & New Zealand Sports Law Association Inc. (ANZSLA)
www.anzsla.com.au

Corporate Profiles

Hoover's
This is a great resource for finding profiles of companies and industries from the United States, United Kingdom, Germany, and many other countries. This is not a free service, but they do let you try it out before committing. See www .hoovers.com.

iWave Information Systems
A subscription service with more than 1,000 U.S. and 300 Canadian corporate profiles that will assist nonprofit organizations in gaining sponsorship. Also provides biographies, major gift announcements, and special interest group articles. Ask for the online 10-minute tour. See www.rpbooks.com.

Sponsorship Agreement Pro Forma

Warning

This document is provided as a sample only and is not a substitute for legal advice. You should seek the advice of a suitably qualified and experienced lawyer before using this document. In particular, you or your lawyer should:

- Check the law in your jurisdiction—make sure this agreement works there.
- Check for changes to the law—law and practice might have altered since this document was drafted or you last checked the situation.
- Modify wherever necessary—review this document critically and never use it without first amending it to suit your needs.
- Remember that every sponsorship is different.
- Beware of limits of expertise. If you are not legally qualified or are not familiar with this area of the law, do not use this document without first obtaining legal advice about it.

You should also read the guidance notes in Chapter 10 before using this sample agreement.

Sponsorship Agreement

This Sponsorship Agreement comprises the attached Schedules, Special Conditions, and Standard Conditions.

Date
Parties

1.   [*] incorporated in [*] of [*] (the Sponsor)
2.   [*] incorporated in [*] of [*] (the Owner).

This Sponsorship Agreement comprises the Standard Conditions, the Schedules, and the Special Conditions.

IT IS AGREED as follows.

Schedule 1
"Sponsor"

Title: _____

Address: _____

Telephone: _____

Facsimile: _____

Email: _____

Schedule 2
"Owner"

*(Identify the sponsee—the legal entity receiving the sponsorship. This must be the proper name of the company or association receiving the funds and controlling the team, event, or venue being sponsored, **NOT** the name of the team, event, or venue, etc.)*

Title: _____

Address: _____

Representative: _____

Telephone: _____

Facsimile: _____

Email: _____

Schedule 3
"Commencement Date"

(Insert when the sponsorship starts.)

_____

Schedule 4

"Term"

(Insert when the sponsorship will end or for how long it will last e.g., "5 years.")

_____
_____
_____
_____
_____

Schedule 5

Option to Renew

(See clause 1.5.)
Does Sponsor have an option to renew? Yes/No
If yes:

- *For what "Period" (Specify an extended finishing date or further term, e.g., 3 years)?*
- *Will the sponsorship fee and other Owner Benefits be the same after renewal? If not, list the new benefits.*

_____
_____
_____
_____
_____
_____
_____
_____
_____
_____
_____

Schedule 6

First Right of Refusal

(See clause 1.6.)
Does Sponsor have a first right of refusal? Yes/No

_____
_____
_____
_____
_____

Schedule 7

"Property"

(Identify the event, team, venue, or other property the subject of this sponsorship.)

_____
_____
_____
_____
_____

Schedule 8

"Sponsorship Category"

(Identify the nature of the sponsorship; e.g., title/ category/official supplier, etc.)

_____
_____
_____
_____

Schedule 9

"Territory"

(Specify the area in which the sponsorship operates, e.g., state, region, country, continent, worldwide, etc.)

_____
_____
_____
_____
_____
_____

Schedule 10

Sponsor Objectives

(See clause 2.1.)

(Be specific: list bottom-line sales objectives, measurable promotional activities, business development targets, etc.)

1. _____
2. _____
3. _____

Schedule 11

Owner Objectives

(See clause 2.2.)

(Be specific—list expected leverage from Sponsor in developing event/sport, target participation or attendance numbers, entry fee and merchandise income, measurable business development targets, etc.)

1. _____
2. _____
3. _____

Schedule 12

"Sponsor Benefits"

(List, in detail, the signage/ tickets/hospitality/advertising credits/merchandising rights, and other benefits that Owner must provide to Sponsor—be precise about amounts, timing, etc.)

1. _____
2. _____
3. _____
4. _____
5. _____
6. _____
7. _____
8. _____
9. _____
10. _____

Schedule 13

"Owner Benefits"

(List, in detail, the sponsorship fee, Contra/in kind benefits that Sponsor must provide to Owner—be precise about amounts, timing, etc.)

1. _____
2. _____
3. _____
4. _____
5. _____
6. _____
7. _____
8. _____
9. _____
10. _____

Schedule 14

Evaluation Criteria

- *Is Media analysis required and, if so, by whom, at whose expense, how regularly, and what details must be provided?*
- *Is Owner obliged to provide reports on mutual marketing activities, demographic information, samples of printed and promotional materials, and, if so, what and when?*
- *Specify, in detail, the level of performance (and how it will be assessed) that is regarded by Sponsor as unacceptable.*
- *Specify the consequences of failing to achieve this level (for example right of termination, reduced fees or benefits).*
- *Specify the level of performance (and how it will be assessed) above which Sponsor's reasonable expectations are exceeded.*
- *Specify the consequences of this level of performance (for example increased sponsorship fee or benefits).*
- *Specify any other relevant evaluation criteria, information, or consequences.*

_____
_____
_____
_____
_____
_____
_____
_____
_____
_____
_____
_____
_____
_____
_____
_____
_____
_____
_____
_____

Schedule 15

"Applicable Law"

(Identify the country or state the laws of which will apply to this Agreement.)

_____

_____

_____

_____

_____

Schedule 16

Owner Marks

(Insert here all trademarks, names, logos, and other artwork that Sponsor is entitled to use under this Agreement. Include artwork. If nothing is listed, Sponsor may use all Owner Marks.)

_____

_____

_____

_____

_____

_____

_____

Schedule 17

Sponsor Marks

(Insert here all trademarks, names, logos, and other artwork that Owner is entitled to use under this Agreement. Include artwork.)

_____

_____

_____

_____

_____

Schedule 18

Use of Owner Marks

(List here the specific purposes for which Owner Marks can be used by Sponsor.)

1. _____

2. _____

3. _____

Schedule 19

Use of Sponsor Marks

(See clause 5.1.)
(List here the specific purposes for which Sponsor Marks can be used by Owner.)

1. _____

2. _____

3. _____

Schedule 20

Promotional & Media Objectives

(See clause 6.3.)
(Be specific—e.g., list target media outlets, promotional events, nature of coverage, etc.)

1. _____
2. _____
3. _____

Schedule 21

Competitors of Sponsor

(See clause 7.1.)

1. _____
2. _____
3. _____

Schedule 22

Competitors of Property

(See clause 7.2.)

1. _____
2. _____
3. _____

Schedule 23

Sponsor's Termination Events

(See clause 9.2.)
(Insert here the circumstances in which Sponsor can terminate this Agreement.)

1. _____
2. _____
3. _____
4. _____
5. _____

Schedule 24

Owner's Termination Events

(See clause 9.3.)
(Insert here the circumstances in which Owner can terminate this Agreement.)

1. _____
2. _____
3. _____
4. _____
5. _____

Schedule 25

Insurance
(See clause 16.)
(Insert here the amount of public liability insurance required to be maintained by Owner and full details of any other insurance required for the purposes of this Agreement.)

Schedule 26

Ambush Strategies
(Include here specific strategies designed to minimize the likelihood of Ambush occurring, such as obligations on Owner to:
- *Prevent or minimize Competitor involvement;*
- *Exercise control of venue access and signage*
- *Impose contractual obligations on bidders for commercial rights not to engage in Ambushing should the bids be unsuccessful*
- *Negotiate broadcasting agreements to provide Sponsor with a first right of refusal to take category exclusive advertising time during broadcasts of the event*
- *Impose ticketing restrictions*
- *Prevent the reuse of tickets or licensed products as prize giveaways*
- *Provide sponsorship fee rebates (be very specific) if serious Ambush occurs, etc.)*

1. Public liability—amount

_____

_____

2. Other:

_____

_____

_____

1. _____
2. _____
3. _____
4. _____
5. _____

Special Conditions

(Insert here any changes to the Standard Conditions and any special conditions not referred to in the Standard Conditions or the Schedules.)

Standard Conditions

1. Sponsorship

1.1 Exclusivity

Sponsor shall be the exclusive sponsor of the Property, in the Sponsorship Category, in the Territory.

1.2 Term

Subject to this Agreement, the sponsorship starts on the Commencement Date and is effective for the Term.

1.3 Consideration

The consideration for this Agreement is the mutual conferring of benefits referred to in clause 1.4.

1.4 Benefits

(a) Sponsor must confer Owner Benefits on Owner; and

(b) Owner must confer Sponsor Benefits on Sponsor,

at the times outlined in, and in accordance with, Schedules 12 and 13.

1.5 Option to Renew

(a) This clause applies if the parties specify "Yes" in Schedule 5.

(b) Sponsor has an option to renew this Agreement for the further Period specified in Schedule 5 if:

(i) Sponsor is not in breach under this Agreement; and

(ii) Sponsor gives notice in writing to Owner no fewer than 3 months before the end of the Term stating it intends to exercise the option.

(c) If Sponsor exercises the option, the provisions of this Agreement (except for this clause 1.5) shall continue in full force and effect for the further Period, subject to any differences in fees or Owner Benefits specified in Schedule 5 for the further Period.

1.6 First Right of Refusal

(a) This clause applies if the parties specify "Yes" in Schedule 6.

(b) Owner must not enter into an agreement with any other person to sponsor the Property in the Sponsorship Category at or immediately after the end of the Term without first offering the sponsorship to Sponsor on the same terms as it proposes to offer to (or as have been offered by) other parties.

(c) If Sponsor declines within 30 days to accept the new sponsorship terms, Owner may enter into an agreement with a third party, but only on the terms offered to, and rejected by, Sponsor.

(d) Sponsor's first right of refusal extends to any revised terms offered to or by third parties after Sponsor declines to accept the initial terms.

1.7 No Assignment Without Consent

(a) Sponsor must not assign, charge, or otherwise deal with Sponsor Benefits without the prior written consent of Owner.

(b) Owner must not assign, charge, or otherwise deal with Owner Benefits without the prior written consent of Sponsor.

(c) This clause does not apply to Owner Benefits or Sponsor Benefits that the parties, on signing this Agreement, agree will be conferred on third parties.

2. Objectives

2.1 Objectives of Sponsor

The primary objectives of Sponsor in entering into this Agreement are:

(a) to associate Sponsor's brand with the Property;

(b) to promote the products and services of Sponsor;

(c) to encourage brand loyalty to Sponsor;

(d) to assist in raising and maintaining Sponsor's corporate profile and image;

(e) to provide to Sponsor marketing leverage opportunities related to the Property;

(f) to promote community awareness of, affinity for, and (if relevant) participation in the Property;

(g) to continually review and evaluate the ongoing success and performance of the sponsorship for maximum commercial advantage to all parties; and

(h) the objectives outlined in Schedule 10.

2.2 Objectives of Owner

The primary objectives of Owner in entering into this Agreement are:

(a) to secure sponsorship funds and other benefits;

(b) to increase the profile, standing, brand value, and (if relevant) participation in the Property;

(c) to promote the profile and corporate image of Sponsor and the use of Sponsor's products and services;

(d) to continually review and evaluate the ongoing success and performance of the sponsorship for the maximum commercial advantage to all parties; and

(e) the objectives outlined in Schedule 11.

2.3 Fulfillment of Objectives

The parties must act at all times in good faith toward each other with a view to fulfilling the objectives outlined in clauses 2.1 and 2.2. This Agreement is to be interpreted in a manner that best promotes the fulfilment of those objectives.

3. Warranties

3.1 Owner Warranties

Owner warrants that:

(a) it has full right and legal authority to enter into and perform its obligations under this Agreement;

(b) it owns the Property (or, if the Property is not legally capable of being owned, it holds rights which effectively confer unfettered control of the Property);

(c) Owner Marks do not infringe the trademarks, trade names, or other rights of any person;

(d) it has, or will at the relevant time have, all government licenses, permits, and other authorities relevant to the Property;

(e) it will comply with all applicable laws relating to the promotion and conduct of the Property; and

(f) throughout this Agreement, it will conduct itself so as not to cause detriment, damage, injury, or embarrassment to Sponsor.

3.2 Sponsor Warranties

Sponsor warrants that:

(a) it has full right and legal authority to enter into and perform its obligations under this Agreement;

(b) Sponsor Marks do not infringe the trademarks, trade names, or other rights of any other person;

(c) it will comply with all applicable laws in marketing and promoting its sponsorship of the Property; and

(d) throughout this Agreement, it will conduct itself so as not to cause detriment, damage, injury, or embarrassment to Owner.

4. Disclosure

4.1 Initial Disclosure

Owner warrants that it has disclosed to Sponsor:

(a) the substance (other than financial details) of all agreements entered into or currently under negotiation with Owner for sponsorship, exclusive or preferred supplier status or other like arrangements relating to the Property; and

(b) all other circumstances which might have a material impact upon Sponsor's decision to enter into this Agreement.

4.2 Continuing Disclosure

Owner must from time to time keep Sponsor informed of:

(a) new sponsorship, exclusive or preferred service or supplier status, or other like arrangements conferred by Owner in respect of the Property;

(b) significant marketing programs and other promotional activities which might provide leverage opportunities for Sponsor; and

(c) research and demographic information held or commissioned by Owner about the Property and its participants.

5. Marks and Title

5.1 Authorized Use

(a) Sponsor may use Owner Marks:

    (i) for all purposes reasonably incidental to obtaining the Sponsor Benefits; and

    (ii) as permitted in Schedule 18.

(b) Owner may use Sponsor Marks;

    (i) for all purposes reasonably incidental to obtaining the Owner Benefits; and

    (ii) as permitted in Schedule 19.

5.2 No Unauthorized Use

(a) Sponsor must not use, or permit the use of, Owner Marks or any other trade or service marks, logos, designs, devices, or intellectual property rights of Owner; and

(b) Owner must not use, or permit the use of, Sponsor Marks or any other trade or service marks, logos, designs, devices, or intellectual property rights of Sponsor,

unless:

(c) authorized by this Agreement; or

(d) with the written consent of the other party.

5.3 Merchandise

(a) Unless permitted in Schedule 18, Sponsor must not manufacture, sell, or license the manufacture or sale of any promotional or other merchandise bearing Owner Marks without Owner's prior written consent.

(b) Unless permitted in Schedule 19, Owner must not manufacture, sell, or license the manufacture or sale of any promotional or other merchandise bearing Sponsor Marks without Sponsor's prior written consent.

(c) All authorized merchandise bearing Owner Marks or Sponsor Marks permitted under this Agreement must be:

    (i) of a high standard;

    (ii) of such style, appearance, and quality as to suit the best exploitation of the Sponsor, Owner, and Property (as the case may be); and

    (iii) free from product defects, of merchantable quality, and suited for its intended purpose.

5.4 Image

The parties must ensure that any authorized use by them of the other's marks or intellectual property rights:

(a) is lawful;

(b) properly and accurately represents those rights;

(c) (in the case of Owner using Sponsor Marks), strictly complies with Sponsor's trademark and logo usage policies current at the relevant time;

(d) is consistent with the other's corporate image; and

(e) (if used in connection with the provision of goods or services) is associated only with goods or services of the highest quality.

5.5   **Enforcement Protection**

The parties must provide all reasonable assistance to each other to protect against infringers of Owner Marks or Sponsor Marks in connection with the Property.

5.6   **Title**

Despite any rights to use another's marks conferred under this Agreement:

(a)   Owner holds all legal and equitable right, title, and interest in and to the Property and all Owner Marks;

(b)   Sponsor holds all legal and equitable right, title, and interest in and to the Sponsor Marks;

(c)   naming, title, and other rights conferred by this Agreement merely constitute licenses to use the relevant Owner Marks or Sponsor Marks (as the case may be) for the purposes of, and in accordance with, this Agreement and do not confer any property right or interest in those marks; and

(d)   the right to use another's marks is non-exclusive and non-assignable.

5.7   **Infringements Incidental to Television Broadcasts, Etc.**

This clause 5 does not prevent any person holding rights to televise or reproduce images associated with the Property from incidentally broadcasting or reproducing Sponsor Marks appearing as or in signage on premises controlled by Owner and relevant to the Property.

5.8   **No Alteration to Broadcast Signal, Etc.**

Owner must not authorize or permit any media rights holder contracted in respect of the Property (for example, the official broadcaster of an event or an authorized Internet site manager or multimedia provider or rights holder), in the exercise of those media rights, to alter any images associated with the Property (for example, by the artificial electronic insertion, removal, or alteration of signage or other images) without the prior written consent of Sponsor.

6.   **Media, Branding, Leverage, Etc.**

6.1   **Media Exposure**

At all reasonable opportunities:

(a)   Owner will use its best endeavors to obtain public and Media exposure of the sponsorship; and

(b)   Sponsor will use its best endeavors to obtain public and Media exposure of the Property.

6.2 Approval

Media releases relating to the sponsorship must:

(a) be issued jointly by the parties; or

(b) not be issued by one party without the consent of the other.

6.3 Promotional Objectives

Owner and Sponsor must use their best endeavors to achieve their promotional and Media objectives outlined in Schedule 20. Sponsor licenses Owner to use Sponsor Marks, and Owner licenses Sponsor to use Owner Marks, for these purposes.

6.4 Leverage

Sponsor has the right at its cost to:

(a) promote itself, its brands, and its products and services in association with the Property; and

(b) engage in advertising and promotional activities to maximize the benefits to it of its association with the Property,

provided that it will not knowingly or recklessly engage in any advertising or promotional activities which reflect unfavorably on the Property, the parties, or any other sponsors of the Property.

6.5 Social Media Policies

Owner must comply, and must procure its employees and contractors to comply, with Sponsor's Social Media policies from time to time in relation to any direct or indirect references to the sponsorship or the Sponsor in Social Media content created or exchanged by or on behalf of Owner, its employees, or contractors.

7. Exclusivity

7.1 Exclusivity Within Territory

(a) If the Sponsorship Category is designed for only 1 sponsor (for example, naming rights or principal sponsorship):

  (i) Sponsor's rights under this Agreement are exclusive within the Territory; and

  (ii) Owner must not enter into any sponsorship or supply arrangements for the Property in the Sponsorship Category within the Territory with any other person.

(b) If the Sponsorship Category is designed for multiple sponsors (for example, official suppliers or Gold Class sponsors) Owner must not, without the prior written consent of Sponsor (which must not be unreasonably withheld), enter into any sponsorship or supply arrangements for the Property in the Sponsorship Category within the Territory with any other person.

(c) The sponsorship categories for the Property must not be redesigned without Sponsor's prior written consent if to do so might affect adversely Sponsor's rights under this clause.

7.2 Competitors

Owner must not within the Territory authorize or permit to subsist:

(a) the provision of any products or services to the Property, in any sponsorship category; or

(b) any association with the Property,

by any Competitor of Sponsor.

7.3 Sponsor Restraint

Sponsor must not enter into any sponsorship or supply arrangements with any Competitor of the Property or the Owner during the Term or within a reasonable time after the end of the Term.

7.4 Injunctions

The parties acknowledge that the restraints referred to in this clause 7 cannot adequately be compensated for in damages and consent to injunctive relief for the enforcement of these restraints.

8. Marketing and Service Delivery

8.1 Marketing Committee

Owner and Sponsor will establish a marketing committee to meet quarterly (or otherwise, as agreed) for the purposes of:

(a) reviewing the progress of the sponsorship and the mutual rights conferred under this Agreement;

(b) evaluating the success of the sponsorship against its objectives;

(c) discussing further opportunities for leverage and cross-promotional activities;

(d) maximizing the ongoing benefits to the parties, implementing promotional strategies for the parties, and identifying new, mutual opportunities; and

(e) maximizing the Sponsor Benefits by:

    (i) identifying actual or potential Ambush activities;

(ii) using their best endeavors to prevent Ambush or minimize its potential impact on the sponsorship; and

(iii) directing implementation of the strategies outlined in Schedule 26.

8.2 Service Delivery

Both Sponsor and Owner must designate a representative to be primarily responsible for the provision of the day to day service and support required by the other party under this Agreement. Until otherwise nominated, the representatives will be the representatives named in Schedules 1 and 2.

8.3 Evaluation

The parties must evaluate the success of the sponsorship in accordance with the criteria outlined in Schedule 14 and with the consequences (if any) outlined in that Schedule.

9. Termination

9.1 Expiry

This Agreement, unless terminated earlier under this clause or extended under clause 1, will continue until the end of the Term.

9.2 Early Termination by Sponsor

Sponsor may terminate this Agreement if any of the following occurs:

(a) Owner fails to provide a Sponsor Benefit, and failure continues for 7 days after Owner receives written notice from Sponsor to provide the benefit.

(b) Owner is Insolvent.

(c) any event outlined in Schedule 23 occurs.

(d) application of the evaluation criteria in Schedule 14 permits termination.

(e) any laws come into operation which in any way restrict, prohibit, or otherwise regulate the sponsorship of, or association by Sponsor with, the Property or the Owner so that:

(i) the benefits available to Sponsor are materially reduced or altered; or

(ii) Sponsor's obligations under this Agreement are materially increased.

(f) for reasons beyond the reasonable control of Sponsor, Sponsor is unable to continue to exploit and enjoy fully the Sponsor Benefits.

(g) any major, public controversy arises in connection with the Owner, the Property, or this Agreement which, in the reasonable opinion of Sponsor, reflects adversely and substantially on Sponsor's corporate image.

(h) any statement, representation, or warranty made by Owner in connection with this Agreement proves to have been incorrect or misleading in any material respect.

(i) the rights conferred on Sponsor under this Agreement are directly or indirectly diminished, prejudiced, or compromised in any way by the reckless acts or omissions of Owner.

(j) Owner has not used its best endeavors to ensure that the exclusive rights conferred on Sponsor under this Agreement are not directly or indirectly diminished, prejudiced, or compromised in any way by the acts or omissions of third parties (for example, by Ambush).

9.3 Early Termination by Owner

Owner may terminate this Agreement if any of the following occurs:

(a) Sponsor fails to provide a material Owner Benefit, and failure continues for 7 days after Sponsor receives written notice from Owner to provide the benefit.

(b) Sponsor is Insolvent.

(c) any event outlined in Schedule 24 occurs.

(d) any major, public controversy arises in connection with the Sponsor or this Agreement which, in the reasonable opinion of Owner, reflects adversely and substantially on Owner's corporate image or upon the Property.

(e) any statement, representation, or warranty made by Sponsor in connection with this Agreement proves to have been incorrect or misleading in any material respect when made.

(f) the rights conferred on Owner under this Agreement are directly or indirectly diminished, prejudiced, or compromised in any way by the reckless acts or omissions of Sponsor.

9.4 Immaterial Breaches

Nothing in this clause entitles a party to terminate this Agreement for trivial or immaterial breaches which cannot be remedied, however this does not prevent termination for regular, consistent, or repeated breaches (even if they would, alone, be trivial or immaterial).

9.5 Method of Termination

A party entitled to terminate this Agreement may do so by notice in writing to the other at the address specified in Schedule 1 or Schedule 2, as the case may be.

9.6 Effect of Early Termination

Termination of this Agreement for any reason shall be without prejudice to the rights and obligations of each party accrued up to and including the date of termination.

10. Re-branding

10.1 Change of Name, Logo, Product, Etc.

If at any time Sponsor changes its name or logo, or wishes to change any Sponsor's product associated with Property, Sponsor may re-brand the sponsorship of the Property provided that, in the reasonable opinion of Owner, to do so will not affect the good name and image of the Property or Owner.

10.2 Costs

Re-branding must be at Sponsor's cost. This includes:

(a) direct costs to Sponsor; and

(b) any costs incurred by Owner directly or indirectly resulting from the re-branding.

11. Governing Law and Jurisdiction

The Applicable Law governs this Agreement. The parties submit to the non-exclusive jurisdiction of the courts of the country or region of the Applicable Law and courts of appeal from them for determining any dispute concerning this Agreement.

12. Relationship of Parties

The parties are independent contractors. Nothing in this Agreement or in the description of the Sponsorship Category shall be construed to place the parties in, and the parties must not act in a manner which expresses or implies, a legal relationship of partnership, joint venture, franchise, employment, or agency.

13. Ongoing Assistance

13.1 Assist Parties

Each party must promptly:

(a) do all things;

(b) sign all documents; and

(c) provide all relevant assistance and information,

reasonably required by the other party to enable the performance by the parties of their obligations under this Agreement.

14. Costs

14.1 Agreement Costs

Each party must pay its own costs of and incidental to the negotiation, preparation, and execution of this Agreement.

14.2 Implementation Costs

Unless otherwise specified as a Sponsor Benefit or Owner Benefit, each party must pay its own signage, advertising, leverage, general overhead, and incidental costs related to the performance of its obligations under this Agreement. Despite this, all signage, artwork, photography, film, video tape, and similar expenses directly or indirectly incurred under this Agreement must be met by Sponsor unless otherwise provided for in the Schedule or Special Conditions.

14.3 Transaction Taxes

Sponsor must also pay all transaction taxes (such as GST, VAT, or similar goods or services taxes) applicable to this Agreement.

15. Notices

Notices under this Agreement may be delivered or sent by post, facsimile, or email to the relevant addresses outlined in Schedules 1 and 2 and will be deemed to have been received in the ordinary course of delivery of notices in that form.

16. Insurance

16.1 Liability Insurance

Owner must effect and keep current:

(a) a public liability insurance policy for an amount not less than the amount specified in Schedule 25 for any single claim for liability of Owner or Sponsor or both for death, personal injury, or property damage occasioned to any person in respect of the Property (including a contractual liability endorsement to cover the obligations of Owner under clause 17);

(b) such other insurance as is specified in Schedule 25; and

(c) if Property is a one-off event (or if the parties specify in Schedule 25), event cancellation insurance in an amount equaling or exceeding the value of Sponsor Benefits.

16.2 Product Liability Insurance

If:

(a) Owner is authorized under this Agreement to manufacture, sell, or license the sale or manufacture of any merchandise bearing Sponsor Marks; or

(b) Sponsor is authorized under this Agreement to manufacture, sell, or license the sale or manufacture of any merchandise bearing Owner Marks;

the party so authorized must effect and keep current a product liability insurance policy for an amount not less than the amount specified in Schedule 25 for any single claim for liability of Owner or Sponsor or both for death, personal injury, or property damage occasioned to any person in respect of the manufacture or sale of the merchandise (for example, for claims relating to a defective product).

16.3 Terms of Policies

All insurance policies effected under this Agreement must:

(a) be wholly satisfactory to Beneficiary;

(b) identify Beneficiary as a named insured;

(c) remain enforceable for the benefit of Beneficiary even if invalid or unenforceable by Payer; and

(d) include full, automatic reinstatement cover at all times during the Term.

16.4 Other Obligations

Payer must:

(a) not violate, or permit the violation of, any conditions of these policies; and

(b) provide insurance certificates and copies of the policies to Beneficiary on its reasonable request.

17. Indemnities and Liability Limitation

17.1 Owner Indemnities

Owner must indemnify Sponsor and Sponsor's officers, employees and agents from and against all claims, damages, liabilities, losses, and expenses related to:

(a) any breach by Owner of this Agreement;

(b) the inaccuracy of any warranty or representations made by Owner;

(c) any wrongful act or omission by Owner (including negligence, unlawful conduct, and wilfull misconduct) in performance of this Agreement;

(d) Sponsor's involvement with the Property (other than losses and expenses incurred solely as a result of Sponsor's decision to invest in the Property);

(e) liabilities for which insurance is required under clause 16.

17.2 Sponsor Indemnities

Sponsor must indemnify Owner and Owner's officers, employees, and agents from and against all claims, damages, liabilities, losses, and expenses related to:

(a) any breach by Sponsor of this Agreement;

(b) the inaccuracy of any warranty or representations made by Sponsor;

(c) any wrongful act or omission by Sponsor (including negligence, unlawful conduct, and wilfull misconduct) in its performance of this Agreement; and

(d) all liabilities for which insurance is required under clause 16.

17.3 Limitation of Liability

To the extent permitted by law, Sponsor's liability to Owner under this Agreement (whether for breach of warranty or otherwise) is limited to the payment of sponsorship fees as and when due.

18. Dispute Resolution

18.1 Mediation

Any dispute or difference about this Agreement must be resolved as follows:

(a) the parties must first refer the dispute to mediation by an agreed accredited mediator or, failing agreement, by a person appointed by the President or other senior officer of the Law Society or Bar Association in the jurisdiction of the Applicable Law;

(b) the mediator must determine the rules of the mediation if the parties do not agree;

(c) mediation commences when a party gives written notice to the other specifying the dispute and requiring its resolution under this clause;

(d) the parties must use their best endeavors to complete the mediation within 14 days; and

(e) any information or documents obtained through or as part of the mediation must not be used for any purpose other than the settlement of the dispute.

18.2 Final Resolution

If the dispute is not resolved within 14 days of the notice of its commencement, either party may then, but not earlier, commence legal proceedings in an appropriate court.

18.3 Contract Performance

Each party must continue to perform this Agreement despite the existence of a dispute or any proceedings under this clause.

18.4 Exceptions to Mediation

Nothing in this clause prevents:

(a) a party from seeking urgent injunctive relief in respect of an actual or apprehended breach of this Agreement;

(b) Sponsor from exercising its rights under sub-clauses 9.2(a)-(c); or

(c) Owner from exercising its rights under sub-clauses 9.3(a)-(c).

19. Confidentiality

The commercial terms of this Agreement are confidential to the parties unless they otherwise agree. However, this does not prevent:

(a) Sponsor or Owner disclosing the existence or the sponsorship to the general public; or

(b) any promotional, marketing, or sponsorship activities authorized or required under this Agreement.

20. Definitions and Interpretation

20.1 Composition

This Agreement comprises these Standard Conditions and the attached Schedules and Special Conditions.

20.2 Precedence

The Special Conditions and the attached Schedules have precedence over these Standard Conditions to the extent of any inconsistency.

20.3 Definitions

In this Agreement, unless the context otherwise requires, terms defined in the Schedules or Special Conditions have the meaning set out there and:

Agreement means this Agreement as amended from time to time.

Ambush means the association by any person, not authorized in writing by Owner, of the person's name, brands, products, or services with the Property or with a party, through marketing or promotional activities or otherwise, whether or not lawful, accurate, or misleading.

Beneficiary means the party for whose benefit an insurance policy must be effected under clause 16.

Competitor means:

(a) in the case of Sponsor:

(i) any person who conducts any business which competes (other than incidentally), directly or indirectly, with any business conducted or services provided by Sponsor or any company related to Sponsor or whose products or services are antithetical to or incompatible with the business, products, or services of Sponsor; or

(ii) any person listed in Schedule 21 or who conducts a business in the industry, or of the nature, described in that Schedule.

(b) in the case of Owner:

(i) any person who conducts any event or offers any product substantially similar to the Property anywhere in the Territory or whose operations are antithetical to or incompatible with the Property; or

(ii) any person or property listed in Schedule 22 or any property or event of the nature described in that Schedule.

Insolvent in respect of a party means one of the following events has occurred:

(a) the filing of an application for the winding up, whether voluntary or otherwise, or the issuing of a notice summoning a meeting at which it is to be moved a resolution proposing the winding up, of the party;

(b) the appointment of a receiver, receiver and manager, administrator, liquidator, or provisional liquidator with respect to that party or any of its assets;

(c) the assignment by that party in favor of, or composition or arrangement or entering into of a scheme of arrangement (otherwise than for the purposes solely of corporate reconstruction) with, its creditors or any class of its creditors.

(d) something having a substantially similar effect to (a) to (c) happens in connection with party or its assets under the Applicable Law.

Media means any of communication to the public at large, whether by radio, television, newspaper, digital media (such as the Internet), or otherwise.

Owner Benefits include additional fees or benefits that accrue to Owner by application of the evaluation criteria in Schedule 14.

Owner Marks means Owner's name and trade or service marks, labels, designs, logos, trade names, product identifications, artwork and other symbols, devices, copyright and intellectual property rights directly associated with the Property. If Schedule 16 is completed, the term is limited to the Owner Marks depicted or listed in that schedule.

Payer means the party obliged to effect an insurance policy under clause 16.

Social Media means a digital application that facilitates the creation and exchange of user-generated information, whether for personal or business purposes, including (for example and without limitation) blogs, wikis, social networks (such as Facebook, YouTube and Twitter), and online media.

Sponsor Benefits may be reduced by application of the evaluation criteria in Schedule 14, and if reduced must be construed accordingly.

Sponsor Marks means Sponsor's name and the marks and other symbols outlined in Schedule 17.

20.4 Currency

References to currency are to the lawful currency of the country or region of the Applicable Law.

20.5 Examples

Examples given in this Agreement do not limit or qualify the general words to which they relate.

Signing Page

By signing, you indicate acceptance of this Agreement (including the standard conditions and the special conditions) on behalf of the entity you represent and you declare your ability to sign this Agreement on behalf of the Sponsor/ Owner (as the case may be).

Signed for and on behalf of Sponsor

Name _____   Signature_____

Capacity_____

Signed for and on behalf of Owner

Name _____   Signature_____

Capacity_____

Index

About the Authors

Kim Skildum-Reid

One of the most highly regarded sponsorship professionals in the world, Kim Skildum-Reid has built her reputation as a sponsorship and marketing thought leader by defining and promoting best practice.

Kim consults to and trains blue chip clients on six continents. Past and current clients include Target Stores, SABMiller, Virgin Group, Dubai Government, Diageo, International Rugby Board, Mazda, Unilever, and ABN Amro.

Her knowledge of sponsorship ranges from high-end theory to down-and-dirty street-fighting tactics, with a strong focus in converting the theoretical into the practical. While many call her methods "innovative" or "visionary," Kim says they are all based on common sense. Her gift is being able to distill complex sponsorship concepts into simple, sensible steps.

It's this rare ability to make the complicated comprehensible that has made her a highly sought-after speaker—both at conferences and in the media.

Kim provides commentary to the world's most respected business media, including *Harvard Business Review, Marketing News (US), CNN, CNBC, Bloomberg, Marketing (UK), Marketing Africa, Marketing Russia, Sponsor Tribune (Netherlands), National Business Review (NZ),* and *SportBusiness.*

Her other books—*The Corporate Sponsorship Toolkit* and *The Ambush Marketing Toolkit*—are considered best in class and are bestsellers in the industry.

Kim's white papers command global industry and academic interest, and her treatise on sponsorship best practice, "Last Generation Sponsorship," has attracted close to a million downloads—and is still climbing. It is required reading for hundreds of university marketing courses and has been reprinted in dozens of magazines in English and eight other languages.

Kim says, "I truly love best practice sponsorship, and helping my clients and the industry get the most from this amazing marketing medium is my mission." Her long-standing commitment to elevating the standards of the industry and informing other practitioners and sponsorship beginners is embodied in her company website, www.PowerSponsorship.com. Its generous sharing of advice and insights has made it one of the most popular sites in the industry, and it is frequently referenced in social media.

Her passion for helping others achieve sponsorship success has led her to translate this knowledge into actionable road maps to help others realize their goals far more efficiently. This fourth edition of The Sponsorship Seeker's Toolkit is another step in Kim's quest to inform, entertain, and, most important, elevate the industry she loves.

Kim can be contacted at admin@powersponsorship.com.

Anne-Marie Grey

Anne-Marie Grey brings more than 30 years of global fundraising and marketing experience and has led fundraising and marketing programs for Share our Strength, UNICEF, and Save the Children before joining UNHCR as Chief of Section, Leadership Giving. Ms. Grey has developed and implemented global sponsorship and CRM programs and partnerships with Procter & Gamble's Pampers and Dawn brands, FC Barcelona, IKEA Foundation, Volvic, The Body Shop, KPMG, Disney, PepsiCo, Coca-Cola, GE, Unilever, Bulgari, and numerous other brands and corporations.

Prior to joining UNICEF, she was the Vice President of Marketing and Strategic Alliances for the United States Fund for UNICEF, where she oversaw the U.S. fund's corporate partnerships and alliances and marketing activities. Anne-Marie held the position of Director, Creative Enterprises and Marketing at Share Our Strength, one of the United States of America's leading antihunger and antipoverty organizations, working with partners that include Evian, American Express, Tyson Foods, Williams-Sonoma, and Coors.

Anne-Marie established Grey O'Keefe and Associates, an international consulting firm specializing in developing strategic alliances between cultural, sporting, and nonprofit organizations and the private sector. Anne-Marie has led the development of public/private partnerships for cultural and nonprofit organizations including Edelman, GAVI Campaign, Operation Smile

International, Save the Children Canada, Children International, Federation of African Women Educationalists, UNHCR, the National Museum of Australia, the Australian National Gallery, the Australian Sports Commission, the Australian War Memorial, and the Australian Healthcare Association.

Anne-Marie studied at Colby College, the Australian National University, the Graduate School of Management at the University of New South Wales, and Monash Mt Eliza.

Anne-Marie can be contacted at agrey@greyokeefe.com.

For More Information

Kim Skildum-Reid

Kim Skildum-Reid runs Power Sponsorship, providing top-level consulting, workshops, in-house training, keynote speaking, books, and extensive online resources to sponsorship professionals worldwide. For more on Power Sponsorship, contact Kim at:

Kim Skildum-Reid
Power Sponsorship
admin@powersponsorship.com
www.powersponsorship.com
Twitter: @KimSkildumReid

Anne-Marie Grey

Anne-Marie Grey is a world-leading expert in bringing causes and corporations together to positively impact society and business through corporate engagement programs that integrate Corporate Social Responsibility, Strategic Philanthropy, Cause Marketing, Communications, and Partnerships. With over 30 years fundraising and marketing experience in corporations, nonprofits, arts organizations, and international organizations, Anne-Marie is available for speaking, training, and strategic advice. She can be contacted at:

Anne-Marie Grey
Grey O'Keefe and Associates LLC
agrey@greyokeefe.com